Introduction to Computer and Digital Forensics
Corporate and Law Enforcement Training System
Volume I, Exercise Manual

Cyber Defense Training Systems, LLC
Sixth Edition

Digital forensics analysis involves much more than becoming a proficient mouse click master. Technical competency involves understanding how the technology works, what it can do, what it cannot do, where and how data is stored, and how to navigate through it when traditional tools of the trade fail to provide access or insight into unique situations. Technical knowledge and skills a computer or digital forensics examiner must possess include efficient use of command lines, understanding how to decode ASCII, EBCDIC and UNICODE, binary, and hexadecimal numbering systems, and how to view and read a variety of file formats and interpret registry entries.

Understanding how hardware, software and firmware interact is necessary for understanding and being able to demonstrate under what conditions, how, where and when data is or may be written to the disk. This is prerequisite knowledge and skill for entering into this profession. Forensic examiners must have a working knowledge of how to search, recover and analyze data, reconstruct deleted, lost and fragmented data, recover passwords, use specific search parameters, how to use various forensic analysis and recovery software and how to report their findings.

On the handling side of forensics, examiners in both the corporate and law enforcement professions must be skilled in, and have strict adherence to, proper evidence handling and chain-of-custody reporting. They must know how to secure an environment and efficiently document and report their findings, all with an understanding of associated laws.

Being technically competent is not enough. Forensic examiners must be familiar with legal issues pertaining to electronic search and discovery. This includes local, state and federal licensing requirements. Some states require a forensic examiner to be licensed. Essentially, the profession of a computer forensic examiner touches every other profession in that it encompasses digital data from various circumstances, occupations and legal jurisdictions. Thus, the forensic examiner must have access to efficient and legally recognized software and hardware tools.

This training program encompasses multiple aspects of this profession. It begins by introducing the basic concepts of what a computer forensic examination is, how to conduct one with validity and accuracy, the best practices of seizing, and proper handling

1

and documentation of each case, and legal considerations. It includes technical aspects of understanding a drive format, operating system interaction and how data is stored on disk so the examiner may know where to look for it. It includes performing a forensic acquisition, indexing, image analysis, password recovery, file reconstruction and final case reporting using both proprietary and open source tools. The information presented in this training system is believed accurate at the time of printing. Current industry practice is researched and incorporated into this material.

This training system was designed to be used in a lecture and hands-on demonstration environment and requires the use of associated case image files and utilizes both commercial and open source forensic acquisition and analysis tools. College and University faculty may acquire the accompanying forensic case image files for this training system by sending an e-mail to:

infoccdn@gmail.com

In the subject line enter: Instructor Forensics Resources.

You may then enter your contact information in the body of the e-mail along with which course you have adopted this material for. Include course name, number, academic institution, address and phone number. You will be contacted on how to acquire the instructor power points and case image files.

Cyber Defense Training Systems LLC
P.O. Box 86
Leslie, Michigan, 49251 USA
lewisja@aim.com

Table of Contents

STATEMENT OF ETHICS AND TERMS OF USE AGREEMENT
Volume I, 6th edition

STUDENT COPY

Digital and computer forensics is a critical profession that requires advanced technical skills and compliance with local, state and federal laws. In the corporate environment, the security professional, as well as the computer examiner must be familiar with these areas. Although some of the exercises and materials included in this program may not be considered a security issue for many organizations, some of the tools presented may be of a concern if used for malicious or non-benevolent purposes.

This program has been designed to enhance the student's ability to recover data in an accurate and uncompromising manner, and to guide the learner in techniques on how to acquire further knowledge in this field dependent upon discovery. Guided exercises and assignments combined with structured exercises will provide additional skills necessary for the learner to be successful and self-sustaining in the field of digital computer forensics and computer examinations.

Each exercise in this curriculum requires a student summary of the material covered. In addition to structured lecture and presentation time, it is expected that many hours of study, research and preparation is required to prepare the learner for the next level of material. Deviation from this may affect learner performance.

The terms of use for this material, including any accompanying case image files or examples are;

1. The student or learner accepts the Statement of Ethics and Terms of Use Agreement. .

2. The student or learner is not permitted to copy or distribute any part of this material.

3. The learner agrees to abide by all expectations of ethical behavior that is representative of a skilled professional.

4. The undersigned further agrees to use the knowledge and skills obtained as a result of the undersigned's participation in this computer forensics program only for lawful and legitimate purposes.

5. The undersigned agrees to the lawful use of knowledge and skills obtained as a result of their participation in this training program and to indemnify, defend and hold harmless the college, its board members, its employees and agents, teachers, professors and instructors, and / or the developers and providers of this material from any and all claims, actions, damages, or liability arising from the undersigned's use of or violation of any of the terms of this agreement, or from the unlawful use of knowledge and skills obtained as a result of the undersigned's participation in this computer forensics training.

I recognize that the field of computer forensics involves knowledge and skills that is not common to traditional computer users. I also understand that the knowledge and skills obtained by participating in a computer forensics curriculum are not to be used in any manner contrary to the legal and ethical standards of this profession. With this understanding I, of my own free will and choice accept the responsibility of maintaining the integrity of this profession by exercising lawful and ethical behavior at all times.

Use of this material is subject to acceptance to the Statement of Ethics and Terms of Use Agreement.

It is important that to realize and accept the responsibility of this Statement of Ethics and Terms of Use Agreement between the student and the Institution before being permitted to use this material.

I accept the Statement of Ethics and Terms of Use Agreement.

Printed Name of Student/Learner:

_____

Signed:

_____

Today's Date: _____ _____

Educational Institution/Organization:

_____

Course Name & Number: _____ _____

STATEMENT OF ETHICS AND TERMS OF USE AGREEMENT
Volume I, 6th edition

INSTRUCTOR COPY
SIGN, DETACH AND GIVE TO YOUR INSTRUCTOR

Digital and computer forensics is a critical profession that requires advanced technical skills and compliance with local, state and federal laws. In the corporate environment, the security professional, as well as the computer examiner must be familiar with these areas. Although some of the exercises and materials included in this program may not be considered a security issue for many organizations, some of the tools presented may be of a concern if used for malicious or non-benevolent purposes.

This program has been designed to enhance the student's ability to recover data in an accurate and uncompromising manner, and to guide the learner in techniques on how to acquire further knowledge in this field dependent upon discovery. Guided exercises and assignments combined with structured exercises will provide additional skills necessary for the learner to be successful and self-sustaining in the field of digital computer forensics and computer examinations.

Each exercise in this curriculum requires a student summary of the material covered. In addition to structured lecture and presentation time, it is expected that many hours of study, research and preparation is required to prepare the learner for the next level of material. Deviation from this may affect learner performance.

The terms of use for this material, including any accompanying case image files or examples are;

3. The student or learner accepts the Statement of Ethics and Terms of Use Agreement. .

4. The student or learner is not permitted to copy or distribute any part of this material.

3. The learner agrees to abide by all expectations of ethical behavior that is representative of a skilled professional.

4. The undersigned further agrees to use the knowledge and skills obtained as a result of the undersigned's participation in this computer forensics program only for lawful and legitimate purposes.

Page 1 of 2

5. The undersigned agrees to the lawful use of knowledge and skills obtained as a result of their participation in this training program and to indemnify, defend and hold harmless the college, its board members, its employees and agents, teachers, professors and instructors, and / or the developers and providers of this material from any and all claims, actions, damages, or liability arising from the undersigned's use of or violation of any of the terms of this agreement, or from the unlawful use of knowledge and skills obtained as a result of the undersigned's participation in this computer forensics training.

I recognize that the field of computer forensics involves knowledge and skills that is not common to traditional computer users. I also understand that the knowledge and skills obtained by participating in a computer forensics curriculum are not to be used in any manner contrary to the legal and ethical standards of this profession. With this understanding I, of my own free will and choice accept the responsibility of maintaining the integrity of this profession by exercising lawful and ethical behavior at all times.

Use of this material is subject to acceptance to the Statement of Ethics and Terms of Use Agreement.

It is important that to realize and accept the responsibility of this Statement of Ethics and Terms of Use Agreement between the student and the Institution before being permitted to use this material.

I accept the Statement of Ethics and Terms of Use Agreement.

Printed Name of Student/Learner:

_____

Signed:

_____

Today's Date: _____   _____

Educational Institution/Organization:

_____

Course Name & Number: _____   __

Page 2 of 2

Forensics Exercise # 1
Self-Test and System Component Identification

OBJECTIVE:

For each student to self gauge their own level of technical competency as preparation for working in the field of computer and digital forensics and to identify those areas where further study is required.

Part 1: <u>Student Self Assessment:</u>

1. Hardware is that part of the computer system that is;

   A. Virtual
   B. Hidden
   C. Physical
   D. None of the above

2. Software is that part of the computer system that

   A. Virtual
   B. Hidden
   C. Physical
   D. None of the above

3. The power supply

   A. Changes DC voltage to AC voltage
   B. Amplifies AC voltage to higher levels
   C. Changes AC voltage to DC voltage
   D. Is optional
   E. None of the above

4. POST is an acronym for

   A. Power Off System Test
   B. Power On Self Test
   C. Power Outage Start Testing
   D. Power Outage Stop Testing
   E. None of the above

5. Which comes first, the POST or the BOOT?

   A. POST   B. BOOT

6. DIMM is a type of _____.

    A. Hard drive
    B. CD-ROM
    C. Thumb Drive
    D. RAM Stick
    E. None of the above

7. ESD protection is not important when working with electronic devices.

    A. True   B. False

8. Binary is a _____ state numbering system.

    A. 2
    B. 8
    C. 10
    D. 16
    E. None of the above

9. The most central electronic component in the PC system is the _____.

    A. Hard disk
    B. BIOS
    C. CPU
    D. CD-ROM
    E. None of the above

10. BIOS is an acronym for _____.

    A. Binary Input Operating System
    B. Binary Input Operating Services
    C. Basic Input Operating System
    D. Basic Input Operating Services
    E. None of the above

11. What is the purpose of the battery in a PC system?

    A. To provide power backup to the power supply
    B. To provide a continuous source of power to the CMOS settings
    C. To provide a continuous source of power to the CPU
    D. To provide a power backup to the keyboard unit
    E. None of the above

12. What is the primary purpose of the crystal clock in a PC system?

   A. To provide a timing reference for internal operations
   B. To provide a timing reference for the date and time settings
   C. Both A and B
   D. None of the above

13. Identify the following components:

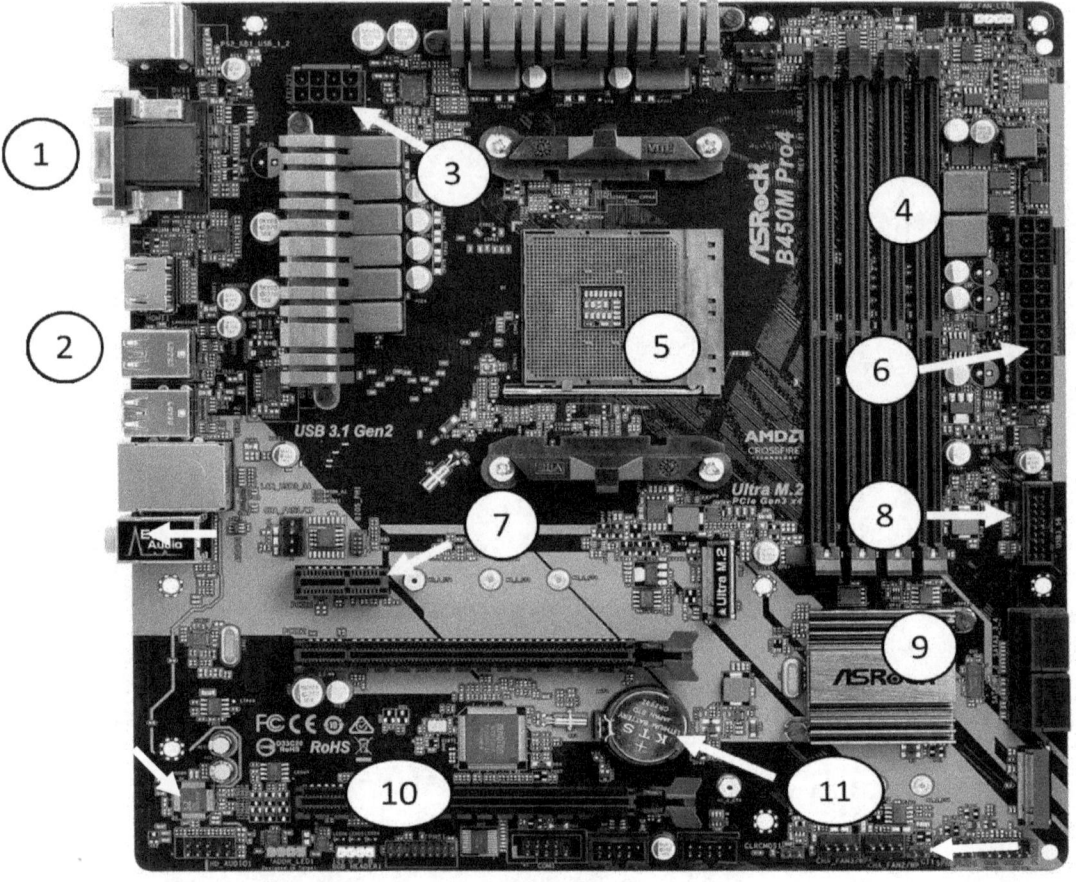

Figure 1-1

1. _____
2. _____
3. _____
4. _____
5. _____
6. _____
7. _____
8. _____
9. _____
10. _____
11. _____

14. Identify the following ports:

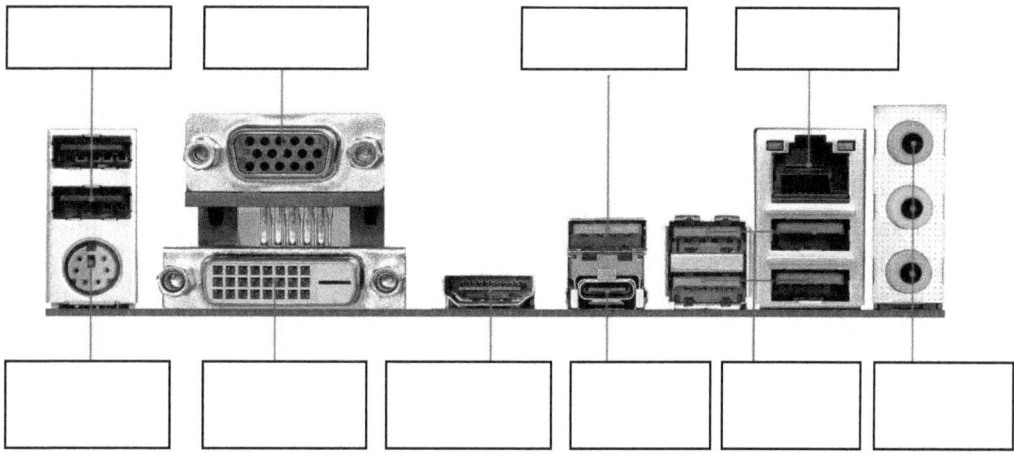

Figure 1-2

15. Five volts (5 V) is used for the;

       A. Motors
       B. Circuitry
       C. Monitor Displays
       D. None of the above

16. Twelve volts (12 V) is used for the;

       A. Motors
       B. Circuitry
       C. Monitor Displays
       D. None of the above

17. List these startup events in order from first to last.

    _____ BIOS POST "Beep tone"

    _____ Power Supply Initializes

    _____ Hardware and Memory check

    _____ Starting Operating System

18. The binary number 1101001 is equal to _____ in octal.

19. The binary number 1101001 is equal to _____ in hexadecimal.

20. The binary number 1101001 is equal to _____ in decimal.

21. The octal number 431 is equal to _____ in decimal.

22. The octal number 431 is equal to _____ in hexadecimal.

23. The octal number 431 is equal to _____ in binary.

24. The hexadecimal number 4FA is equal to _____ in binary.

25. The hexadecimal number 4FA is equal to _____ in octal.

26. The hexadecimal number 4FA is equal to _____ in decimal.

27. RAM is an acronym for _____ _____ _____.

28. 1 Kilobyte is equal to approximately

    A. 1000 bytes
    B. 1,000,000 bytes
    C. 1,000,000,000 bytes
    D. 1,000,000,000,000 bytes
    E. 1.44 bytes
    F. None of these

29. 1 Megabyte is equal to approximately

    A. 1000 bytes
    B. 1,000,000 bytes
    C. 1,000,000,000 bytes
    D. 1,000,000,000,000 bytes
    E. 1.44 bytes
    F. None of these

30. 1 Gigabyte is equal to approximately

    A. 1000 bytes
    B. 1,000,000 bytes
    C. 1,000,000,000 bytes
    D. 1,000,000,000,000 bytes
    E. 1.44 bytes
    F. None of these

31. 1 Terabyte is equal to approximately

    A. 1000 bytes
    B. 1,000,000 bytes
    C. 1,000,000,000 bytes
    D. 1,000,000,000,000 bytes
    E. 1.44 bytes
    F. None of these

32. 1 Petabyte is equal to approximately

    A. 1000 bytes
    B. 1,000,000 bytes
    G. 1,000,000,000 bytes
    H. 1,000,000,000,000 bytes
    I. 1.44 bytes
    J. None of these

33. A CPU without a heat sink will have a similar effect as a/an

    A. Television without a remote control
    B. Boat without a GPS system
    C. Engine without a radiator
    D. Car without a radio

34. The unit of electrical pressure is referred to as a/an

    A. Amp
    B. Ohm
    C. Volt
    D. Tesla

35. The system will not boot from the hard drive. After booting from the CD, the contents of the hard drive, (files and directories) can be accessed. The most likely cause is:

    A. The hard drive is completely defective.
    B. The hard disk controller is defective.
    C. The CD drive is defective.
    D. POST is corrupted.
    E. None of these are accurate.

36. You power up the system and it boots correctly, however, 30 minutes later the system freezes. You power off the system and reboot, but the system will not work. You wait 20 - 30 minutes and try again. This time the system boots. Again, 30 minutes later the system freezes. This is behavior is consistent. The most likely cause is:

    A. The operating system crashes every 30 minutes.
    B. The power system is faulty.
    C. The CD drive is defective.
    D. The microprocessor is having a thermal failure.
    E. None of these are accurate.

37. The system power on button is depressed. The following symptoms are present:

    1. The power supply fan does not spin
    2. The hard disk spins
    3. The CD drive seeks
    4. A single beep
    5. The OS loads

The most likely cause of this is;

    A. A defective microprocessor.
    B. A defective fan in the power supply.
    C. The power supply is not supplying the proper voltages to the rest of the system.
    D. The CD drive and hard disk were still spinning from when the system was powered down before.
    E. There is nothing wrong.

38. Pin one on a ribbon cable is identified by a _____.

    A. Black dot on the end of the cable
    B. Colored strip on the edge of the ribbon cable
    C. There is no way to tell

39. Windows 9x is based upon the _____ file system.

    A. NTFS
    B. HPFS
    C. NFS
    D. DOS
    E. None of the above

40. Windows 10 is based upon the _____ file system.

        A. NTFS
        B. HPFS
        C. NFS
        D. DOS
        E. None of the above

41. List in order of operation;

      ___ Format Hard Disk
      ___ Partition Hard Disk
      ___ Install Operating System
      ___ Install User Applications

42. .ini is an abbreviation for an _____ file.

43. .dll is an abbreviation for a _____ file.

44. The command for opening the Registry editor is _____.

45. The Registry is organized into five components called _____.

        A. Files
        B. Data
        C. Packets
        D. Hives
        E. Keys

46. List in order of release;

      ___ Windows 98
      ___ DOS
      ___ Windows 3.1
      ___ Windows XP
      ___ Windows Server 2016
      ___ Windows 10

47. Linux and Windows XP use the same file system structure.

        A. True   B. False

48. What on a disk drive consists of a minimum of one or more sectors?

      _____

49. You purchase a new advanced video graphics card. You install it and discover an exclamation point under the Device Manager for that device. This is an indication that;

    A. The device driver installed correctly
    B. The device driver was not installed
    C. The device driver installed however there may be a problem
    D. None of the above because there are no exclamation point options under the Device Manager

50. The Registry is a _____ used by Windows to store both hardware and software configuration information, user preferences, and setup information.

    A. Hardware device
    B. Text file
    C. Spreadsheet file
    D. Database
    E. None of the above

51. When changes in Windows are made, including in the Control Panel or the Device Manager, the registry is / is not automatically modified.

    A. Is   B. Is not

52. Enter the exact command with switch settings to turn off the System, Hidden and Read Only attributes on a system file with the name system1.sys.

_____

53. FAT32 allows for how many bits of addressing? _____

54. FAT16 allows for how many bits of addressing? _____

55. FAT12 is used on which storage device?

    A. CD ROM
    B. DVD
    C. Hard Disk
    D. None of the above

56. How many bits are in 4 nibbles? _____

57. A single transistor or other electronic switch is needed to create a single bit in memory.

    A. True   B. False

58. Figure 1-3 is a Window of;

    A. Text file directory structure
    B. Spreadsheet file directory structure
    C. Registry tree structure
    D. None of the above

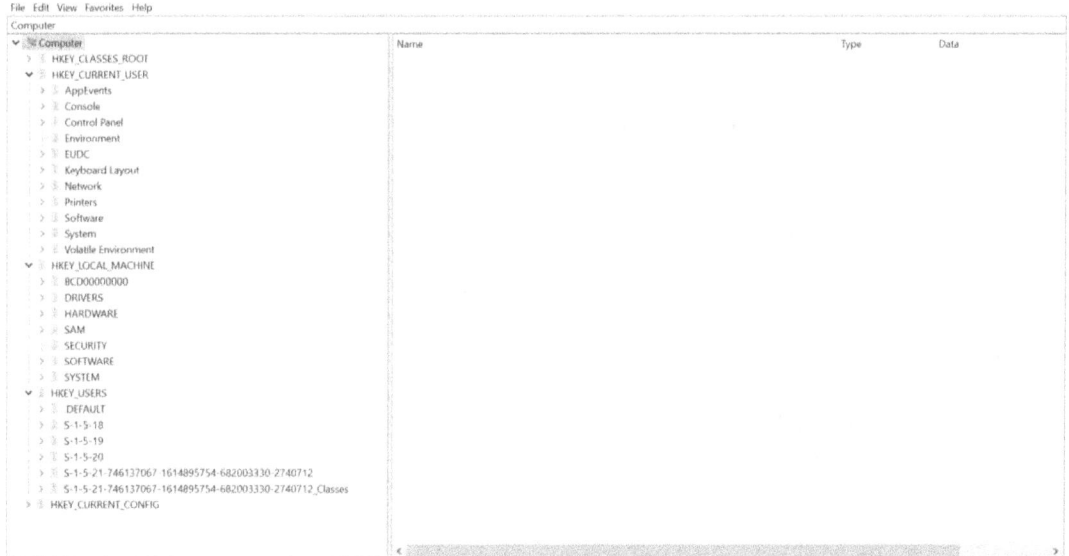

Figure 1-3

59. Files called initialization files are used to store _____ information that Windows uses.

    A. Configuration
    B. Backup
    C. Restore
    D. Word document information
    E. None of the above

60. Which type of memory requires constant refreshing?

    A. Static
    B. ROM
    C. Dynamic
    D. None of the above

61. You desire to view the hidden files in a directory and you type "DIR /A:H". Will this command syntax work?

    A. Yes   B. No

62. IDE is a type of;

    A. CD / DVD / Hard disk interface
    B. Monitor interface
    C. Keyboard interface
    D. USB interface
    E. None of the above

63. SATA is a type of;

    A. CD / DVD / Hard disk interface
    B. Monitor interface
    C. Keyboard interface
    D. USB interface
    E. None of the above

64. The command to partition your hard disk is

    A. Format
    B. Delete
    C. FDISK
    D. None of these

65. The first partition on a hard disk is known as the _____ partition.

    A. Extended
    B. Secondary
    C. Primary
    D. Alternate
    E. None of these

66. DDR memory is

    A. Slower than non DDR memory
    B. The same speed as non DDR memory
    C. Twice as fast as non DDR memory
    D. DDR memory has no speed

67. A set of several parallel lines connecting two devices is known as a

    A. Car
    B. Bus
    C. Boat
    D. Plane
    E. None of the above

68. The Windows swap file can exist on a compressed volume.

    A. True
    B. False

69. Identify the type of interface cable. _____

Figure 1-4

70. Identify the type of port. _____

Figure 1-5

71. RJ-11 connectors are used to connect PC's to what type of interface?

    A. Ethernet
    B. Phone Modem
    C. Serial Port
    D. Parallel Port
    E. None of the above

72. Identify both types of interfaces.

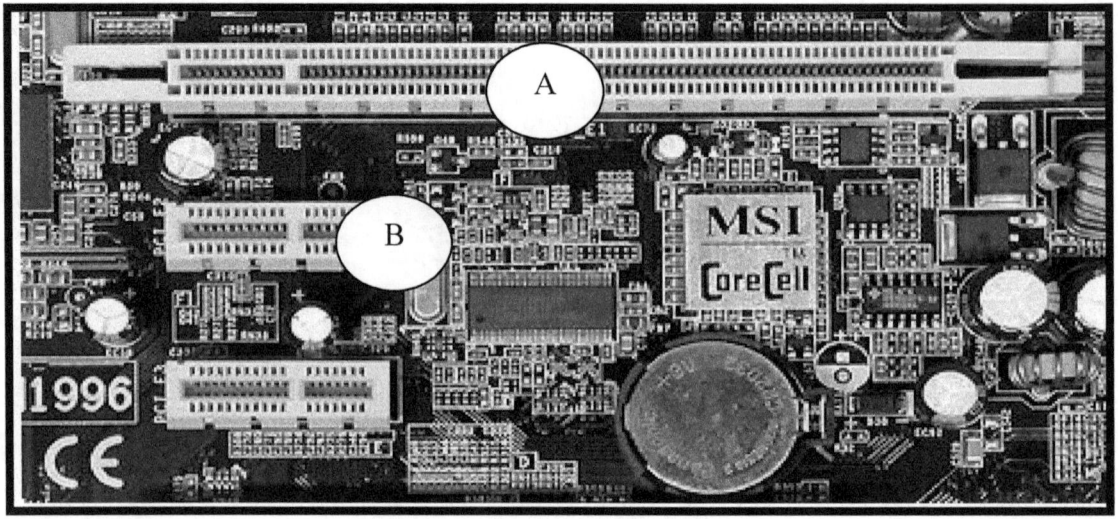

Figure 1-6

A. _____   B. _____

73. The name of the software program that allows a hardware peripheral to effectively function is known as;

    A. Gaming program
    B. Video graphic application
    C. Operating system file
    D. Device Driver
    E. None of the above

74. You install a new graphic accelerator card. You just paid $300 for it. After installing into the appropriate slot you power up the system and the graphics are just as bad as they were before you installed the new card. What is the most likely problem?

75. You create a text file that is 1024 bytes in logical size. The file system uses 2K size clusters. Writing this file to disk will require the use of _____ cluster/s.

    A. 1
    B. 2
    C. 3
    D. 4
    E. 5

76. The text file identified in the previous question will have approximately how much RAM slack written to the disk?

    A. 1 K
    B. 2 K
    C. 3 K
    D. 4 K
    E. 5 K

77. ECC is used for

    A. Identifying hardware failures and fixing them
    B. Identifying software that is compatible with Apple Systems
    C. Identifying software that was compiled
    D. Identifying errors in a file and recovering them

78. Starting a computer in a controlled manner is known as a;

    A. Hard boot
    B. Cold boot
    C. Safe Boot
    D. POST
    E. None of the above

79. A collection of software tools that permits a hacker to establish a stealth method of maintaining access on a system is known as a _____.

    A. Virus
    B. Cluster
    C. Backdoor
    D. Batch file
    E. None of the above

80. The speed of modern day CPUs is measured in:

    A. Milliseconds
    B. Nanoseconds
    C. Kilohertz
    D. Gigahertz

81. AGP is an abbreviation for _____ _____ _____.

82. PCI is an abbreviation for _____ _____ _____.

83. ESD is an abbreviation for _____ _____ _____.

84. Which command makes a file read only?

    A. attrib +r "filename"
    B. read_only +r "filename"
    C. read_status /y "filename"
    D. readonly /y "filename"
    E. attrib /r "filename"

85. If you have data on a hard drive that you want to repartition, what should you do before performing this operation?

    A. Run the scandisk utility
    B. Run the chkdsk utility
    C. Format the hard drive
    D. Issue the sys c: command
    E. Backup all files

86. A disk has four platters. The surface of each platter consists of 400 tracks. How many cylinders are there on this disk? _____

    A. 200
    B. 400
    C. 800
    D. 1600
    E. None of the above

87. Amp is a unit of measure of _____

    A. Voltage
    B. Current
    C. Resistance
    D. Power

88. Voltage is measured;

    A. Across a component with the power applied
    B. Across a component with no power applied
    C. In series with a component with the power applied
    D. In series with a component with no power applied
    E. None of the above

89. Current is measured;

   A. Across a component with the power applied
   B. Across a component with no power applied
   C. In series with a component with the power applied
   D. In series with a component with no power applied
   E. None of the above

90. Resistance is measured;

   A. Across a component with the power applied
   B. Across a component with no power applied
   C. In series with a component with the power applied
   D. In series with a component with no power applied
   E. None of the above

91. The system will not boot from the CD drive. After booting
    from the hard drive, the contents of the CD drive, (files and
    directories) can be accessed. The most likely cause is:

   A. The CD disk controller is defective.
   B. The hard disk device driver has been corrupted.
   C. RAM is corrupted.
   D. A non-system disk is in the CD drive.
   E. None of these are accurate.

92. Using the attached ASCII Character Encoding Chart complete the
    following, identifying the hexadecimal equivalents. Include the space as a
    character.

Computer & Digital Forensics

_____

93. RAID is an acronym for

   _____ _____ _____ _____ _____

94. SSD is an abbreviation that represents a type of _____.

   A. RAM Stick
   B. Video Monitor
   C. Hard Disk Drive
   D. CD or DVD
   E. None of these are accurate.

27

95. A USB thumb drive is a storage only device, it cannot be used to boot an operating system.

   A. True   B. False

96. Which type of hard drive would you put in a typical laptop?

   A. 5400 RPM 2.5″
   B. 5400 RPM 3.5″
   C. SSD
   D. USB Flash Drive

97. A client system will not connect to the rest of the network. The IP address of the client is consistently 169.254.0.220. The problem is most likely;

   A. The incorrect operating system has been installed
   B. The monitor interface is impaired
   C. TCP/IP settings are not set to search for a DHCP server
   D. The local firewall is preventing the system from obtaining a DHCP address

98. The maximum data transfer rate of SATA revision 3.0 is;

   A. 1.5 Gb/s
   B. 150 MB/s
   C. 3.0 Gb/s
   D. 6.0 Gb/

99. A user's time and date keeps resetting to January 1, 2000. Which of the following is the most likely cause?

   A. The BIOS needs to be updated
   B. Windows needs to be updated
   C. The Windows Date and Time Properties window needs to be modified.
   D. The lithium battery needs to be replaced.

100. The minimum number of hard drives necessary to implement RAID 5 is;

   A. Two
   B. Five
   C. Three
   D. Four

Your total score of questions answered correctly. _____ of 100
Review the correct answers with your instructor. Your instructor may ask you to
provide this score.

SCORING GUIDELINE
Based on Average Computer Technicians Skills

Above 90%	-Exceptional technical knowledge
Between 80 and 89%	-High level of technical knowledge
Between 70 and 79%	-Above average technical knowledge
Between 60 and 69%	-Average technical knowledge, needs review
Between 50 and 59%	-Below average technical knowledge, needs additional training or review
Less than 50%	-Lacking adequate technical skills, needs additional training

ASCII CHARACTER ENCODING

HEX ASCII Code	ASCII Char Char	HEX Code	ASCII Char	HEX Code	ASCII Char	HEX Code	
00	NUL	20	SP	40	@	60	
01	SOH	21	!	41	A	61	a
02	STX	22	"	42	B	62	b
03	ETX	23	#	43	C	63	c
04	EOT	24	$	44	D	64	d
05	ENQ	25	%	45	E	65	e
06	ACK	26	&	46	F	66	f
07	BEL	27	'	47	G	67	g
08	BS	28	(	48	H	68	h
09	HT	29	)	49	I	69	i
0A	LF	2A	*	4A	J	6A	j
0B	VT	2B	+	4B	K	6B	k
0C	FF	2C	'	4C	L	6C	l
0D	CR	2D	-	4D	M	6D	m
0E	SO	2E	.	4E	N	6E	n
0F	SI	2F	/	4F	O	6F	o
10	DLE	30	0	50	P	70	p
11	DC1	31	1	51	Q	71	q
12	DC2	32	2	52	R	72	r
13	DC3	33	3	53	S	73	s
14	DC4	34	4	54	T	74	t
15	NAK	35	5	55	U	75	u
16	SYN	36	6	56	V	76	v
17	ETB	37	7	57	W	77	w
18	CAN	38	8	58	X	78	x
19	EM	39	9	59	Y	79	y
1A	SUB	3A	:	5A	Z	7A	z
1B	ESC	3B	;	5B	[	7B	{
1C	FS	3C	<	5C	\	7C	|
1D	GS	3D	=	5D	]	7D	}
1E	RS	3E	>	5E	^	7E	~
1F	US	3F	?	5F	_	7F	DEL

Forensics Exercise # 2
Introduction to Basic Hashing Operations

OBJECTIVE:

This is an introduction to hashing operations. Your instructor should have presented and demonstrated the concept of file hashing operations. The objective of this exercise is to provide the student the opportunity to run a hashing operation on a file, modify the file, run the hashing operation again and observe the hash value change. Later exercises in this volume will provide the opportunity to advance skills and understanding in this subject.

OVERVIEW:

The student will create a text file and run a hashing operation against that file. The hash value will then be recorded. The student will then alter the contents of the text file and run a second hashing operation against it and record the hash value. The values of both operations will then be compared.

STEPS:

1. Perform a Google search for the best download location for the file MD5 or another MD5 hashing program. Download and install on your student system.

2. Create a text document with a minimum of three lines of text. The student is to determine what text is to be inserted into the document. Save the document to the Desktop with the file name of Hash1.txt.

3. Initialize the MD5 hashing program and select the document that was created in step 2. Run the hashing algorithm against this file and record the hash value below.

    Hash value: _____

4. Open the text document that was created in step 2 and modify only one character within that file. Save the file with the name Hash2.txt.

5. Again, initialize the same MD5 hashing program and select the newly modified text document. Run the hashing algorithm against this file and record the hash value below.

    Hash value: _____

6. Are the output values of both hashing operations the same?

7. Explain why the outputs are different. Be specific!

8. Rename the file Hash2.txt to Hash3.txt. Do not open the document or modify the contents of this file.

9. Again, initialize the MD5 hashing program and select the Hash3.txt text document. Run the hashing algorithm against this file and record the hash value below.

   Hash value: _____

10. Compare the output values from all three hashing operations.

    Are any of them the same?   Yes_____   No _____

    Explain why or why not!

    Are there any differences?   Yes _____   No _____

    Explain why or why not!

STUDENT SUMMARY:

    1. What did you learn from this exercise?

    2. What is the significance of a hash value to the computer forensic examiner?

    3. How does performing a hashing operation on the copy of a file support validate the integrity of the file as compared to the original?

Evaluators Review of Learners Performance

1   2   3   4   5

Forensics Exercise # 3
Hashing and Bit Steam Image Correlation

OBJECTIVE:

This is an introduction to comparing a bit-stream image acquisition to a file hash before and after. Your instructor should have presented and demonstrated the concept of bit-stream imaging. The objective of this exercise is to provide the student the opportunity to create a bit-stream backup of a media device and then run a hashing operation on a selected file within that backup. This exercise is in preparation for a forensic acquisition of a media device or evidence drive and how the hash values will and must be exact for it to be deemed forensically sound.

OVERVIEW:

The student will take a small media device such as a flash drive and create a bit stream backup of that device. Once the backup image has been created, a selected file will be exported from the contained backup image and its hash value will then be compared with the original still housed on the media device.

The difference between this and the previous exercise is that the original file had a hash value computed on it, then it was slightly modified, then the hashing algorithm was run against it a second time to demonstrate different hash values. This exercise will demonstrate a bit-steam image across an interface from one device to another, then the hash values compared.

STEPS:

Note: Any reputable bit stream imaging software, including the Linux dd command, will suffice for this exercise. This exercise uses Terabyte Drive Image Backup and Restore Suite.

1. Perform a Google search for the best download location for the Terabyte Drive Image Backup and Restore Suite, or a similar program.

2. Attach a flash drive or other small media device to the student system. Make sure the attached media device has several files on it.

3. Initialize the Terabyte Drive Image Backup and Restore Suite software as shown below. Note that this software tool has a 30-day trial license.

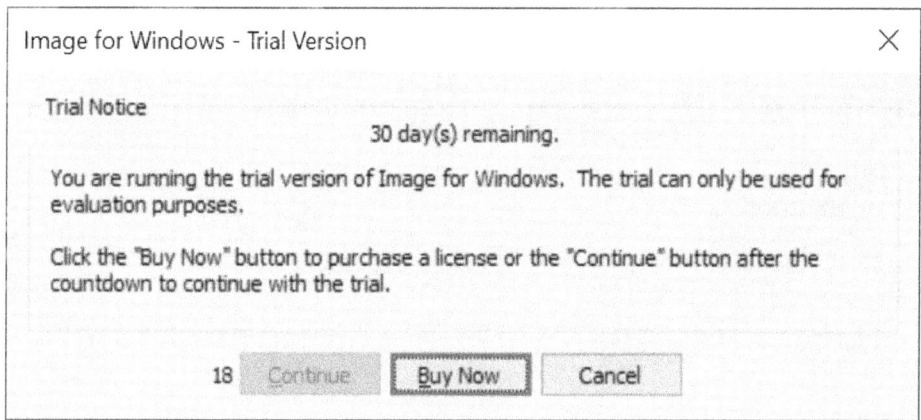

Figure 3-1

4. Complete the installation process until you are presented with the Image for Windows (x64) GUI as shown below.

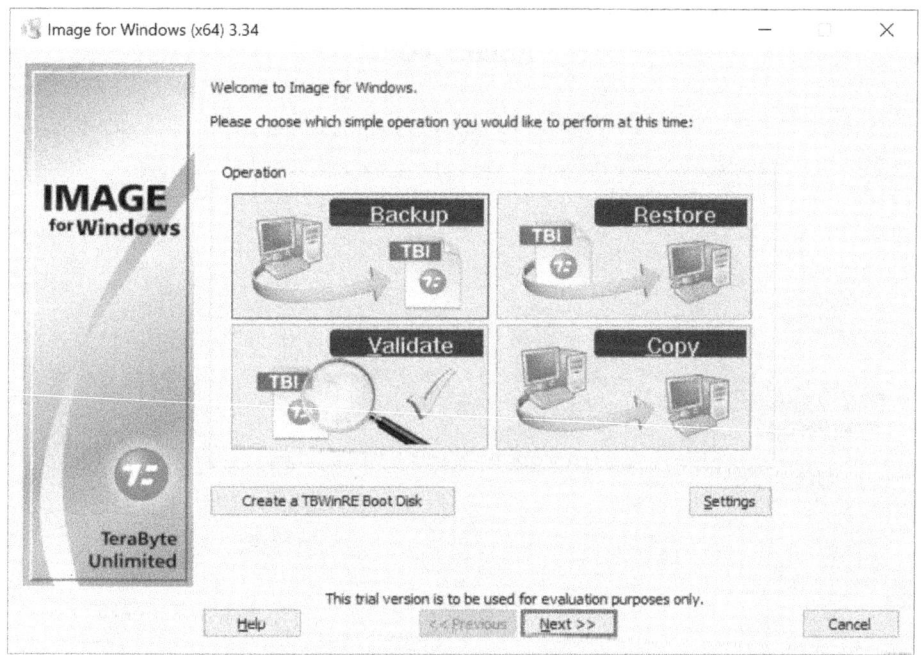

Figure 3-2

5. Select the 'Backup' option and navigate to the target media device.

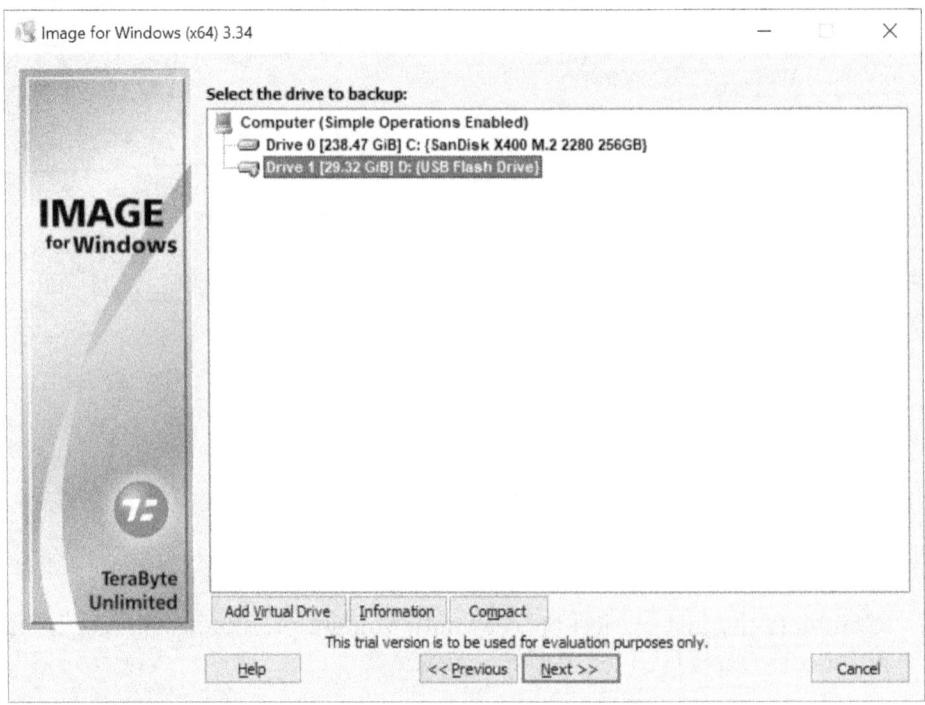

Figure 3-3

6. Select 'Next'. Verify you have selected the intended media device. Then select 'Start'.

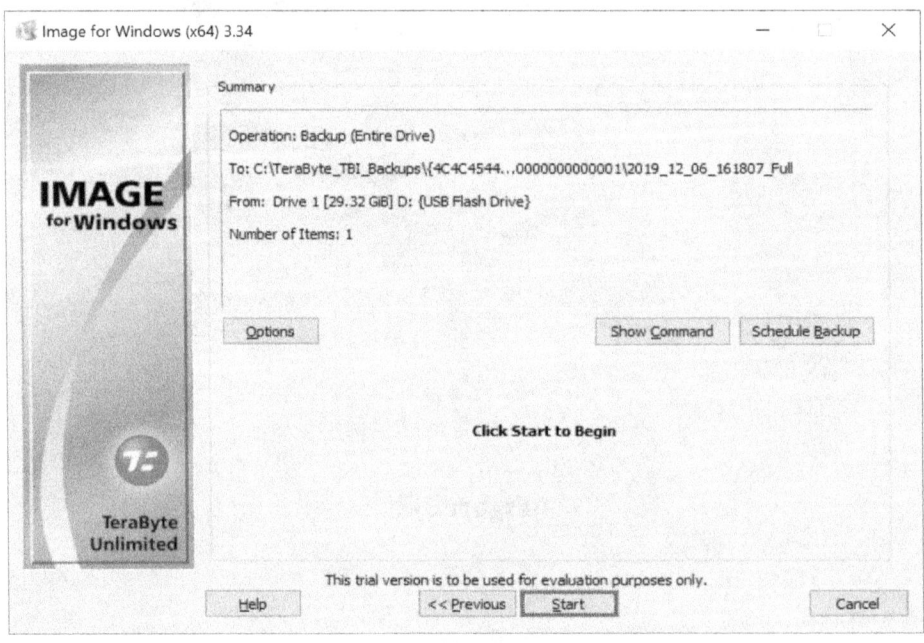

Figure 3-4

7. The Creating image process will begin.

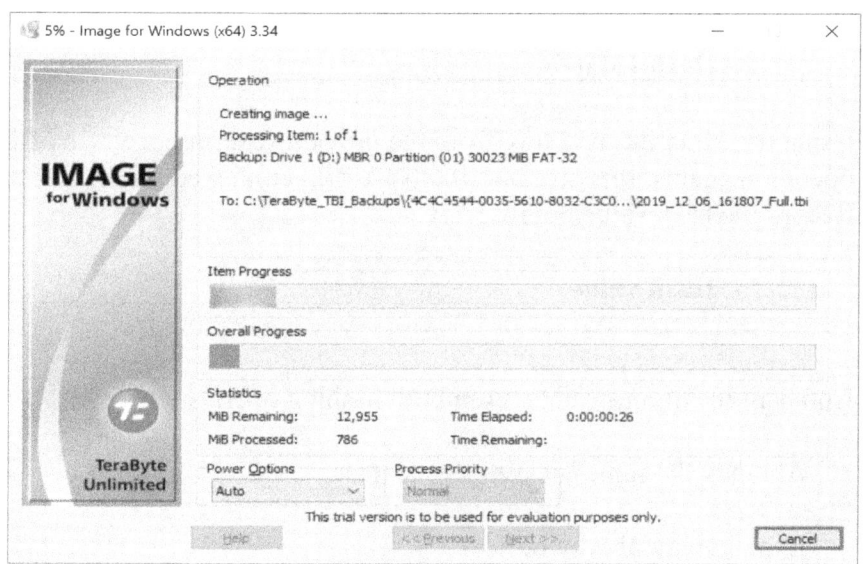

Figure 3-5

8. The next item that will appear, if all operations were successful, will be the 'Validating Image' window. Allow this to complete. You should see the 'Operation' window that, if the bit-stream image transfer was successful, will present the message 'The backup has completed successfully'.

9. The Image for Windows (x64) GUI will appear again. Select the 'Restore' option and navigate to where the backup image was stored. By default, it will be in the c:\Terabyte.... Directory.

10. Expand the backup image file until you identify a file of your choice. For this example, we selected the 2016_Scori... .pdf file. Left click on a file on your system and drag it to your student Desktop.

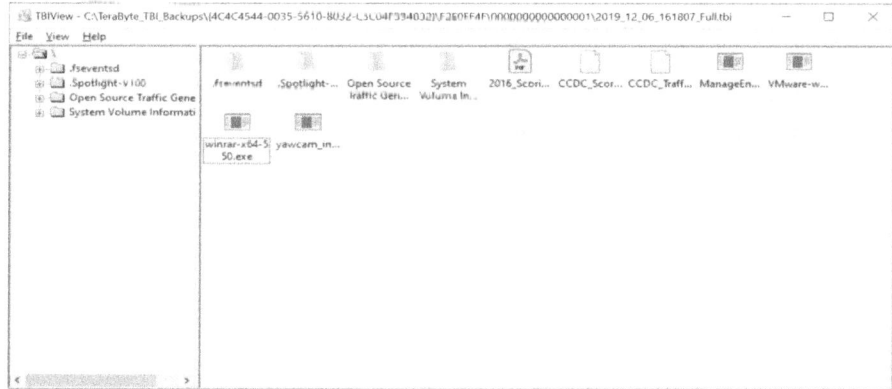

Figure 3-6

11. Using the MD5 hashing tool from the previous exercise, run a hashing operation against this exported file. Record the hash value below.

Hash value: _____

12. Using the MD5 hashing tool from the previous exercise, run a hashing operation against this original file that is still contained on the target media. Record the hash value below.

Hash value: _____

13. Compare the output values from both hashing operations.

      Are they the same?   Yes_____   No _____

      Explain why or why not!

      Are there any differences?   Yes _____   No _____

      Explain why or why not!

STUDENT SUMMARY:

   1. What did you learn from this exercise?

   2. How does demonstrating and understanding hashing operations validate the results of a computer forensic examination?

Evaluators Review of Learners Performance

      1   2   3   4   5

Forensics Exercise # 4
Visual Data Mapping Using SequoiaView

OBJECTIVE:

To better understand file size and associations of data files contained within a particular media. The Sequoia View drive-mapping program should have demonstrated to you.

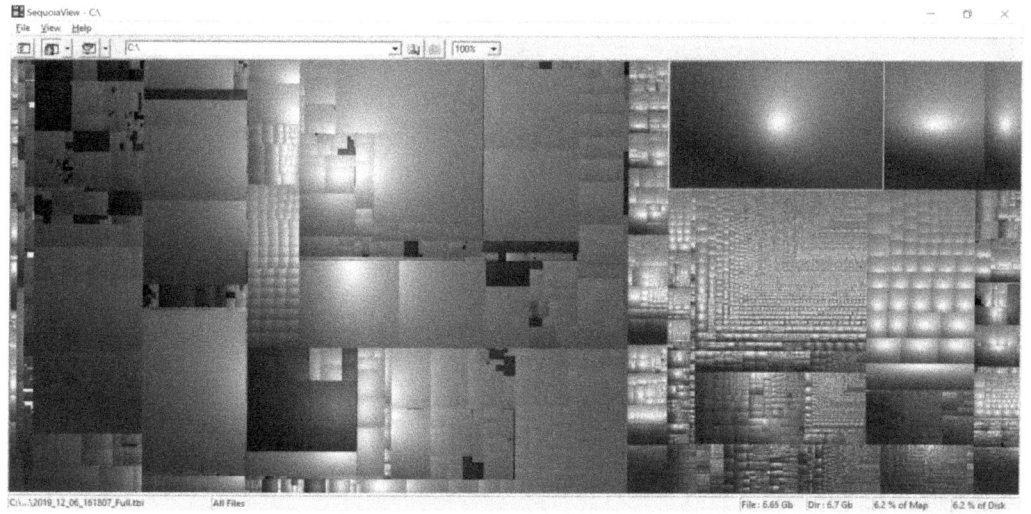

Figure 4-1

STEPS:

1. Perform a search for and download the Sequoia View software-mapping tool.

2. Install the program on your student learning system. Accept all the defaults until the application is successfully installed.

3. Start the program and select the C: drive to and begin scanning process as shown in Figure 4-2 below. Make sure you are at the root of the C: drive.

Figure 4-2

4. Once the scanning process has completed the default installation directory for SequoiaView should be displayed similarly as shown in Figure 4-3 below.

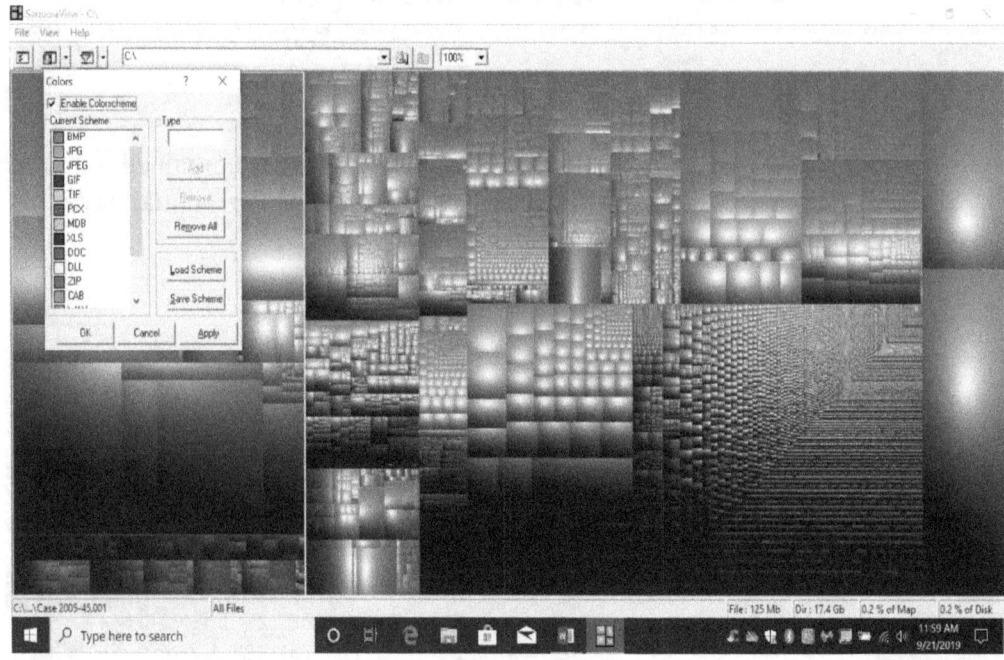

Figure 4-3

5. Select the Color Scheme filter option as shown above to enable color associations to various file types. You will notice that different file types have different color associations. This is to permit a more perceptive view of how many files and their associated sizes are a part of each operating system.

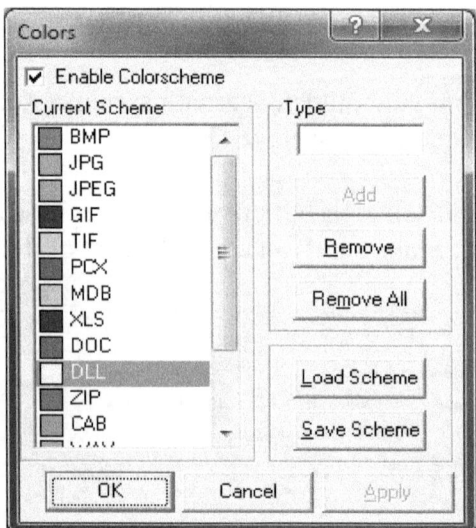

Figure 4-4

6. Also notice the directory path as identified at the top of the Sequioa View window. The default path is the c: drive.

7. Move the cursor over the various shaded boxed areas and identify the specific directory paths. Each file has an associated directory.

8. Navigate the cursor around the various boxes and answer the following questions:

Identify the two largest file sizes on this media and state their sizes. You can right click on the file to display the Properties option.

                 File Names   File Sizes

    a. _____   _____

    b. _____   _____

State the purpose of each of these files!

        File a: _____

        File b: _____

What is the date created for the largest file? _____

    a. What is date modified for that file? _____

    b. What is the date accessed for that file? _____

9. Select the File pull down option on the menu toolbar.

10. Select the Save as Bitmap option. Save the bitmap image to your Desktop.

11. Navigate SequoiaView to a different storage device such as a USB thumb drive or a CD-ROM if available. Navigate around this storage device viewing the different files and folders as you previously did in the above steps.

12. What do you notice about the file presentations from this smaller device? Are there fewer files?

Note: There are fewer files on thumb drive or CD-ROM than there are on a media with an operating system running on it.

13. Select the Filters button on the SequoiaView toolbar. The following window should appear.

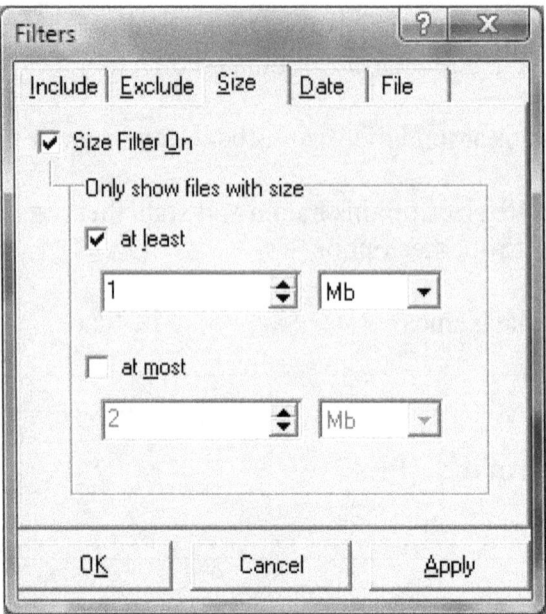

Figure 4-5

14. Select the Size tab, click on the "Size Filter On" and "at least" buttons as shown in Figure 4-5 above.

15. Select at least 1 MB for file size and click the "Apply" button.

    a.   What happened to the SequoiaView screen?

16. Select the Size tab again and change the "at least" option to 2 MB. Then click the "Apply" button.

    a.   What happened to the SequoiaView screen?

17. Repeat these steps several times until you identify several of the largest files on the disk or storage device.

18. Return to the File Filters window and uncheck the "at least" button and check the "at most" button.

19. Set the "at most" option to 1 MB.

    a.   What happened to the SequoiaView screen?

20. Repeat these steps several times until you identify several of the smallest files on the disk or storage device.

STUDENT SUMMARY:

A. How can this tool be useful to you in learning about disk structures?

B. How can this tool be useful to you in examining a disk drive?

Evaluators Review of Learners Performance

1   2   3   4   5

Forensics Exercise # 5
View Hidden Sessions on CD-ROM Media Using ISOBuster and FTK Imager

OBJECTIVE:

To learn how to identify and recover hidden information on a CD or DVD, or information written with an unknown format on a CD-ROM disk.

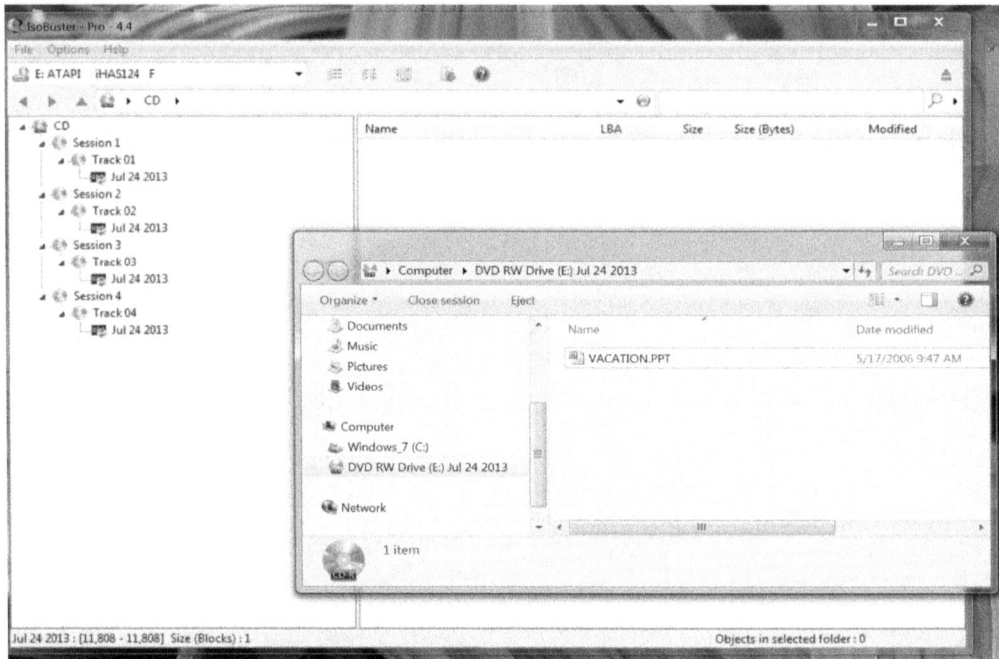

OVERVIEW:

Operating systems are designed to display only usable information. However, not all information on a hard disk, CD-ROM or other device is recognized by the operating system as important to the user. The Windows operating system includes numerous files that are hidden by default.

There are various software tools available that permit additional writing to a CD after the initial session has been written, thus ignoring the previous session. With newer operating systems, the task is to write a file or group of files to the CD, then close the session and eject the CD. ISO Buster is a software tool that will display hidden, discarded or incomplete session information from a CD-ROM or other storage device. ISO Buster can be downloaded from web site: http://www.isobuster.com

PART I

STEPS:

1. If you do not have ISOBuster installed on your computer perform a search for a reputable site, download, and install it.

2. Your instructor should have provided you with a special CD-ROM disk. Consider this disk confiscated from the desk of an employee that is suspected of violating the corporate acceptable use policy. If you do not have a CD-ROM disk that has hidden sessions on it, you may need to create one.

3. Insert the disk into the CD-ROM drive and, using Explorer, view the contents of the disk. You should see the last files that were written, but not the first (Figure 5-1).

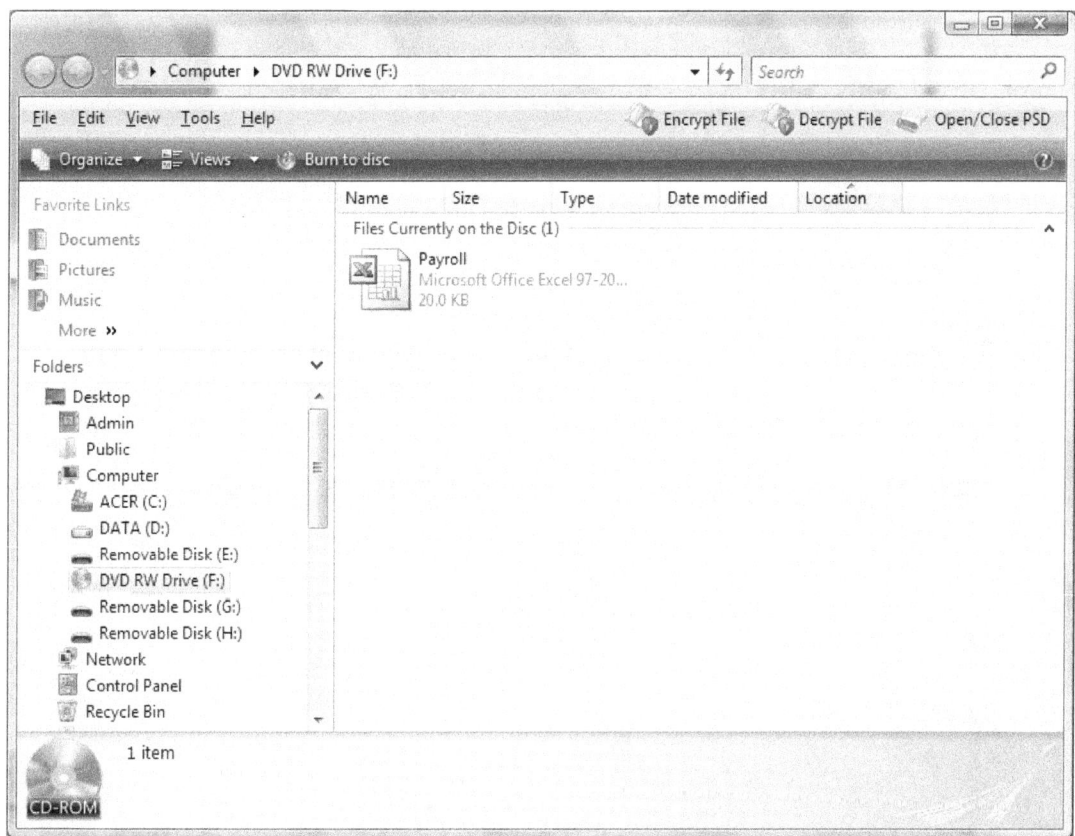

Figure 5-1

4. What file or files were displayed?

5. After viewing the contents of the CD or DVD, close Explorer.

6. Initialize the ISOBuster program and navigate to the CD or DVD drive. ISOBuster should reveal several several sessions on the CD/DVD. How many sessions are identified?

7. Create a folder on the Desktop and title it 'Extracted Files'. Inside the Extracted Files folder, create a folder for each session as shown in Figure 5-2.

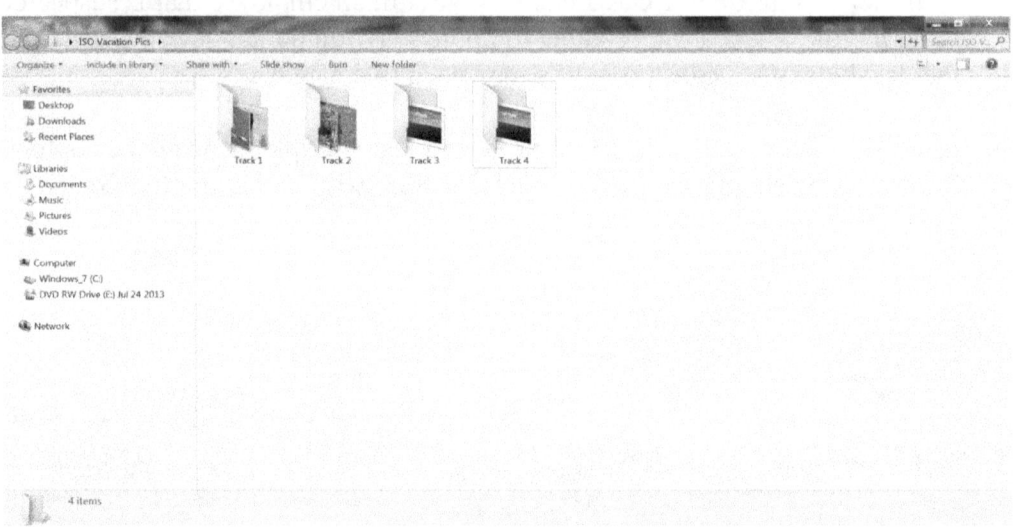

Figure 5-2

8. Right click and select Extract from the pull down menu as shown in Figure 5-3 below. Select the first file in session one, hold the shift key and then select the last file of that same session. All files in that session should be highlighted.

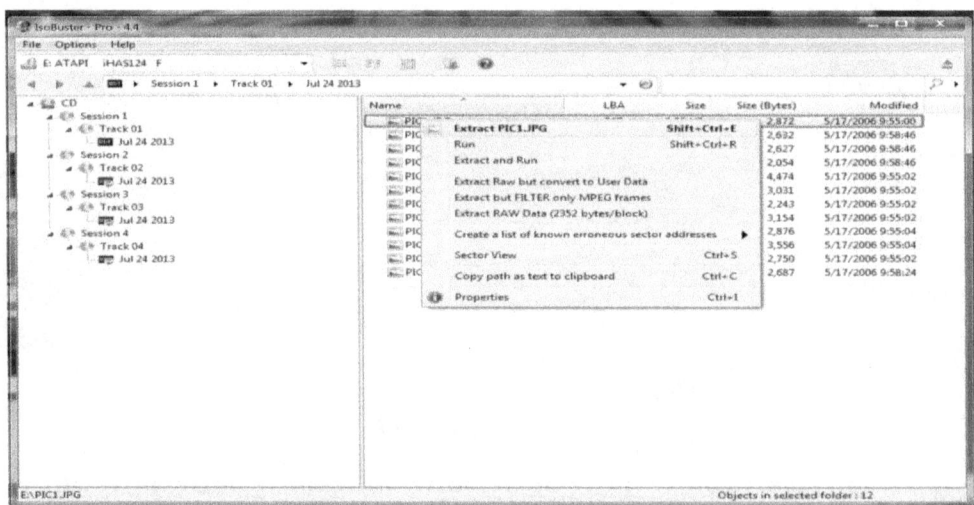

Figure 5-3

9. Export (Extract) your selected files to the Extracted Files, track 1 folder. Repeat this step for each track, exporting to their respective folders.

   At this point each extracted file can be examined either visually or by using WinHex or some other file viewing tool.

   For safe practice when dealing with files of unknown origin the extracted file should not be initialized on the forensic examination system. Sometimes hidden files contain malicious software that you do not want on your system. In actual practice in the field the file should be taken to an isolated system that was built and maintained specifically for the opening of files of unknown origin.

10. Navigate to the hard disk drive and view the system, active and other partition information. Navigating through System Reserved under Partition 01 reveals the bootmgr, recycle bin, boot and system volume information folders.

   How many partitions do you see on your hard disk? _____

   Identify the name of each partition:

   _____

   _____

   _____

   _____

   _____

11. Expand the System Reserved option under the first active partition. It should look similar to that of Figure 5-4 below.

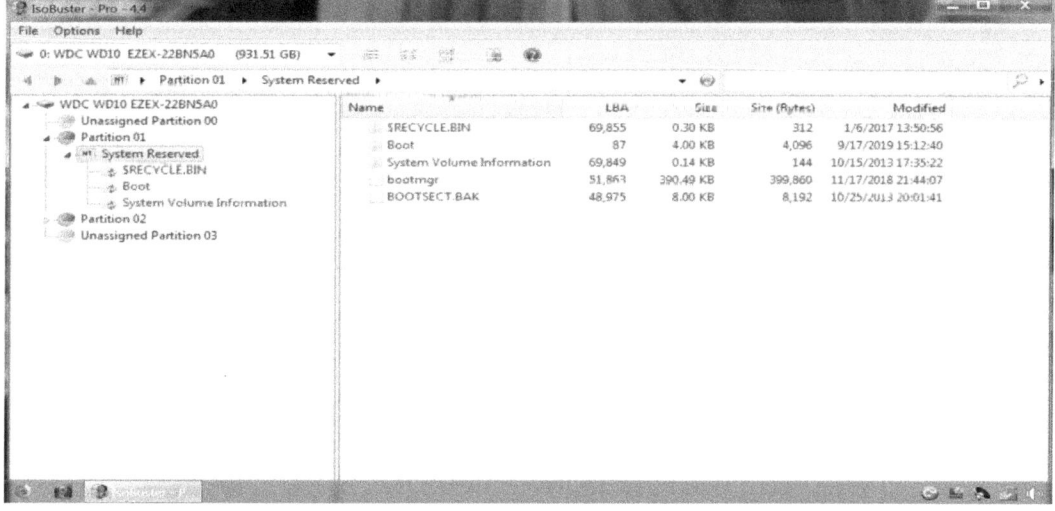

Figure 5-4

47

12. What is the purpose of the bootmgr?

_____

_____

13. Record the following for the bootmgr file:

LBA	Size	Size (Bytes)	Modified
_____	_____	_____	_____

14. What would cause the bootmgr file to have a different size than its original size from when the operating system was installed?

_____

_____

15. What command, commands or tools could you use to edit the bootmgr?

_____

_____

PART II
Viewing Hidden Files on CD/DVD using FTK Imager

This portion of the exercise introduces FTK Imager, a widely used, professionally and legally recognized forensic tool.

16. The FTK Imager program should be installed on your student system. If it is not, obtain a copy from your instructor or download it from www.accessdata.com.

17. Ensure the CD/DVD from Step # 3 is still in the CD drive.

18. Initialize FTK Imager. You should observe all media devices that are connected to your student system. See Figure 5-5 below for an example.

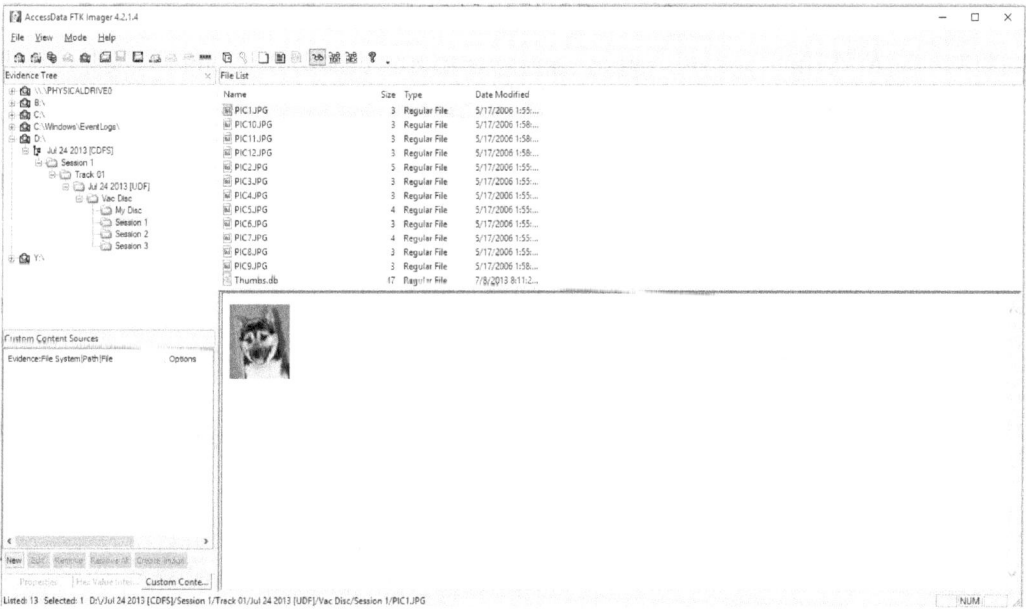

Figure 5-5

19. Navigate to the CD drive and expand the sessions.

Do you observe the same number of sessions as identified in Part I of this exercise?

One of the benefits of using FTK Imager is that it can be executed from a flash drive without having to install it on a system. You will become more proficient with FTK Imager in a future exercise where it will be utilized to acquire a hash validated bit stream image of a target media that will then be forensically examined.

STUDENT SUMMARY:

1. What did you learn from this exercise?

2. Consider, as a corporate computer examiner, that you have been presented with several CD or DVD media and instructed to examine each of them and discover their contents. Answer and explain the following:

   A. What type of system should you insert these disks into? (Select one the options below)

      a. Your $10,000 forensic examination system.
      b. The system that is to be examined
      c. An alternate system that was built just for this purpose

   B. Research and explain the following:

      a. What is a macro file is and how does it relate to Excel and other types of files.

      b. What risks or dangers may be involved in opening a recovered file on a specially created forensic system?

C. Answer the following questions:

    a. Provide two examples of how a hidden macro might damage a forensic examination system?

    b. Is it possible that a hidden macro could open a back door to your computer forensic examination system?

    c. If this happened, would your computer forensic examination system be compromised from a legal perspective?

    d. If your computer forensic examination system was compromised, how could you recover your forensic examination to be considered exact?

Evaluators Review of Learners Performance

1   2   3   4   5

Forensics Exercise # 6
Protecting Forensic Examination Systems by
Disabling Auto Run Features

OBJECTIVE:

To better understand how to protect forensic examination systems from malicious auto run files. This exercise focuses on Windows based operating systems.

OVERVIEW:

You may not have access to all of the operating systems identified in this particular exercise so you may perform these steps on the operating system that is available to you. There are several methods of disabling auto run features. Each operating system has unique methods for accomplishing this. There are several methods to enable or disable the auto run or auto play features of an operating system. A few of them are presented here.

Part A. Disabling Windows Auto run using the Keyboard

Step 1: Determine if your system has auto run features enabled by inserting a CD-ROM disk that has an auto run program on it. If auto run is enabled on your system, continue to Step 2. If it is not enabled on your system, enable it or have your instructor provide directions on how to do so.

Step 2: Insert the CD-ROM or DVD disk used in Step 1 into the drive.

Step 3: Immediately after inserting the CD-ROM or DVD disk press down and hold the shift key while the CD-ROM disk is spinning up. This will allow the CD or DVD to be recognized as installed, but it will not load anything from it.

Step 4: Did the CD-ROM auto run startup files on the CD-ROM disk?

Yes   No

Step 5: If desired or necessary, restore your operating system to its original auto run setting.

Part B. This Part Applies only to Windows 95/98/Me/XP operating systems.

Step 1: Determine if your system has auto run features enabled by inserting a CD-ROM disk that has an auto run program on it.

Step 2: Right click on the My Computer icon and select properties.

Step 3: Select the Device Manager tab.

Step 4: Select the CD-ROM folder.

Step 5: Select the entry for the CD-ROM drive and select Properties.

Step 6: Select the Settings tab and turn either on or off the Auto insert notification option and select OK.

Step 7: Click OK again.

Step 8: Insert a CD-ROM disk into the CD-ROM drive. If Step # 1 identified that the system you are using had auto run features enabled, did the CD-ROM not auto run startup files on the CD-ROM disk?

Step 9: If desired, restore your operating system to its original auto run setting.

Part C. Windows 7 and 10 Operating Systems

This part of the exercise requires use of the Regedit program. Verify with your instructor if you are to perform these steps.

Step 1: Open the Registry editing program by clicking on Start and selecting the Run option.

Step 2: Enter the Regedit command in the Run window. When the User Account Control window appears asking if you want to allow this app to make changes to your device, select 'Yes'.

Step 3: Navigate to the HKEY_LOCAL_MACHINE/System/ CurrentControlSet/Services/Cdrom key.

Step 4: Change the Autorun value to the opposite binary value, a '1' will enable auto run and a '0' will disable it. See Figure 6-1 on the next page.

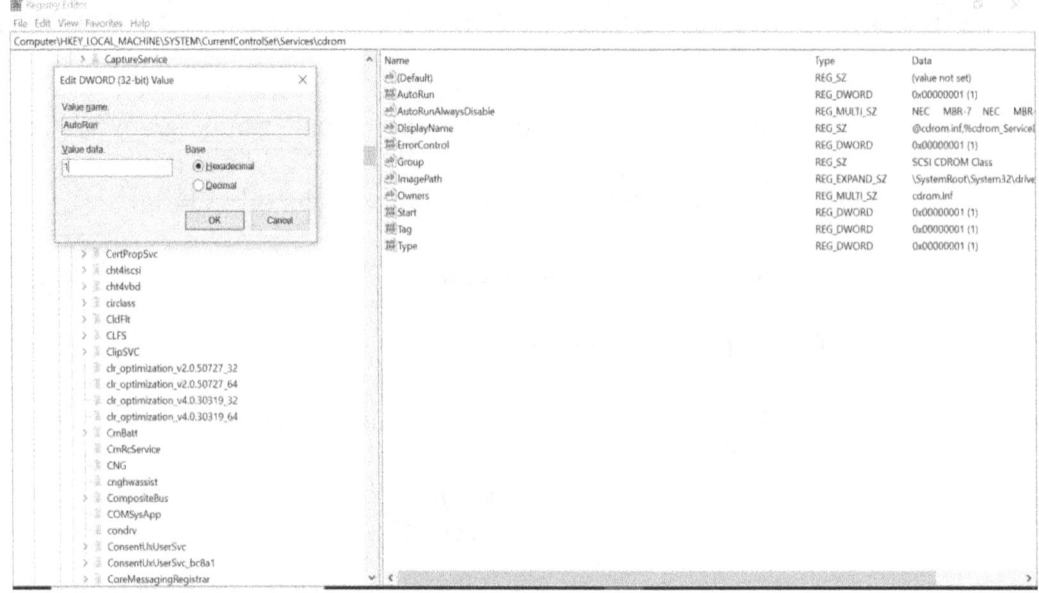

Figure 6-1

Step 5: Exit out of the Registry editor program.

Step 6: Insert a CD-ROM disk into the CD-ROM drive. Did the auto run file initialize?

　　　　　　　　Yes　　　　　　　　　　No

Step 7: If desired or necessary, restore your operating system to its original auto run setting.

Part D: Create an Auto run Disable File

Step 2: Open Notepad and enter the following into the open text file:

> REGEDIT4
> [HKEY_LOCAL_MACHINE\SOFTWARE\Microsoft\
> WindowsNT\CurrentVersion\IniFileMapping\Autorun.inf]
> @="@SYS:DoesNotExist"

Step 3: Save the file as File Name NOAUTO.REG, the Save as Type to "All Files", and the Encoding as ANSI.

The resulting file save should look like that of Figure 6-2 on the next page.

54

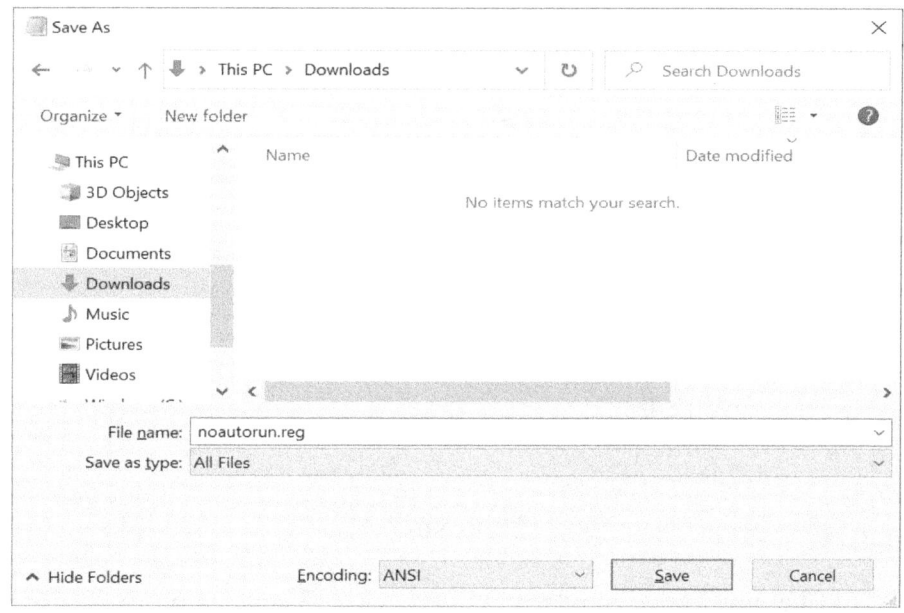

Figure 6-2

Figure 6-3

A new icon will appear with the registry image and the title 'noautorun'. This new file will permit the quick use of disabling CD/DVD auto run features on your operating system.

Step 4: Double click the noautorun.reg file. The User Account Control window appears asking if you want to allow this app to make changes to your device. Select the 'Yes' option. The following window should appear.

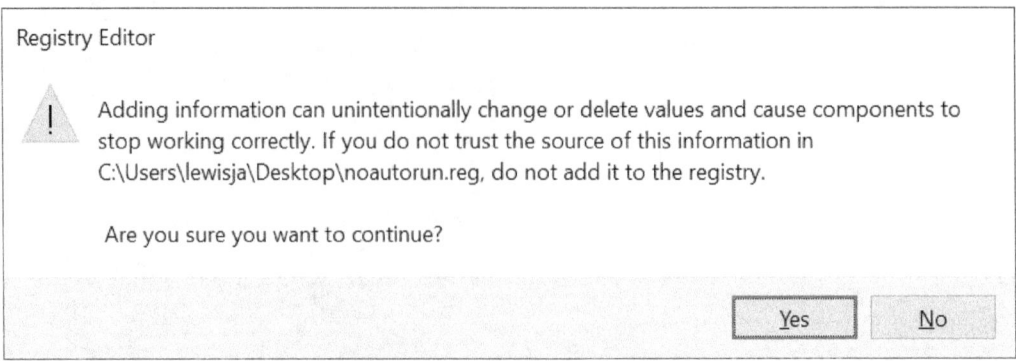

Figure 6-4

Step 5: Clicking Yes will update the Registry to disable auto run. Verify with your instructor if you are to actually perform this step.

Step 6: If you selected Yes, insert a CD-ROM disk into the CD-ROM drive and verify it works properly.

Step 7: If desired or necessary, restore your operating system to its original auto run setting.

Part E. Using the Command Shell

Step 1: Select the Run window in the lower left of the Windows student display and enter the command 'Autoplay'. The following window should appear.

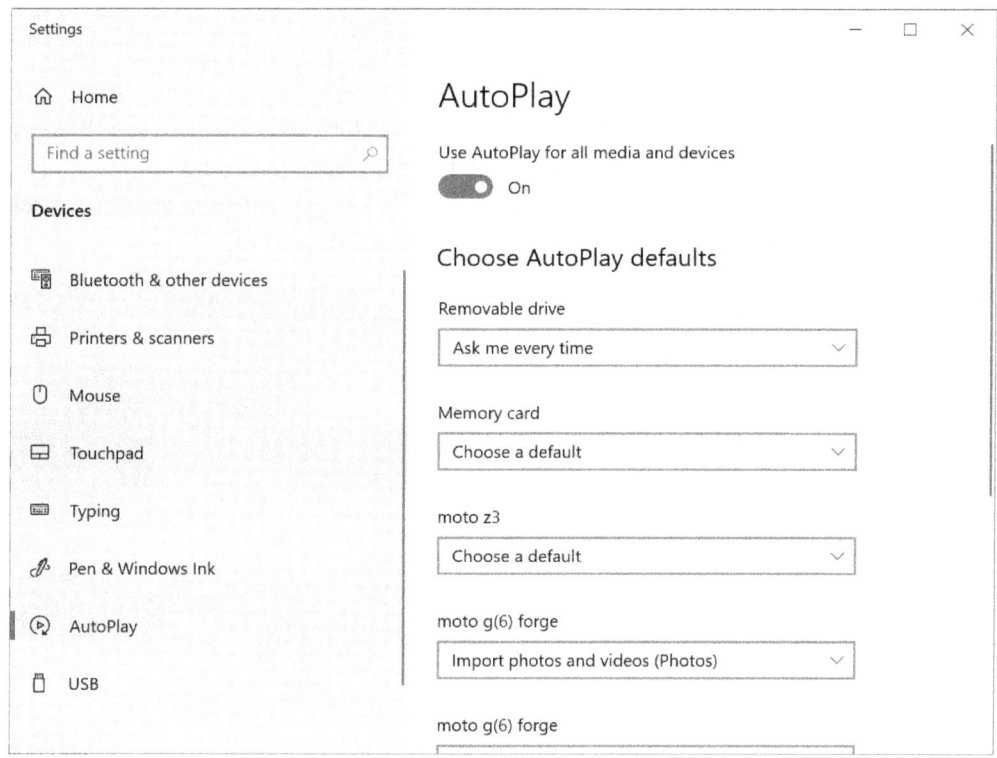

Figure 6-5

Step 2: View the selections available under the Removable drive option. Select the 'Ask me every time option.

Step 3: Exit the Auto Play window and insert a CD with an auto run file on it.

Step 4: Were you prompted to allow the program to run?

STUDENT SUMMARY:

1. What did you learn from this exercise?

2. Explain three ways how malicious software started by an auto run file can be a problem for the forensic examiner. Consider the consequences of explaining to your employer or client how malicious software from the system under examination infected your forensic examination system.

    A.

    B.

    C.

Evaluators Review of Learners Performance

1   2   3   4   5

OBJECTIVE:

To better understand the importance of the bootmgr file and to view it.

OVERVIEW:

There are several methods to view the bootmgr file, both command line and GUI based tools. The first view will be with the command line.

Step 1:   Open a command window on your system and enter the command bcdedit.exe. For later versions you may need to enter the bcdedit command in the search window and when the command option appears in the upper toolbar, right click and select 'Run as Administrator'.

Step 2:   When the command executes, you will see the following information below.

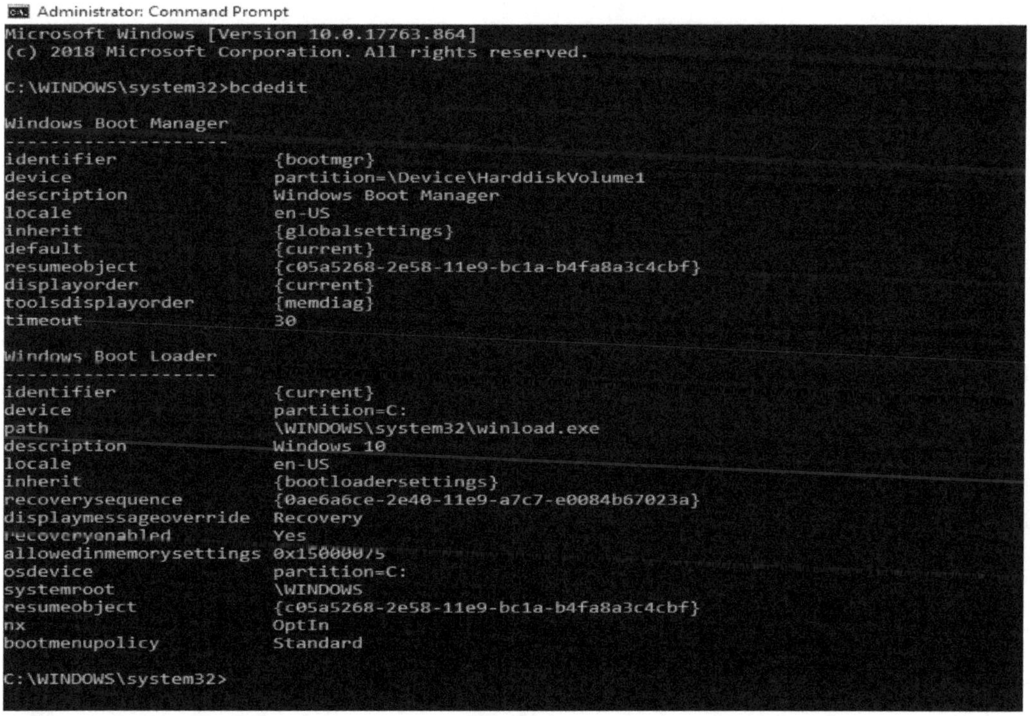

```
Administrator: Command Prompt
Microsoft Windows [Version 10.0.17763.864]
(c) 2018 Microsoft Corporation. All rights reserved.

C:\WINDOWS\system32>bcdedit

Windows Boot Manager
--------------------
identifier              {bootmgr}
device                  partition=\Device\HarddiskVolume1
description             Windows Boot Manager
locale                  en-US
inherit                 {globalsettings}
default                 {current}
resumeobject            {c05a5268-2e58-11e9-bc1a-b4fa8a3c4cbf}
displayorder            {current}
toolsdisplayorder       {memdiag}
timeout                 30

Windows Boot Loader
-------------------
identifier              {current}
device                  partition=C:
path                    \WINDOWS\system32\winload.exe
description             Windows 10
locale                  en-US
inherit                 {bootloadersettings}
recoverysequence        {0ae6a6ce-2e40-11e9-a7c7-e0084b67023a}
displaymessageoverride  Recovery
recoveryenabled         Yes
allowedinmemorysettings 0x15000075
osdevice                partition=C:
systemroot              \WINDOWS
resumeobject            {c05a5268-2e58-11e9-bc1a-b4fa8a3c4cbf}
nx                      OptIn
bootmenupolicy          Standard

C:\WINDOWS\system32>
```

Figure 7-1

59

Step 3: Take a screenshot of the bcdedit output. Save this for later comparision.

Step 4: Perform a search and download and install Visual BCD Editor.

Step 5: Initialize Visual BCD Editor as shown below. Click on the {bootmgr} option.

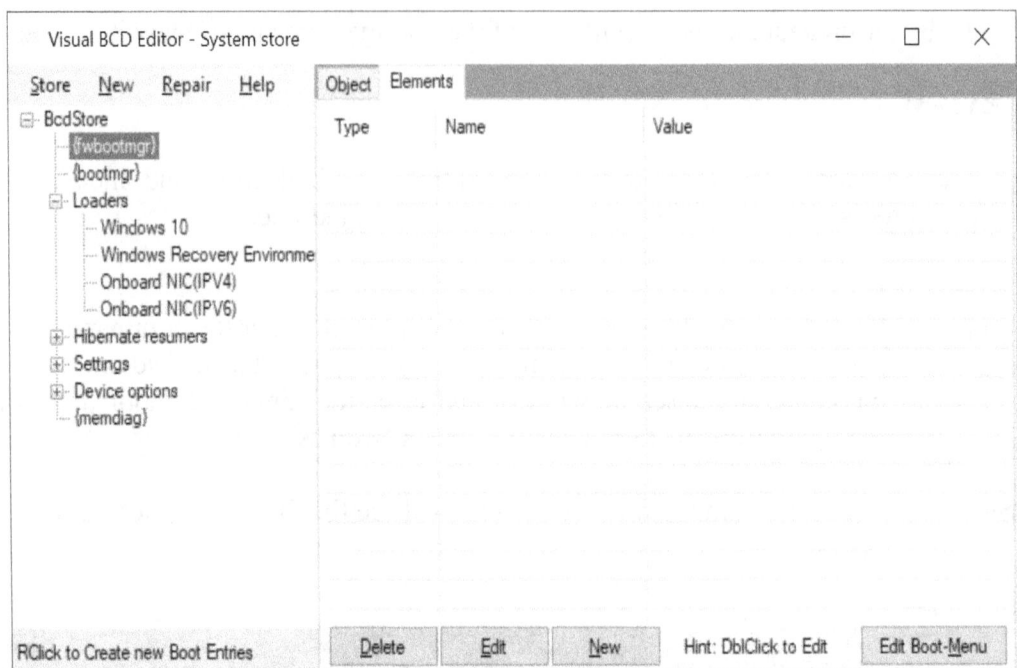

Figure 7-2

Step 6: Complete the following for the Visual BCD Editor view for your student system.

        Application Device   _____

        Application Path   _____

        Description   _____

        Timeout   _____

Step 7: Expand the Loaders option. Complete the following:

    Identify the options under the Loaders path.

               _____

               _____

               _____

               _____

               _____

Step 8: Expand the first option. The title of this option will correspond to the operating system you are using. See Figure 7-3 below as an example.

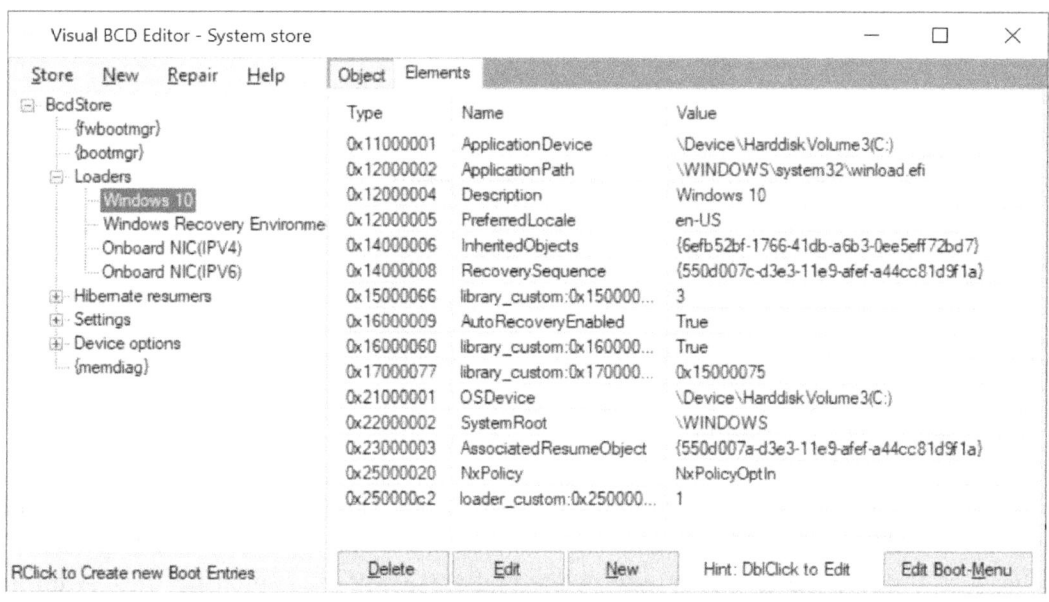

Figure 7-3

Step 9: Complete the following:
Application Device _____
Application Path _____

Step 10: Why is the application device and application path different from that in question # 6? Explain and be specific!

Step 11: How could this information be significant in a forensic examination of a hard drive?

Step 12: Compare the information provided from the Visudal BCD Edit view to that of the bcdedit.exe command output. They should be identical! Are they?

STUDENT SUMMARY:

1. What did you learn from this exercise?

2. What is the purpose of the Windows Registry?

3. Consider the following scenario:

   An employee has been using their office computer for malicious purposes. The employee suspects their activities may have been noticed by their employer and decide to delete and erase any incriminating files. After all files have been erased, what recourse does the corporate computer examiner have to try to discover actions taken on the computer?

Evaluators Review of Learners Performance

1   2   3   4   5

Exercise # 8
Locate Encrypted Files on Disk

OBJECTIVE:

To understand how specific file structures can be identified and exported on a storage device.

OVERVIEW:

There are several methods for identifying password protected files on a disk. Using forensic examination software is one method for locating. Individually hunting for them is another. There are automated programs that will scan for files noting specific signature patterns such as embedded hash values. One such program for automated detection is Passware Encryption Analyzer. Passware Encryption Analyzer should have been demonstrated to you by your instructor.

PART I
Locate and Recover Encrypted Files

Step 1: Download Password Encryption Analyzer and Passware Kit Business Demo and install them on your student workstation.

Step 2: On your Desktop, create a Word 2016 file. Encrypt it with a two alpha character password. Do not include numbers or special characters. The demo version of Passware Kit that we are going to use in this exercise has a one-minute password recovery limitation. Therefore, for demonstration purposes it is imperative that your file only contain two alpha characters.

Step 3: Move your newly created password protected Word file to somewhere else on the drive. The root directory, the System 32 folder, or some other location would be good.

Step 4: Run the encryption analyzer program. Was your password protected file located?

Step 5: Right-click on your password protected .docx file and select the Recover Password option. The Recover File Password window will appear with the selected file name.

A recovery options window will appear and under the Structure tab you will be asked if you have any information about the password of the file, such as if it contains a dictionary word, a non-dictionary word, or if you know nothing about the file. Select the 'Other' option.

Step 6: Select the 'Settings' tab and set the length to 2 – 2 and the 'Letters' option. Since you created the password and know the parameters, this will speed up the recovery process. In a corporate environment, the password policy would dictate the parameters for this setting.

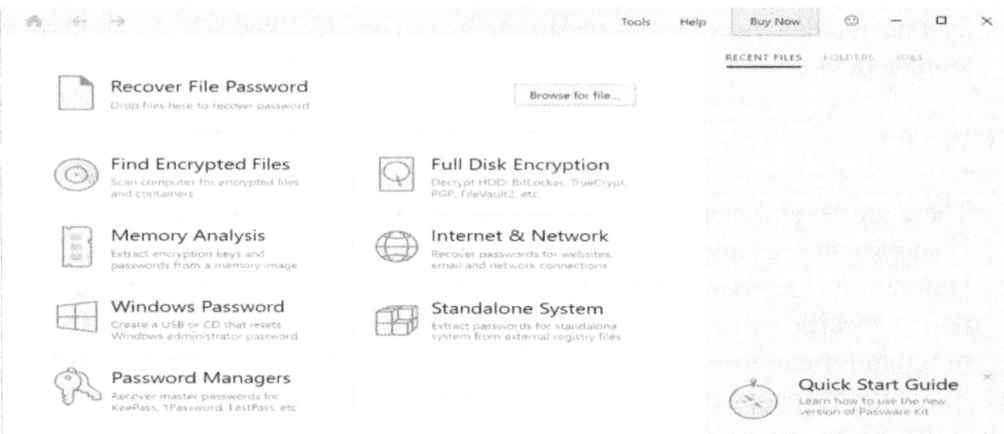

Figure 8-1

Step 7: Click the 'Recover' option. The brute force recovery process will begin.

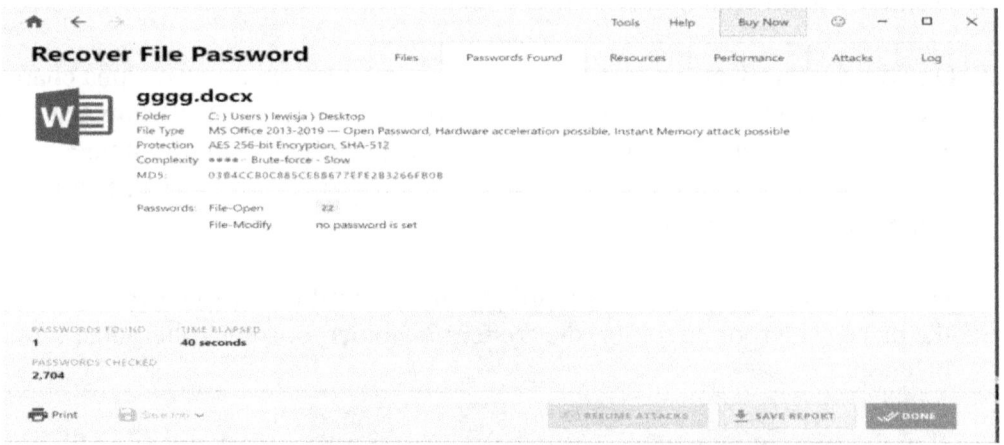

Figure 8-2

Step 8: Was your password recovered?   Yes   No

Step98: How long did it take for your password to be recovered? _____

Step 10 Close the Passware Encryption Analyzer program.

Step 11: Your instructor should now provide you with a folder titled 'Test Folder'. This folder contains several files titled gggg.docx, Word1, Word2 and Word3. Do not password protect these three files. See Figure 8-3 below.

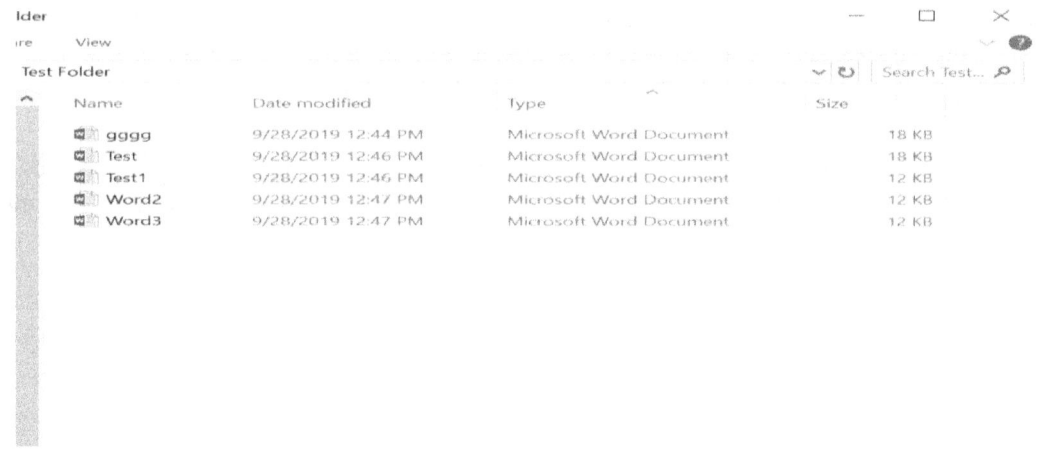

Figure 8-3

Step 12: Initialize Passware Encryption Analyzer.

Step 13: Uncheck all Scan options. Select 'Selected Drives and Folders' option and Navigate to the Test Folder.

Step 14: Click Scan. You should see the following display.

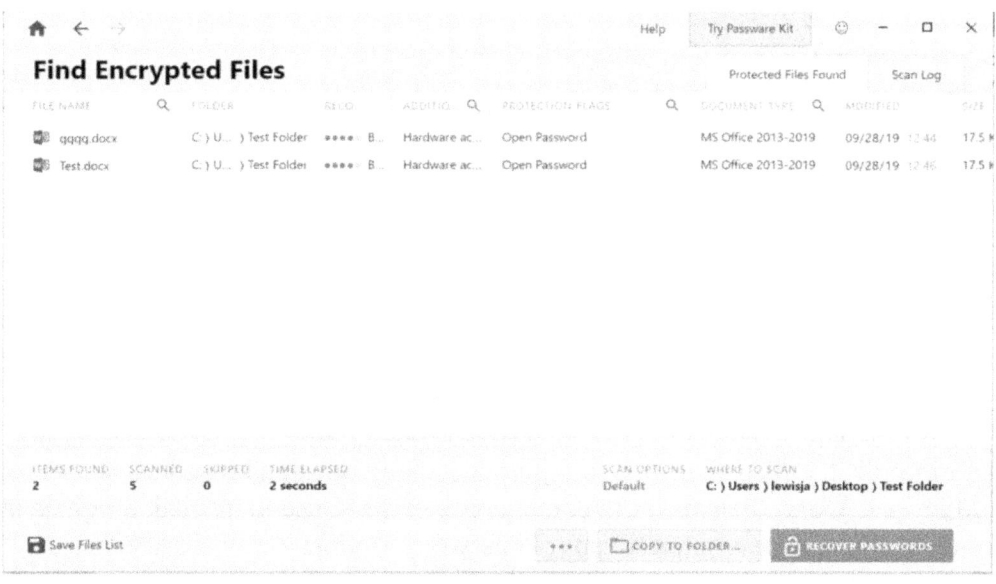

Figure 8-4

Step 15: Were only the encrypted files identified?   Yes   No

PART II
Locate and Recover Encrypted Files

Step 16: Create a Word document and apply a two-character password, using only lower case characters. Put some text inside the document then hide this document somewhere on your student system, like in a subdirectory.

Step 17: With another student, exchange seat positions and using the techniques used in this forensics exercise, locate and extract the password of the hidden file, and answer the following questions:

    a. What is the name of the file you discovered? _____

    b. What is the password of the file you discovered? _____

    c. What text was inside the password-protected file?

    _____

    _____

    _____

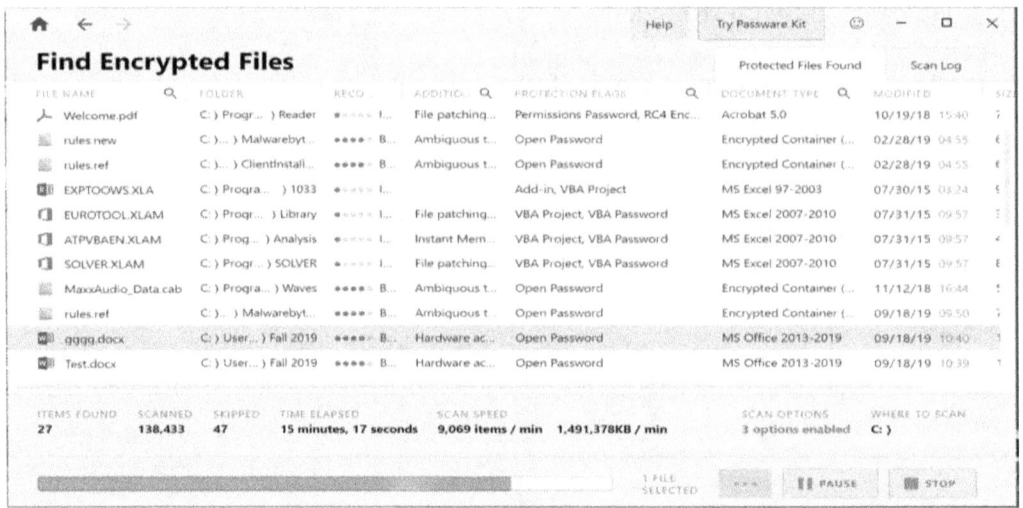

Figure 8-5

As an example, the files identified in Figure 8-5, gggg.docx and test.docx were created using Microsoft Word 2016 and both contain passwords. Once identified, a right-click on the file invokes a window with a 'Recover Password' option. Passware also has a password recovery tool that can be used with this program.

STUDENT SUMMARY:

1. What did you learn from this exercise?

2. Explain how password protected files are identified as being encrypted.

3. Identify two components of an effective password policy for your organization that would provide reasonable protection of company documents that contain IP (Intellectual Property).

Evaluators Review of Learners Performance

1   2   3   4   5

Forensics Exercise # 9
Examining Small Media Devices Using WinHex

OBJECTIVE:

To become familiar with how data on a disk can be located by a string search using any hex editing tool, regardless of how the operating system views it.

OVERVIEW:

Computer and digital forensic examiners must have a working knowledge of the internals of a computer system. This includes system board, adapter boards, peripheral devices, connectors and jumpers. While working in the field as a computer examiner you will encounter a wide range of technologies both new and old. Configuration of systems for computer and forensic examiners is necessary for accurate, effective and non-damaging handling of systems and peripherals. The WinHex editor can be downloaded from the web site: http://www.x-ways.net/winhex/.

STEPS:

1. Insert a small capacity media device such as a thumb drive into the student system. The purpose for selecting a small capacity media is to reduce the amount of time searching through hundreds of thousands of pages on a larger media.

2. Using Notepad or Wordpad create a text file on this media and save it with the name WinHexFile1.txt. Place a copy of this file on the student Desktop for future reference.

3. Visit several websites and save several pages from each to the target media. Include some.pdf files and other formats.

4. Delete the WinHexFile1. This media will now be treated as evidence.

5. Remove the media and write protect it if it has write protection capability or place a write blocker on it if available. If a write blocker is not available, for demonstration purposes, proceed without one.

6. Insert the media back into disk drive.

7. Open Win Hex, select Tools, Open Disk, then select the target media.

8. Click on Search function – select Text

9. Enter any word from the text file you created into the search window and click OK.

10. Did you find the word from the deleted text file? You should have. Explain why or why not!

    If you did not find the word you searched for try to discover why. It may be because you saved the file in a Word 2007 or above format which does not store text information in raw native ASCII or Unicode as previous versions.

11. Close Win Hex

12. Go to 'My Computer' and right click on the device, select Format – then Quick Format

13. Open Win Hex again

14. Select the same media device and search for same word as in step # 9.

    Did you find the words you searched for?

    What happened and why?

15. Go to my computer, right click on the device and select format.

16. Open Win Hex and perform same word search.

    Did you find the words you searched for?

    What happened and why?

17. Scroll down until you see a repeating pattern of hex values. This is the format pattern for the particular type of media. Various media devices use different format patterns. There would be nothing of evidentiary or intellectual value in this pattern.

18. Exit WinHex.

19. Create a Word 2016 or above text file and title it WinHexFile2.docx. Copy and paste the same text from the WinHexFile1.txt backup file into the WinHexFile2.docx file. Save the file on the target media.

20. Open WinHex and navigate to the target media. Perform the same search string on this media as you did with previous steps.

        Did you find the words you searched for?

        What happened and why?

21. Explain the different results from all three of the search operations above. Why were some search strings able to identify the words while others were not.

STUDENT SUMMARY:

1. What did you learn from this exercise?

2. How could WinHex aid the computer examiner when dealing with search strings on media? (Hint: consider the difference in time required between using WinHex and creating a bit stream image and then indexing that image as is done with other forensic software).

Evaluators Review of Learners Performance

        1   2   3   4   5

Forensics Exercise # 10
Comparing File Structures Using WinHex

OBJECTIVE:

To demonstrate how various text editing tools such as Word, Wordpad, Notepad, etc, provide additional formatting information to text files and the various information leakage resulting from formatting.

OVERVIEW:

You are to create several files using different text editors. You will then view those files without the native text editor and using debug.

STEPS:

1. Open Notepad with a file name of File1.txt

   Insert the following text into the File1.txt file:

   ABCDEFGHIJKLMNOPQRSTUVWXYZ
   0123456789
   This is the end of the file!

   Close File1.txt and save on either a blank media or the Desktop.

2. Open Wordpad with a file name of File2. Use the default filename extension.

   Insert the following text into the File2.txt file:

   ABCDEFGHIJKLMNOPQRSTUVWXYZ
   0123456789
   This is the end of the file!

   Close File2 and save in the same location as File1.txt

3. Open Microsoft Word with a file name of File3. Use the default filename extension. Save the file as a Word 2003 document if possible.

   Insert the following text into the File3.txt file:

   ABCDEFGHIJKLMNOPQRSTUVWXYZ
   0123456789
   This is the end of the file!

   Close File3 and save in the same location as File1 and File2.

4. Open Microsoft Word with a file name of File4. Use the default filename extension. Select Tools, Options, Security. Enter a two character password such as zz, ww, dd, etc. Save this file as a 2016 or later document.

   Insert the following text into the File4.txt file:

   ABCDEFGHIJKLMNOPQRSTUVWXYZ
   0123456789
   This is the end of the file!

   Close File4.

5. Initialize the WinHex program. Open each file and navigate throughout the file and view the information contained within.

   a. What similarities do you notice among the files?

   b. What differences do you notice among the files?

   c. How can you tell what type of file you are looking at by what WinHex shows in the hex window? (Hint: Take a look at the Metadata).

6. Based upon this file information, what type of file are you dealing with?

   ```
   00000000   D0 CF 11 E0 A1 B1 1A E1  00 00 00 00 00 00 00 00   ÐÏ.à¡±.á........
   00000010   00 00 00 00 00 00 00 00  3E 00 03 00 FE FF 09 00   ........>...þÿ..
   00000020   06 00 00 00 00 00 00 00  00 00 00 00 12 00 00 00   ...............
   00000030   00 00 00 00 00 00 00 00  00 10 00 00 77 08 00 00   u..........w...
   ```

7. Based upon this file information, what type of file are you dealing with?

   ```
   00000000   50 4B 0304 14 00 06 00  08 00 00 00 21 00 10 DA   PK...............
   00000010   00 00 00 00 00 00 00 00  3E 00 03 00 FE FF 09 00   ........>...þÿ..
   00000020   06 00 00 00 00 00 00 00  00 00 00 00 12 00 00 00   .................
   00000030   75 08 00 00 00 00 00 00  00 10 00 00 77 08 00 00   u..........w...
   ```

STUDENT SUMMARY

1.   What did you learn from this exercise?

2.   What does the hex pattern 55 AA indicate on a hard disk drive?

3.   Explain the difference between Notepad and Word Pad. Under what conditions or circumstances would a user create a Notepad file as opposed to a Word document?

Evaluators Review of Learners Performance

1   2   3   4   5

73

Forensics Exercise # 11
Reconstruct Damaged or Corrupted Excel Files

OBJECTIVE:

To recover damaged or corrupted Excel and Word files using both manual recovery and automated tools.

OVERVIEW:

You will be provided with a corrupted Microsoft Excel and Word 2016 file. You will manually recover it using WinHex, and recover it using automated recovery software.

PART I – Excel File Recovery

STEPS:

1. You have been provided an Excel 2016 file with a corrupted header. The file name is 'ExcelCorruptedFile 1'. Make a copy of this file and name it 'ExcelCorruptedFile1Copy'.

    Note: In a real forensic examination, reconstruction or recovery, you should never work on the original. Make a copy of it and name it something to indicate it is a copy of the original. The example provided above is to use the word 'Copy' in the file name.

2. Try to open the 'ExcelCorruptedFile1Copy' File using Excel. You should receive an error message. (Error messages and amount of information vary depending upon how much of the header is corrupted).

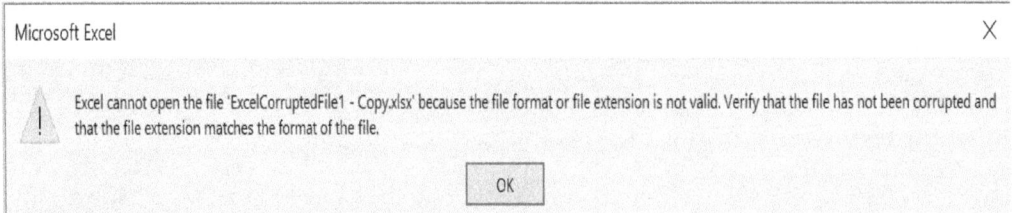

Figure 9-1

3. Click 'Ok'. The file should terminate trying to open.

4. Open Excel 2016 and create another file and save it as 'ReferenceFile1'.

5. Open WinHex and load both files, 'ExcelCorruptedFile1Copy' and 'ReferenceFile1'.

6. Examine the 'ExcelCorruptedFile1Copy' file header. What do you see that may be of a concern?

_____

7. Examine the 'ReferenceFile1' file header. What do you see different between both file headers?

_____

8. Switching between both file tabs in WinHex, reconstruct the corrupted file with the same hexadecimal byte sequence for the first two lines of the non-corrupted file.

9. Once you have recreated the file header, save the newly reconstructed file and minimize WinHex.

10. Try to open the reconstructed file.

Does the file open? _____

What words are contained in the body of the document?

_____

_____

Congratulations! You have opened this file by manually reconstructing the header.

11. There are automated file reconstruction programs available online for Microsoft Office products. Locate one that will reconstruct an Excel 2016 file and download it to your student system.

12. Using steps previously performed, create your own corrupted Excel 2016 file by altering the first two lines of the header using WinHex. Save the newly created and corrupted file MyCorruptedFile.xlsx.

13. Run the reconstruction program on the MyCorruptedFile.xlsx and identify the following:

    a. What automated recovery tool did you locate?

    _____

b. Was it effective in recovering a corrupted Excel 2016 file with a corrupted header?

Note: If you were not successful in recovering the corrupted file, notify your instructor.

PART II – Word File Recovery

You will be provided with a corrupted Microsoft Word 2016 file. You will manually recover it using WinHex, and recover it using automated recovery software.

Steps:

14. You have been provided with a corrupted Word 2016 file with the filename of CorruptedFile1.docx. If you do not have this file, contact your instructor. Place this file into a folder titled 'Corrupted Files'.

15. Make a copy of this file and name it 'CorruptedFile1Copy'.

Note: In a real forensic examination, reconstruction or recovery, you should never work on the original. Make a copy of it and name it something to indicate it is a copy of the original. The example provided above is to use the word 'Copy' in the file name.

16. Try to open the CorruptedFile1Copy file using Microsoft Word 2016 (or 2019 if that is what is available to you.) You should receive an error message. (Error messages and amount of information vary depending upon how much of the header is corrupted). You should receive the following error message.

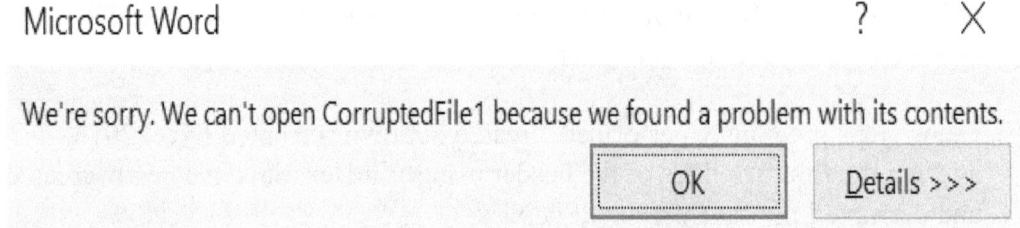

Figure 9-2

17. If you receive the above message, select Ok. You should be presented with the next window.

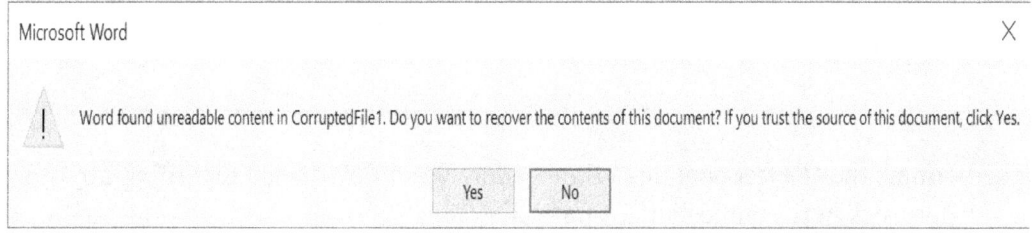

Figure 9-3

Select 'No'. For educational purposes as we do not want Microsoft Word to try to recover the file, we want to demonstrate how to do it manually. Not all automated recoveries are successful.

18. Open Word 2016 and create another file and save it as 'ReferenceFile1'.

19. You should have WinHex on your Desktop. Open the WinHex program. Select 'File', 'Open', then navigate to 'CorruptedFile1Copy.docx', then select 'Open' in the 'Open Files' window.

20. Repeat the previous step and open the 'ReferenceFile1' file.

21. Your WinHex window should have both file tabs displayed as shown below in Figure 9-4.

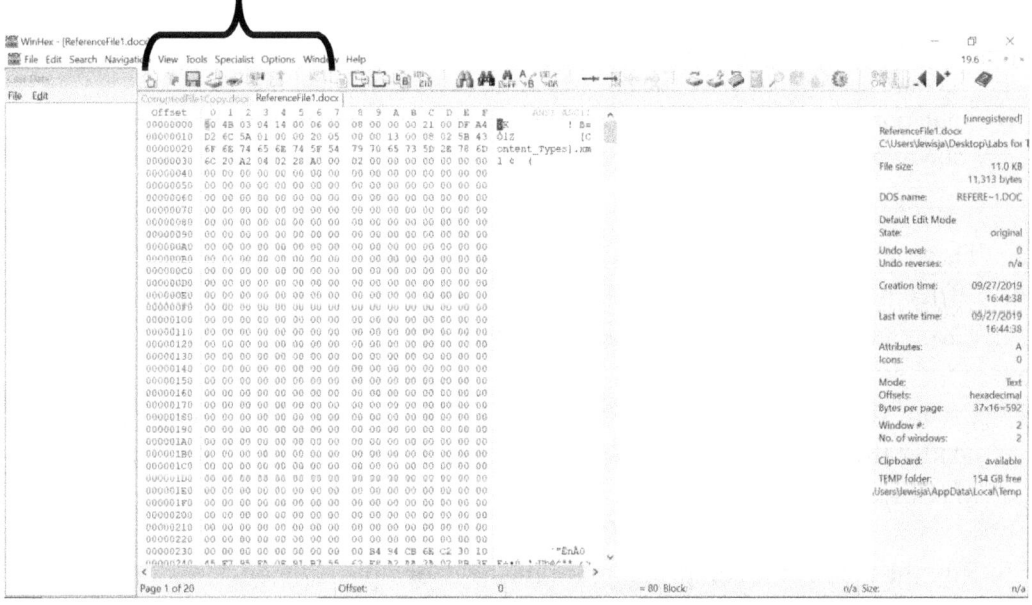

Figure 9-4

22. Examine the 'CorruptedFile1Copy file header. What do you see that may be of a concern?

_____

23. Examine the 'ReferenceFile1' file header. What do you see regarding any differences between headers of both files?

_____

24. Switching between both file tabs in WinHex, reconstruct the corrupted file with the same hexadecimal byte sequence for the first two lines of the non-corrupted file.

25. Once you have recreated the file header, save the newly reconstructed file and minimize WinHex.

26. Try to open the reconstructed file.

      Does the file open? _____

      What words are contained in the body of the document?

      _____

      _____

      Congratulations! You have opened this file by reconstructing the header.

      NOTE: Files in this exercise were created using Microsoft Word 2016. If you reconstruct a Word 2016 file, Word 2007 or earlier will not open it. If this is your situation, perform an Internet search for a suitable Word document viewer program, download it and verify the file will open.

27. There are automated file reconstruction programs available online for Microsoft Office products. Locate one that will reconstruct a Word 2016 file and download it to your student system, or ask your instructor for a copy.

28. Create your own corrupted Word 2016 file by altering the first two lines of the header using WinHex. Save the newly created and corrupted file MyCorruptedFile.docx.

29. Run the reconstruction program on the MyCorruptedFile.docx and identify the following:

      a. What automated recovery tool did you locate?

      _____

b. Was it effective in recovering a corrupted Word 2016 file with a corrupted header?

If you were not successful in recovering the corrupted file, notify your instructor.

STUDENT SUMMARY:

1. What did you learn from this exercise?

2. Consider three ways that a text file could have a corrupted header.

   a. _____

   b. _____

   c. _____

Evaluators Review of Learners Performance

1   2   3   4   5

Forensics Exercise # 12
Identifying File Types by Extension

OBJECTIVE:

To become familiar with the large number of file extension types and how to recognize them.

OVERVIEW:

During a computer forensic evaluation, you are very likely to encounter file types which are unknown to you. You are to provide a description for the following file header types. You must also understand that just because a file has a particular extension does not mean that is the true format of that file. Often the metadata of that file must be examined to provide additional insight into what created the file. One technique to confuse the application believed to be able to open a file it created is to change the extension, thus it may appear corrupted to the user and the application will not recognize it.

This particular exercise is optional and at the discretion of the instructor.

STEPS:

1. Do a search on-line for web sites that identify file extensions. A good web site to visit is www.filext.com.

2. Identify each file type by extension.

FILE TYPE	FILE EXTENSION
_____	png
_____	gif
_____	tif;tiff
_____	bmp
_____	csv
_____	art
_____	jpg;jpeg

_____	pcx
_____	wmf
_____	emf
_____	dwg
_____	psd
_____	rtf
_____	xml
_____	html;htm;
_____	php3;php4;
_____	phtml;shtml
_____	eml
_____	dbx
_____	pst
_____	xls.
_____	doc;doc;
_____	xls;
_____	dot;
_____	ppt;
_____	xla;
_____	ppa;
_____	pps;
_____	pot
_____	mdb;mda;mde;mdt

_____ wpd

_____ eps.or.ps;ps;eps

_____ pdf

_____ qdf

_____ pwl

_____ zip

_____ rar

_____ gz

_____ bz2

_____ arj

_____ wav

_____ avi

_____ ram

_____ rm

_____ mpg;mpeg

_____ mov

_____ asf

_____ mid

STUDENT SUMMARY:

1. What did you learn from this exercise?

Evaluators Review of Learners Performance

1   2   3   4   5

Exercise # 13 Examining the Registry for Forensic Information

OBJECTIVE:

To examine the Windows registry for use and configuration information that may be beneficial in a forensics examination.

OVERVIEW:

If there were to be a comparison to computer system hardware where the CPU is the brain of the hardware, the Windows Registry could be considered the brain of the operating system. The Registry is a dynamically created database, meaning, that it only exists when the opearating system is loaded. When the operating system is not loaded, the Windows Registry is not one large file, but a set of independent and discrete files known as Hives. Each Hive is hierachly structured in a tree like structure consisting of a root key (known as the Hive) of the tree, subkeys and their respective values.

The registry hives and their respective locations are identified as follows:

HKEY_LOCAL_MACHINE\SYSTEM	*\system32\config\system*
HKEY_LOCAL_MACHINE\SAM	*\system32\config\sam*
HKEY_LOCAL_MACHINE\SECURITY	*\system32\config\security*
HKEY_LOCAL_MACHINE\SOFTWARE	*\system32\config\software*
HKEY_USERS\UserProfile	*\winnt\profiles\username*
HKEY_USERS.DEFAULT	*\system32\config\default*

Steps:

1. What version of Windows operating system are you using?

   a. Windows 7
   b. Windows 10
   c. Other _____

2. Open Internet Explorer (Not Edge or any other browser at this point). Navigate to three or four web addresses. After you have browsed several websites, close Internet Explorer.

3. Open or create several Microsoft Word documents and then close them. Repeat this for Excel and Power Point.

4. If your instructor has not provided you with a copy of the program ROT-13, perform an Internet search and download it.

5. Enter the 'Regedit' command in the Windows Search box located on the bottom right of the toolbar.

6. As stated, some versions of Windows have more hives than others. Identify the specific hives on your system.

HKEY_____

HKEY_____

HKEY_____

HKEY_____

HKEY_____

HKEY_____

7. Expand the HKEY_CURRENT_USER hive and spend just a few minutes getting familiar with some of the subkeys. When you are done, collapse the hive back to the original 4 or 6 hives.

8. Expand the HKEY_CURRENT_USER hive again and navigate to the following path:

HKEY_CURRENT_USER\Software\Microsoft\Windows\Winlogon\PasswordExpiryNotification

Is there a 'NotShownReason' value?   Yes   No

If Yes, right click on it and identify the contents here.

_____

9. How does the above value in this specific key relate to your login information for this particular operating system?

10. Collapse the registry key back to the original hive configuration.

11. Expand the HKEY_CURRENT_USER hive again to the following path:

HKEY_CURRENT_USER\Software\Microsoft\Windows\CurrentVersion\Explorer\User Assist

You should see several subkeys with various non-distinguishing names. Open some of these subkeys until you find one with a count subkey that contains various value names that are also non-distinguishing.

NOTE: Do not modify any of the data presented in this window. Inputting an incorrect value could cause the operating system to crash or freeze.

12. Selecting only one at a time, right-click on one of the value names, select Modify. The Value Name will appear in an 'Edit Binary Value' window. Highlight the Value Name, right click and select 'Copy'. For example, the value name you select may be,

P:\Hfref\Choyvp\Qrfxgbc\Jbeq 2016.yax

13. Open the ROT-13 Encoder / Decoder program and paste the copied value name into the 'Enter Text Here' window.

14. Click on the Encrypt/Decrypt option. What appears in the Encrypted/Decrypted text window?

_____

15. Collapse the hive back to the root configuration.

16. Expand the HKEY_CURRENT_USER hive to the following location;

    HKEY_CURRENT_USER\Software\Microsoft\Windows\CurrentVersion\Explorer
    \ComDlg32\OpenSavePidlMRU\docx

17. You should see several subkeys that are identified with various file extensions such as .docx, .pdf, .xlxs, .pptx, etc, as shown in Figure 13-1 below.

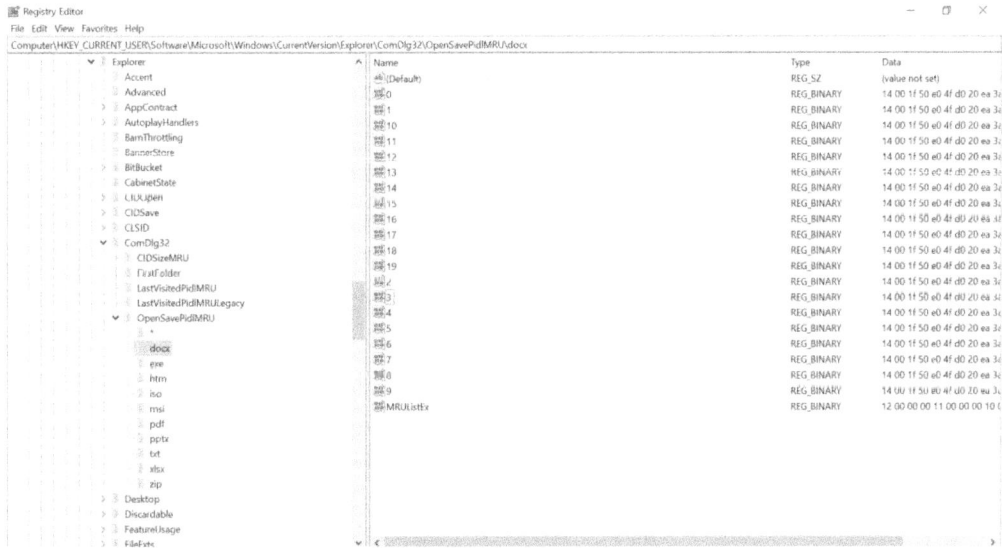

Figure 13-2

18. Open one of the more familiar named subkeys such as .docx. Are several value names presented in the right window?

Yes   No

19. If yes, select one, right click on it, and select Modify. The Edit Binary Value window will appear as shown below.

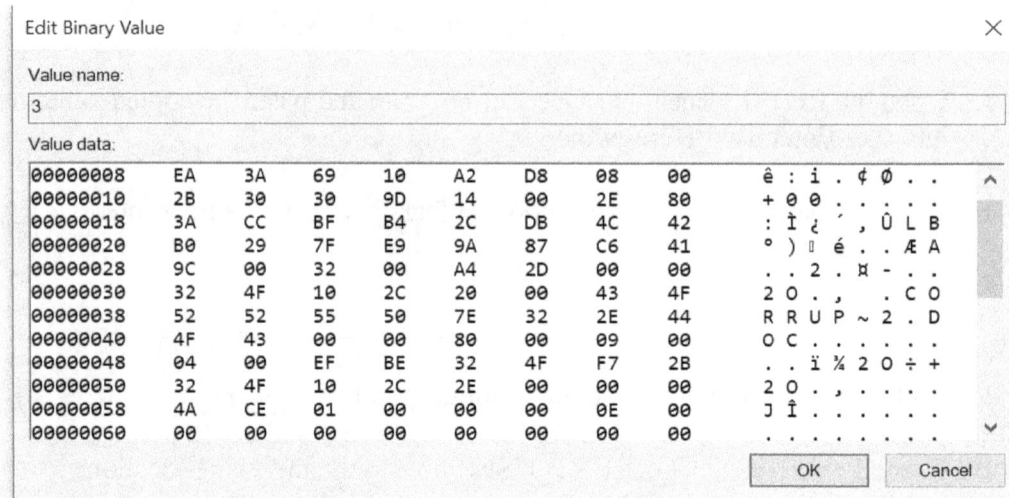

Figure 13-3

20. Can you identify any of the Microsoft Word file names you opened or created previously in this exercise, or from prior use on this system? If yes, identify their names below. If not, notify your instructor.

.docx files

_____

_____

_____

21. Repeat these steps for the .xlsx, .pptx or any other subkey values you desire to examine. Identify them below:

.xlsx files

_____

_____

_____

.pptx files

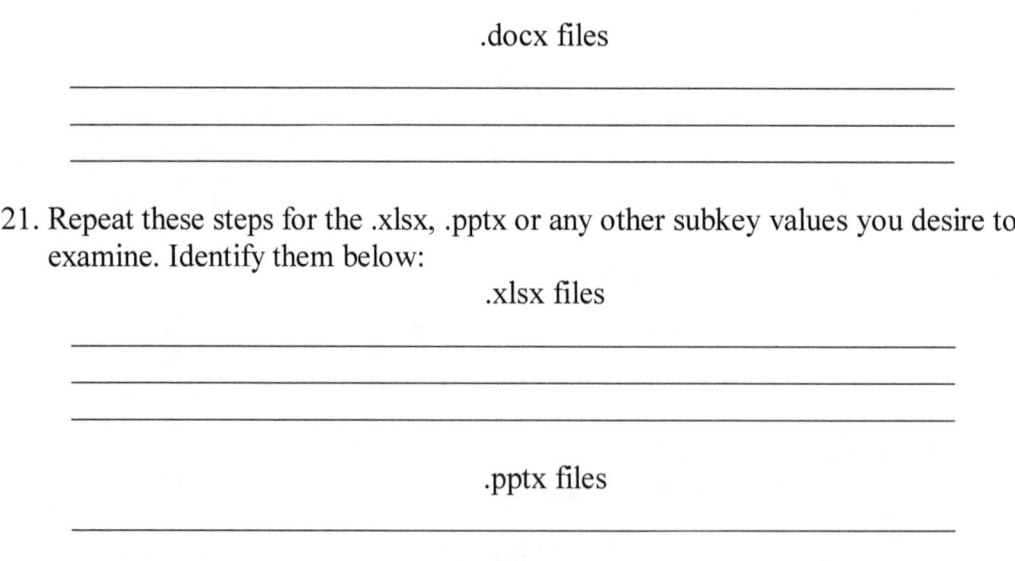

_____

_____

_____

.Other file extensions

_____

_____

_____

_____

22. Navigate to the following registry key;

HKEY_CURRENT_USER\Software\Microsoft\Internet Explorer\TypedURLs

23. Can you identify the websites you entered previously, and / or other websites visited by this system?

Yes   No

24. Identify a few of these websites:

a. _____
b. _____
c. _____
d. _____
e. _____

25. Navigate to the following registry key:

HKEY_LOCAL_MACHINE\SYSTEM\CurrentControlSet\Enum\USBSTOR

a. How many USB devices are identified as having been connected to this system? _____

b. List them as shown in Figure 13-4.

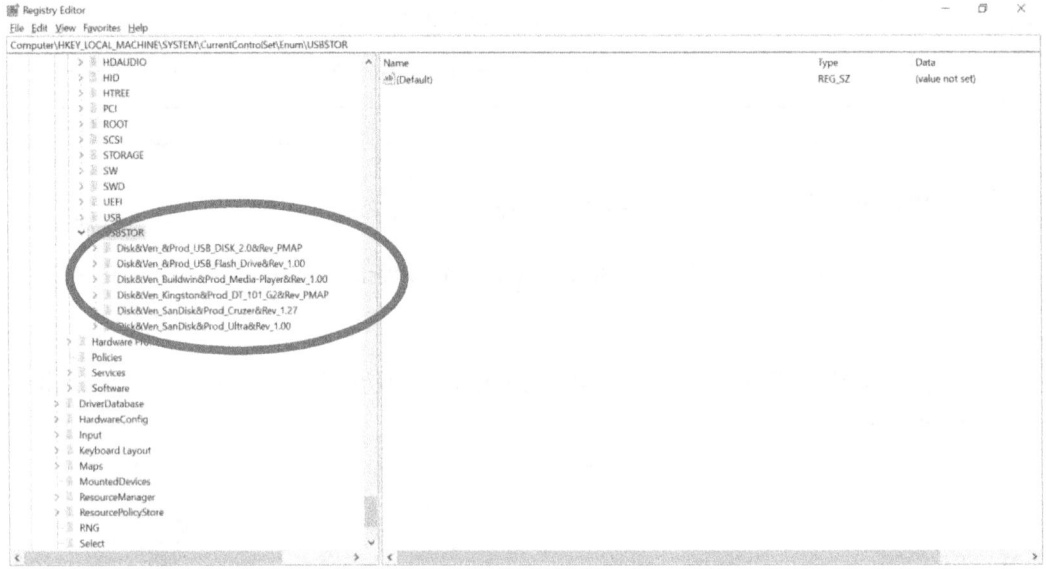

Figure 13-4

USBSTORE

_____

_____

_____

_____

_____

_____

26. Expand one of the media devices identified under USBSTORE as shown in Figure 13-5 on the next page.

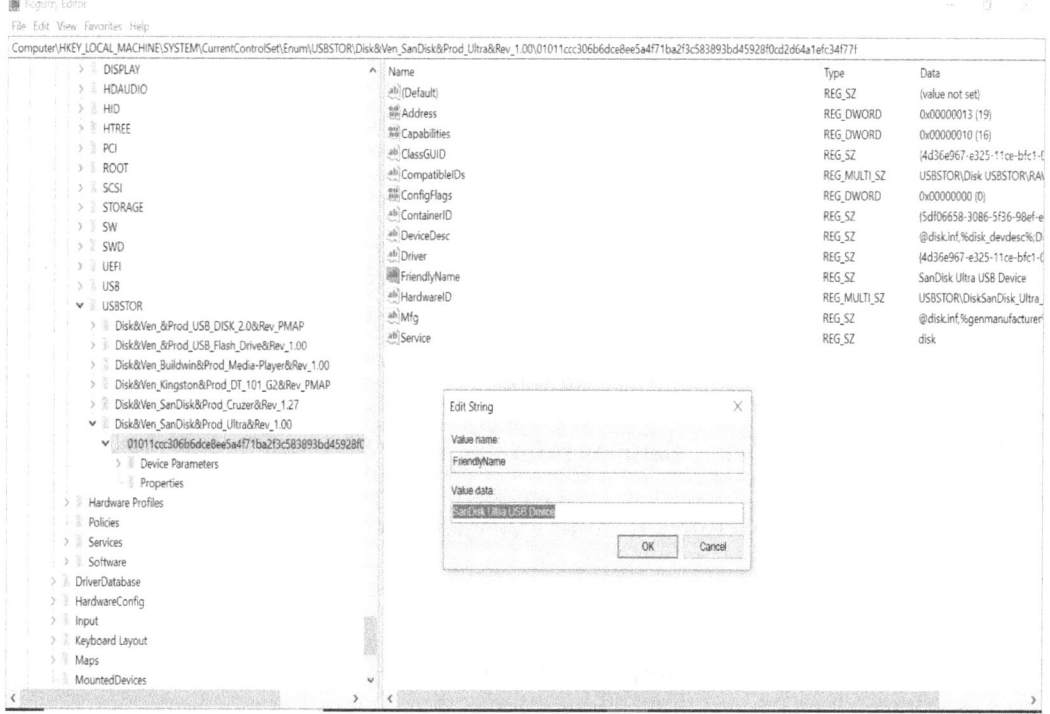

Figure 13-5

27. From the media device you selected under USBSTORE, identify the following information from the subkey values:

       Friendly Name   _____

       MFG   _____

       DeviceDesc   _____

   b. What impression do you have regarding the role and information contained within the registry?

28. Close the Registry Editor.

NOTE: This next step may not be fully functional on the latest versions of Windows operating systems.

29. Open MRUBlaster. Identify the four options available.

      a. _____

      b. _____

      c. _____

      d. _____

30. Select the Settings option. How many options are identified as being able to be cleaned? _____

31. Select the Go to Plugins option. What cleaning options are available under Plugins?

      a. _____

      b. _____

32. Select the Back to Main Menu option.

33. Select Settings, Delete Settings from Registry. What message is presented?

34. Close the Delete Settings from Registry window without selecting Ok.

35. Select and run the Scan option.

How many total items were identified as being able to be cleaned? _____

36. Select the Show Results option.

      a.   What type of information has MRUBlaster identified as being able to be eliminated?

37. Select the Main Menu option.

38. Select Scan, then Clean Now. You should be presented with the following window.

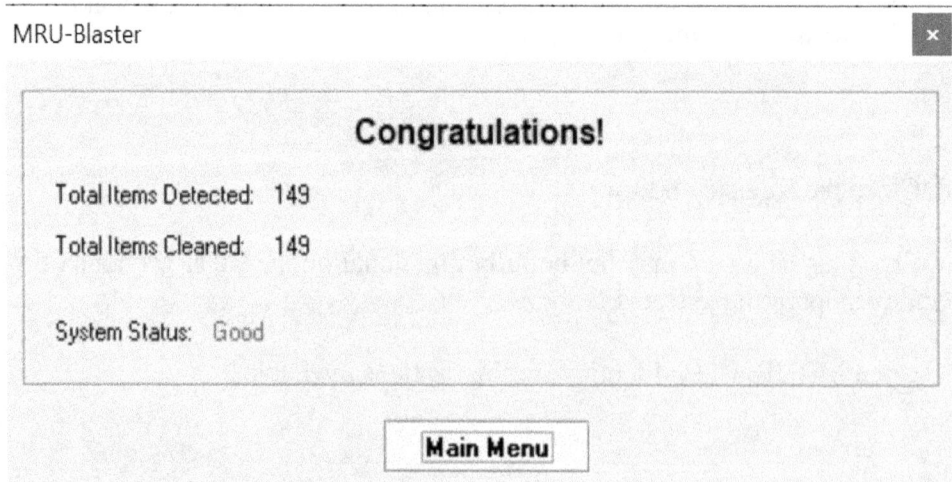

Figure 13-6

90

39. Close and exit MRUBlaster.

40. Open the registry again by entering the regedit command in the search window.

41. Reexamine the registry again and identify any differences from when you first examined the registry and now by viewing the same registry keys as you did in previous steps.

STUDENT SUMMARY:

1. What did you learn from this exercise?

2. You have examined an employee's hard drive and discovered there are no registry entries. Identify two likely scenarios that might cause this.

   a. _____

   b. _____

3. Perform a search and identify two other registry cleaning tools.

Name of Registry Cleaning Tool	Download Location	Performance Specifications	Free or Purchase

Evaluators Review of Learners Performance

1   2   3   4   5

Forensics Exercise # 14
Identifying and Recovering Password Protected Files

EXERCISE CURRENTLY UNDER REVISION

See instructor for addendum

Forensics Exercise # 15
Forensics Known Plaintext ZIP File Password Recovery

EXERCISE CURRENTLY UNDER REVISION

See instructor for addendum

Forensics Exercise # 16
Introduction to Media Imaging using FTK Imager

OBJECTIVE:

To install the FTK Imager program, and create a bit stream image of a target media in preparation for performing a forensic examination.

OVERVIEW:

You are provided with a copy of the FTK Imager program. Installation and use of it should have been demonstrated to you. FTK Imager is a software bit stream data acquisition tool that creates a forensically sound duplicate of the original target media. It is used as a media acquisition tool that will calculate a hash value on each individual files and folders, and the entire image for validation of bit-by-bit validation against the original.

PART I – INSTALL FTK IMAGER

STEPS

1. The FTK Imager version 4.1.1.1 installation program should be provided to you. Place it on the Desktop of your student system.

Figure 16-1

2. Right-click on the installation icon as shown above, and select 'Run as Administrator'. You will be presented with the following screen as shown in Figure16-2. Select the 'Yes' option.

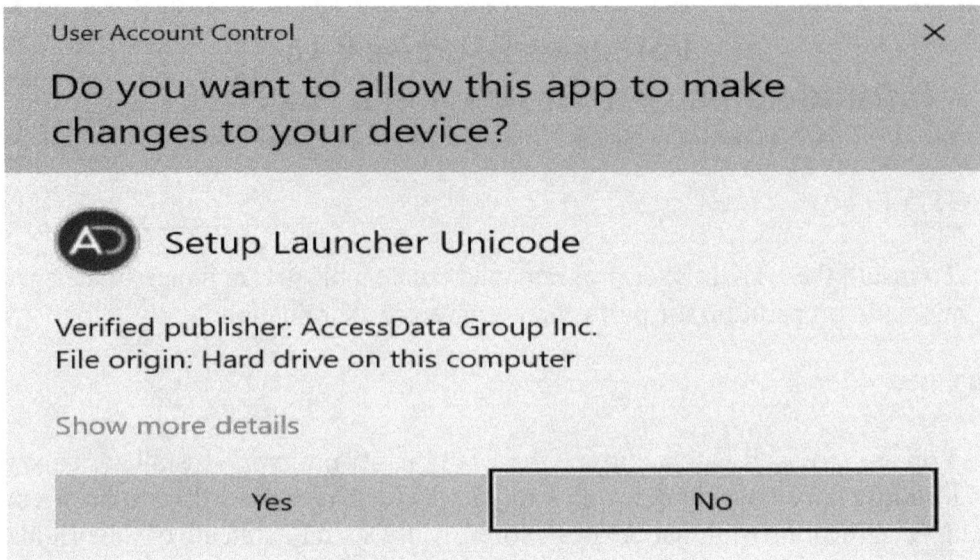

Figure 16-2

3. The Installation process will begin.

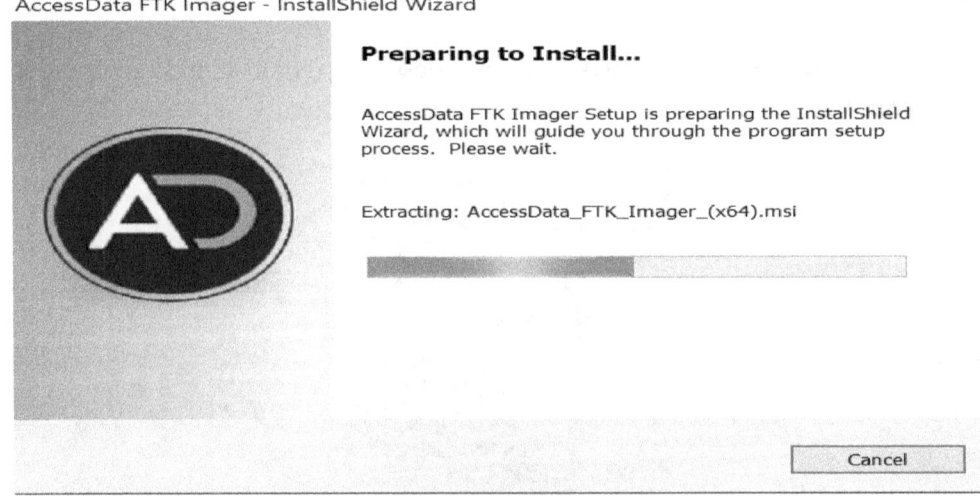

Figure 16-3

4. When the Setup has completed, the InstallShield Wizard window will be presented. Select 'Next'.

Figure 16-4

5. The End-User License Agreement window will appear. Review the terms and conditions when you are ready, select the 'I accept the terms in the license agreement' radial button and click 'Next'.

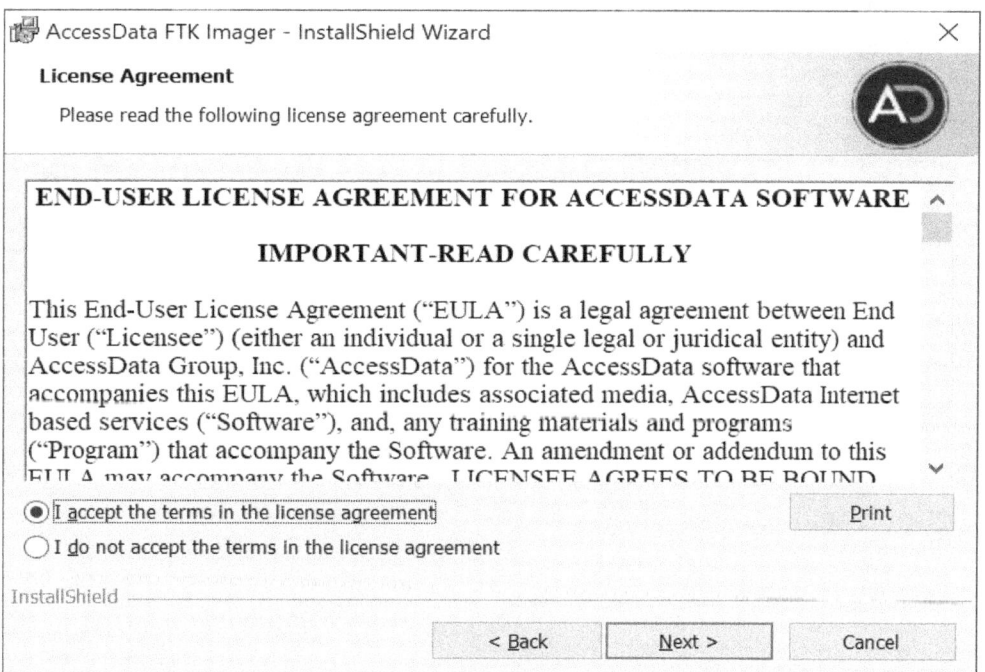

Figure 16-5

6. When the Destination Folder component of the InstallShield Wizard window appears, accept the default destination C:\Program Files\AccessData\.

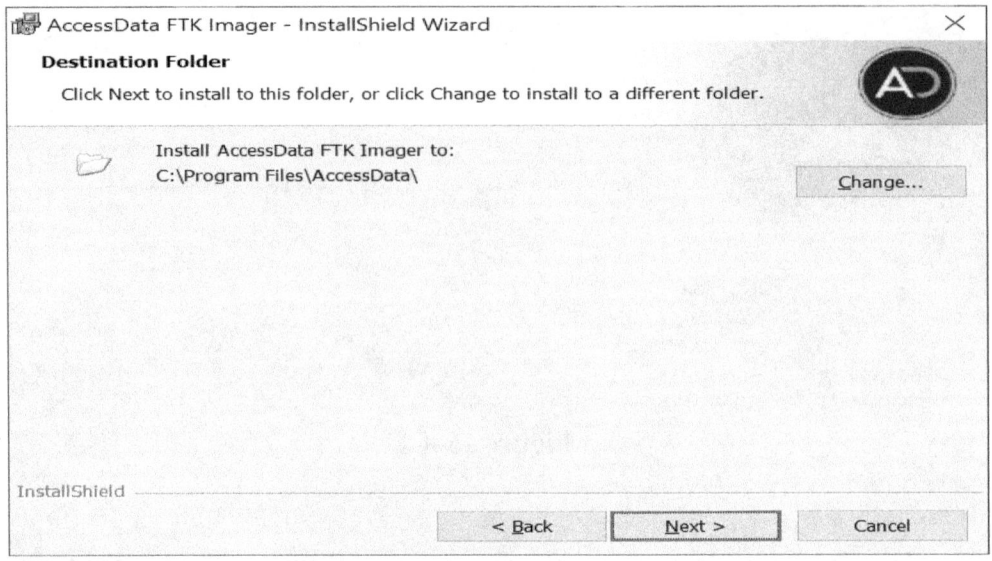

Figure 16-6

7. Your installation setup sequence will be prepared at this point to complete. Select the 'Install' option.

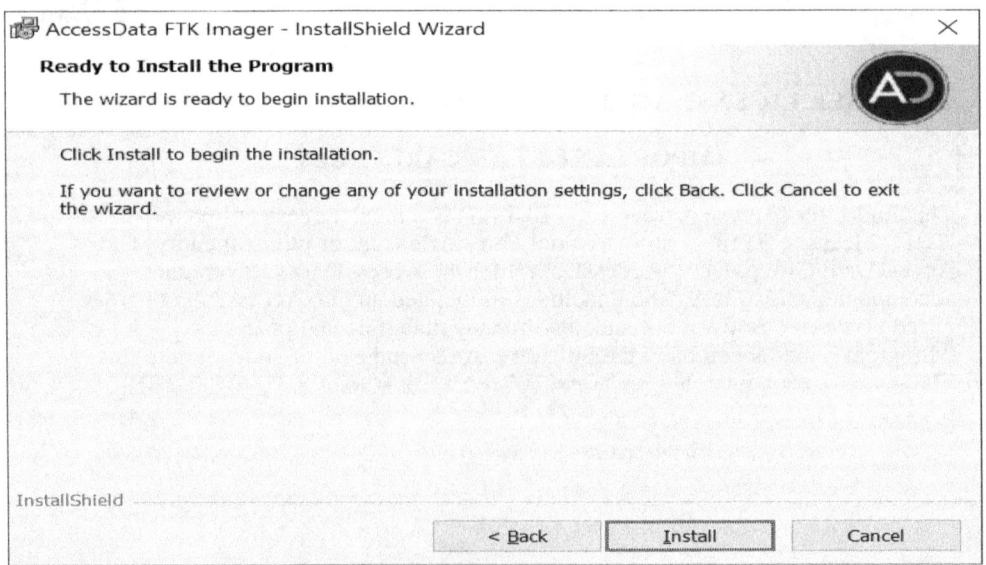

Figure 16-7

8. The FTK Imager files will now be installed per the installation parameters.

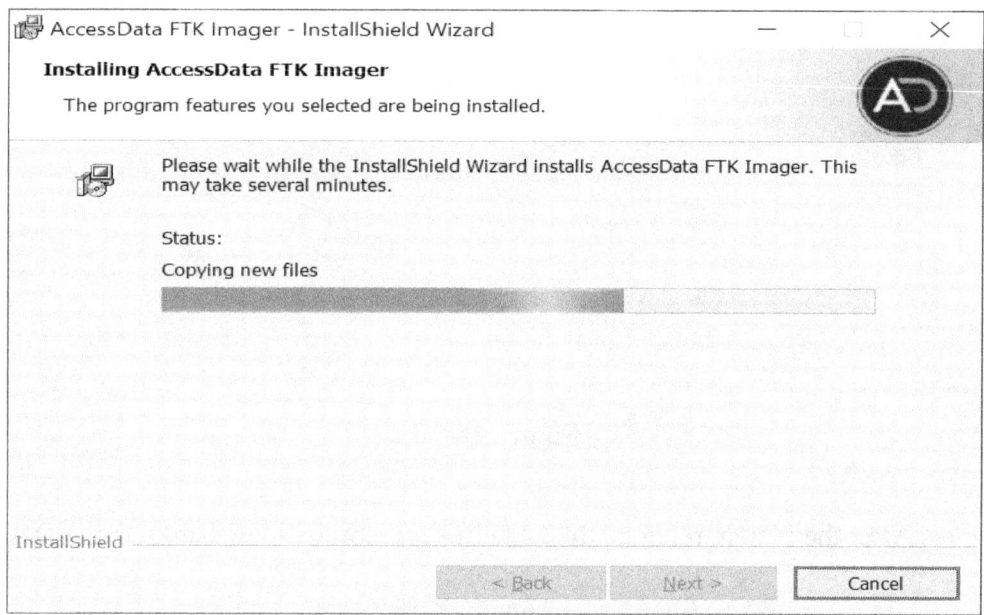

Figure 16-8

9. You should receive this message; select the 'OK' option to allow the system to reboot. Make sure you save and close any open files on your system.

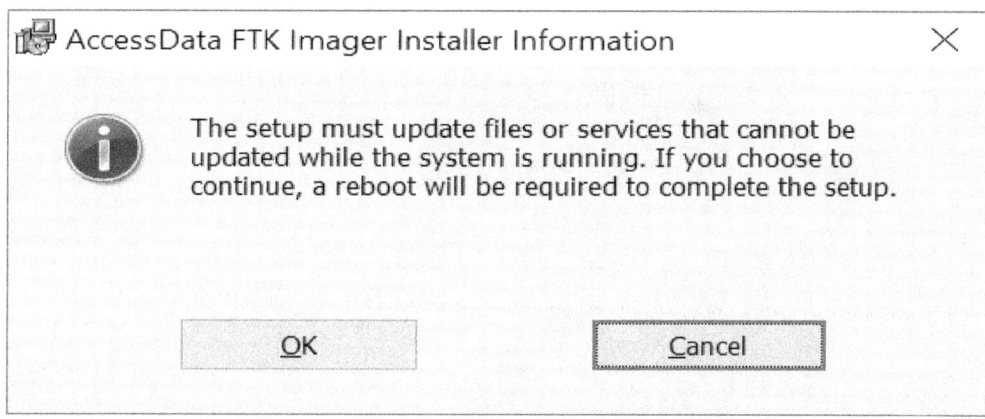

Figure 16-9

10. Select 'Yes' to restart the system.

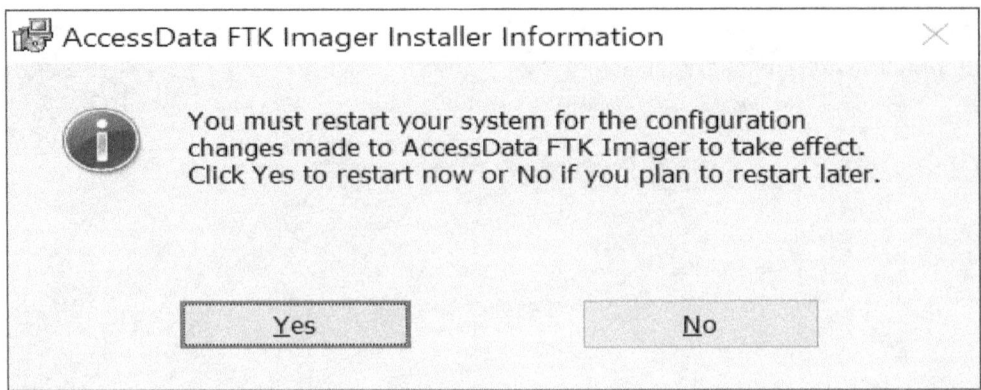

Figure 16-10

11. After the system reboots, the FTK Imager icon will be visible on the Desktop.

Figure 16-11

PART II Creating a Forensically Sound Image Using FTK Imager

You have just installed the FTK Imager program on your system. You will now create a forensically sound bit-stream image of a target media using FTK Imager version 4.1.1.1. or later. Your student system should have a write blocker installed. If it does not have one, notify your instructor.

STEPS

1. Your instructor should provide you with a target media that you are to create a FTK image file from. If you do not have one, see your instructor for instructions on how to create one.

2. Insert the target media into the write blocker.

3. Initialize FTK Imager by right clicking on the icon and selecting 'Run as Administrator'. You will be presented with a User Account Control window asking if you want this program to make changes to your system. Select 'Yes'.

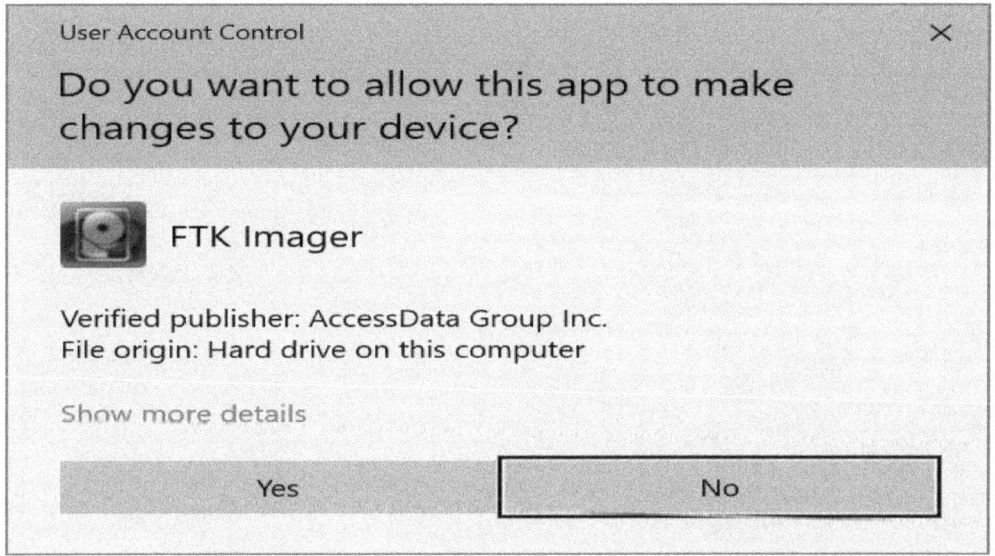

Figure 16-12

4. The FTK Imager program will initialize. You should see the following window as shown in Figure 16-13. NOTE: Some versions of FTK Imager have a slightly different graphical user interface. If you are using a different version, this is ok as the options are the same.

99

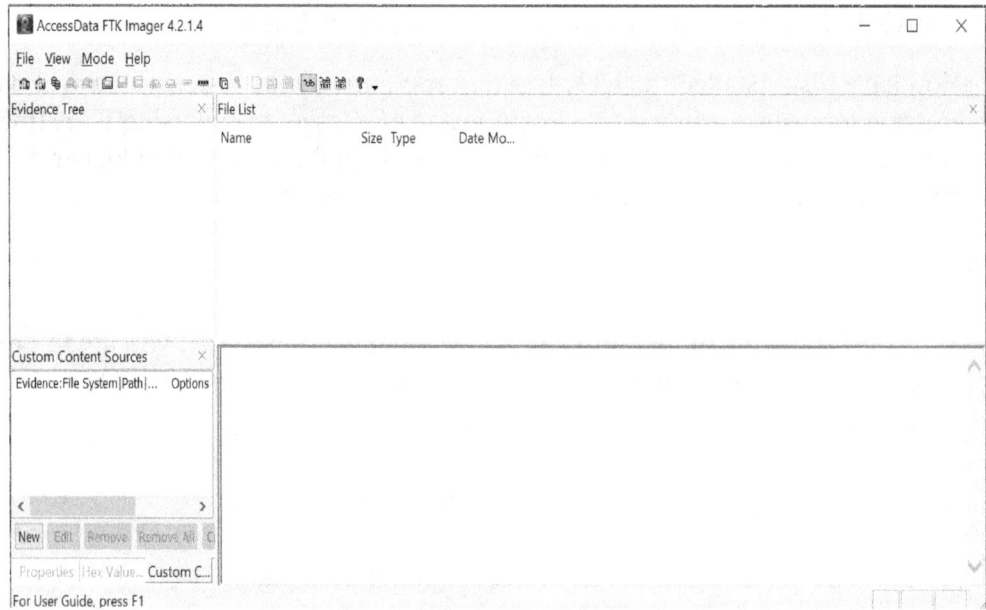

Figure 16-13

5. Select File, and then Create Disk Image.

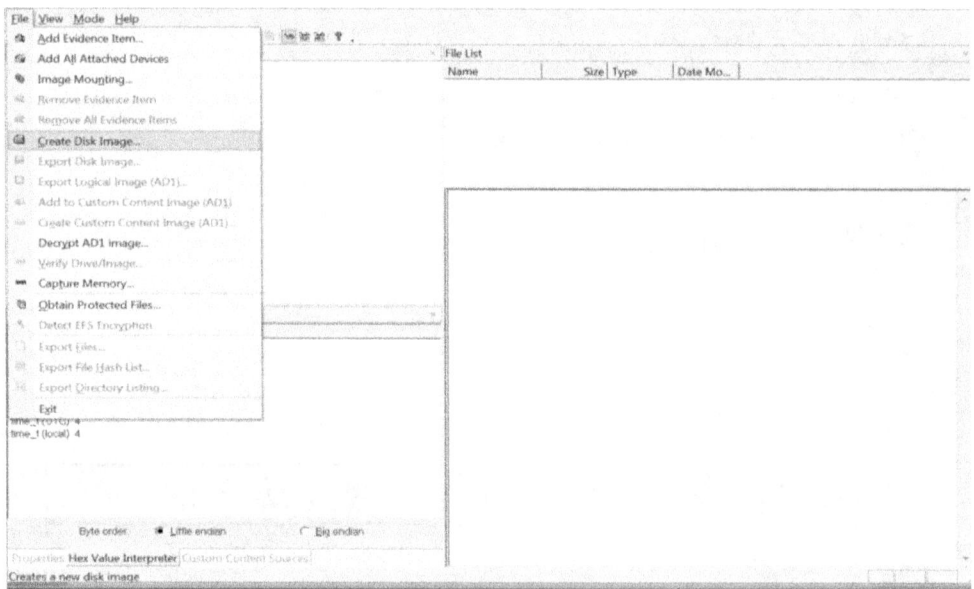

Figure 16-14

6. Select the Source Drive. This should be the small media device identified by your instructor. Whatever device you select, the receiving media will need to be at least the same size or larger. For example, if you select a 32 GB flash drive, you will need space on the Desktop or another flash drive slightly larger than 32 GB.

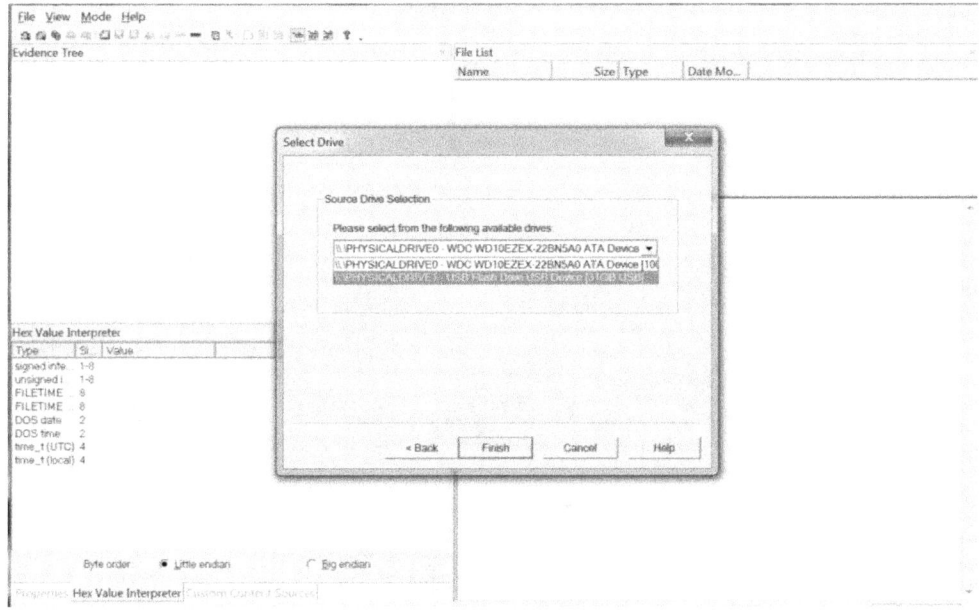

Figure 16-15

7. Select the Add Image option. This invokes the image source as the target to destination location. This is a critical step and forethought should be given as where to store and analyze the image about to be created.

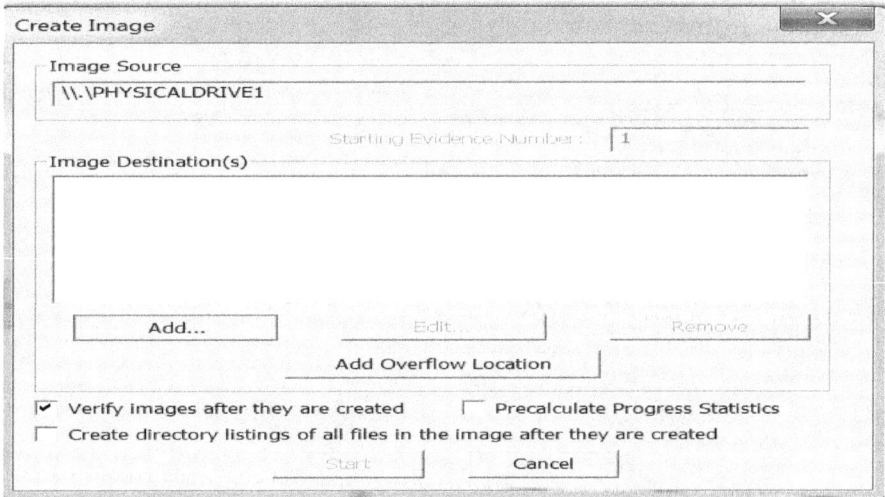

Figure 16-16

8. Select 'Raw' as the Destination Image Type. The Raw option provides the same functionality as the Linux dd command. This option will acquire the target data in a 100% bit-by-bit acquisition. See Figure 16-17.

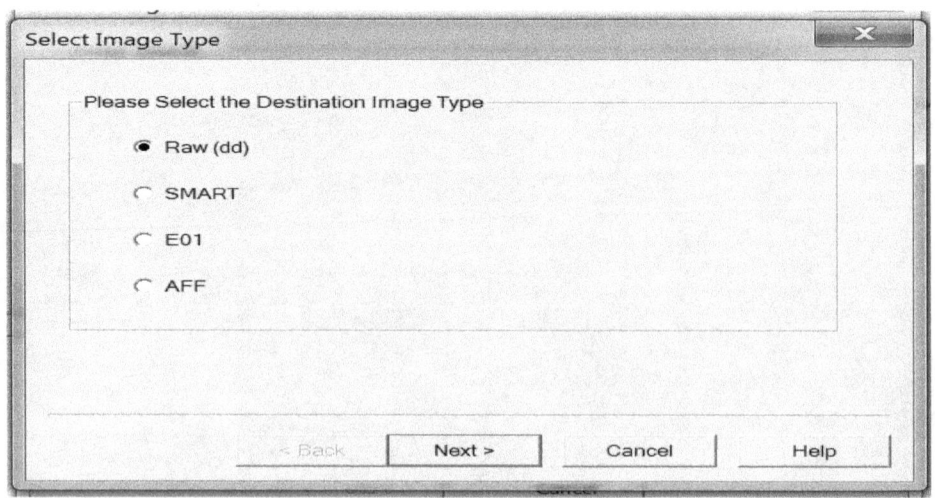

Figure 16-17

9. Configure the Evidence Item Information window as shown below. As stated in a previous step, this requires a predetermined policy on how to name and identify case image files. A forensics examiner must be diligent in maintaining integrity involving all aspects of a forensic examination, including date, time, examiner, target media, descriptions, and any other information relevant to the case or situation that initiated the forensic examination. An accurate naming and storage convention is vital to maintaining accuracy and administrative controls regarding future access and isolation from other case analyses.

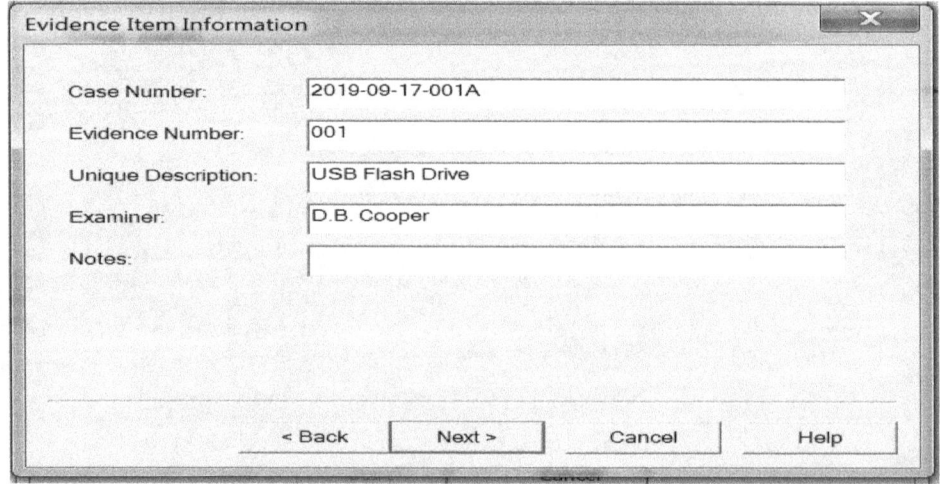

Figure 16-18

10. Once the image destination has been identified, navigate to it using the Browse option. This is where the bit-stream image will be stored for analysis. Then select 'Next'.

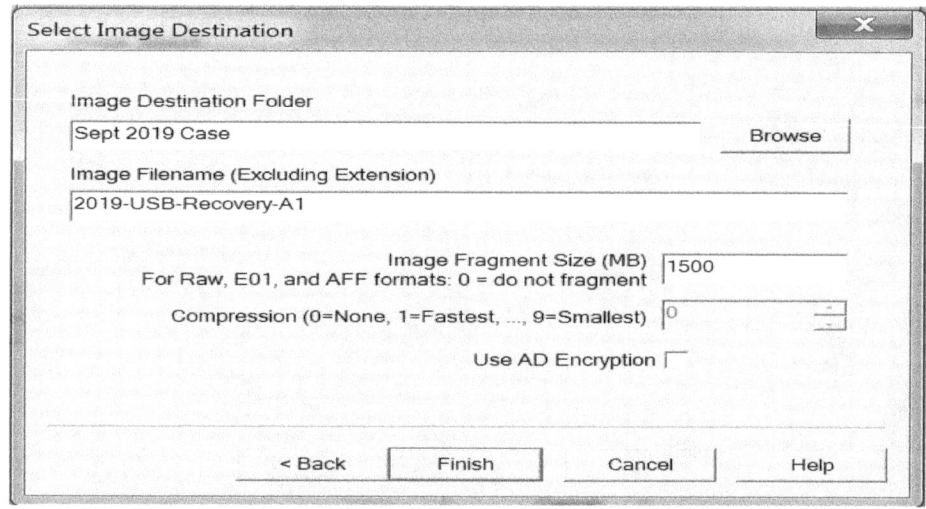

Figure 16-19

11. Verify the Create Image configuration parameters are correct, including 'Image Source', and the 'Verify images after they are created'. Select Start and the bit stream data acquisition process will begin.

Note: Forensic examiners often work with multiple cases and acquisitions. This step is where the examiner validates their administrative and organizational maintenance of the images they work with. An efficient naming convention for storing acquired images is a vital component not only for maintaining integrity of the examination, but also for demonstrating adherence to chain of custody requirements.

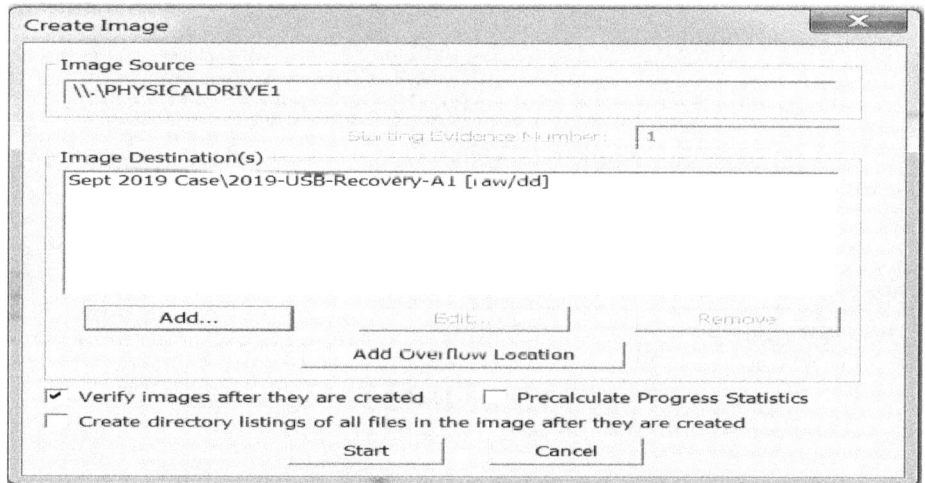

Figure 16-20

12. The Creating Image window will display the Progress time line. Depending on the speed of the interface and the size of the image, this may take a significant

103

amount of time. Some very large drives that are full to capacity may take an entire day or longer to create and verify. See Figures 16-21 and 16-22 below.

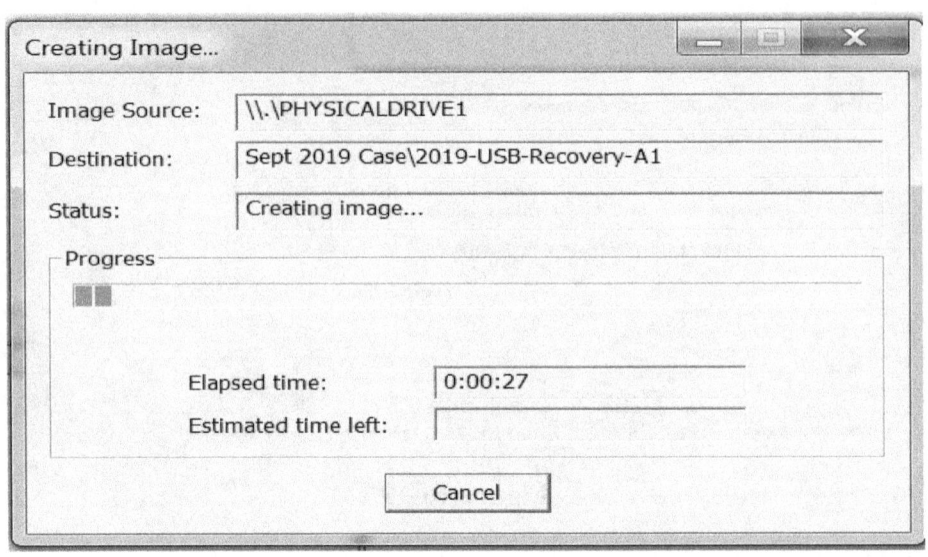

Figure 16-21

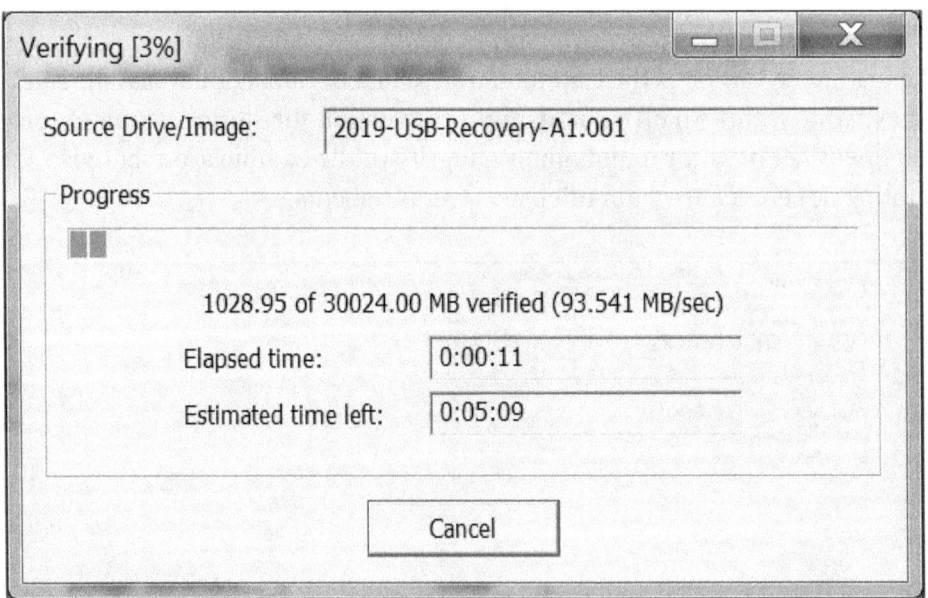

Figure 16-22

13. Once the image has successfully created and verified, the Status window will display 'Image created successfully' as shown in Figure 16-23 below.

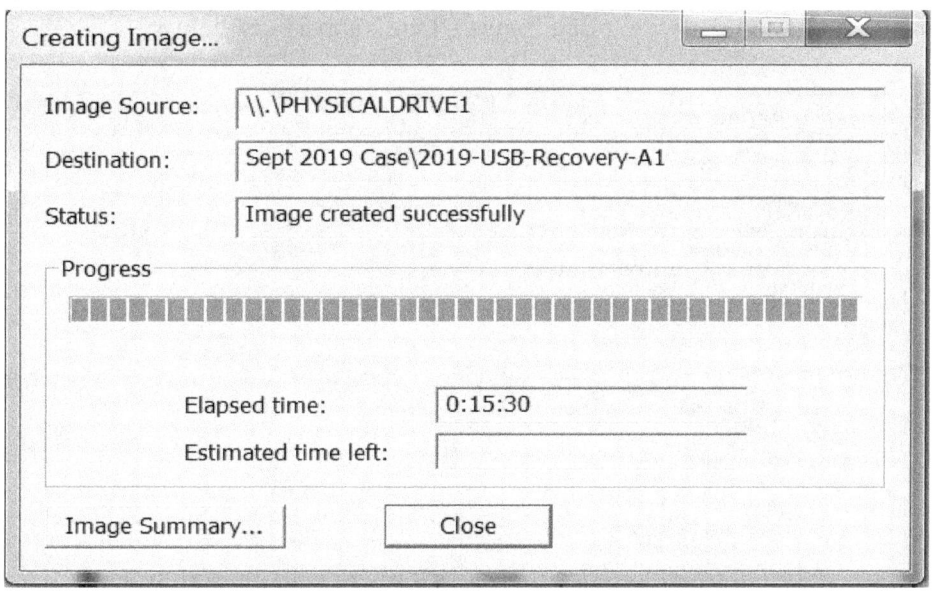

Figure 16-24

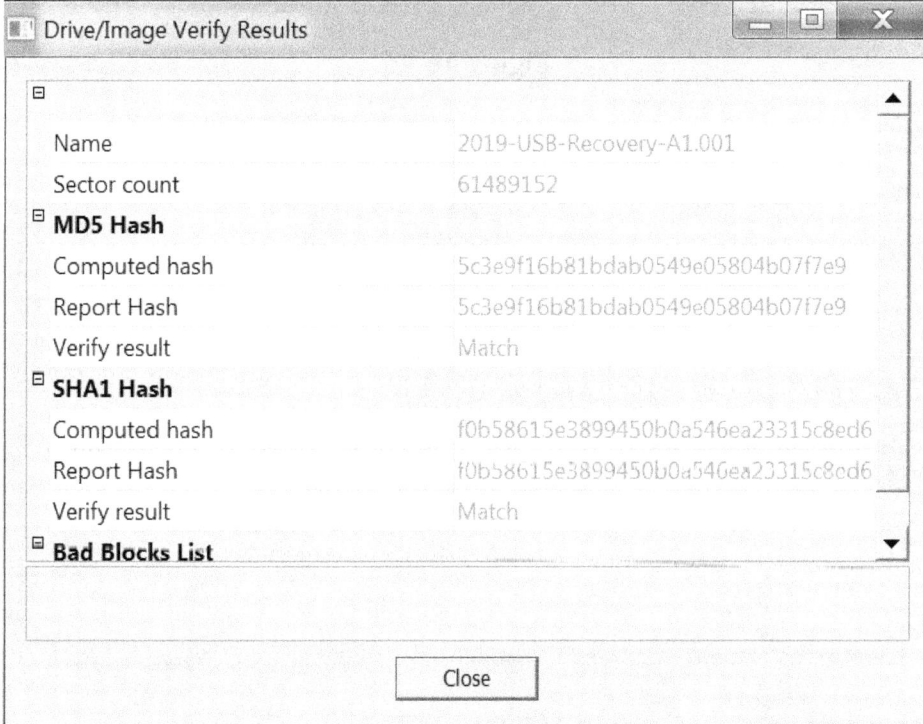

Figure 16-25

14. Selecting the 'Image Summary' option will display the acquired image data, such as drive geometry information and created image. Note that the image was created as individual file segments. These image segments will be chained together as one representative whole when imported into the forensic examination software. See Figures 16-26 and 16-27 below.

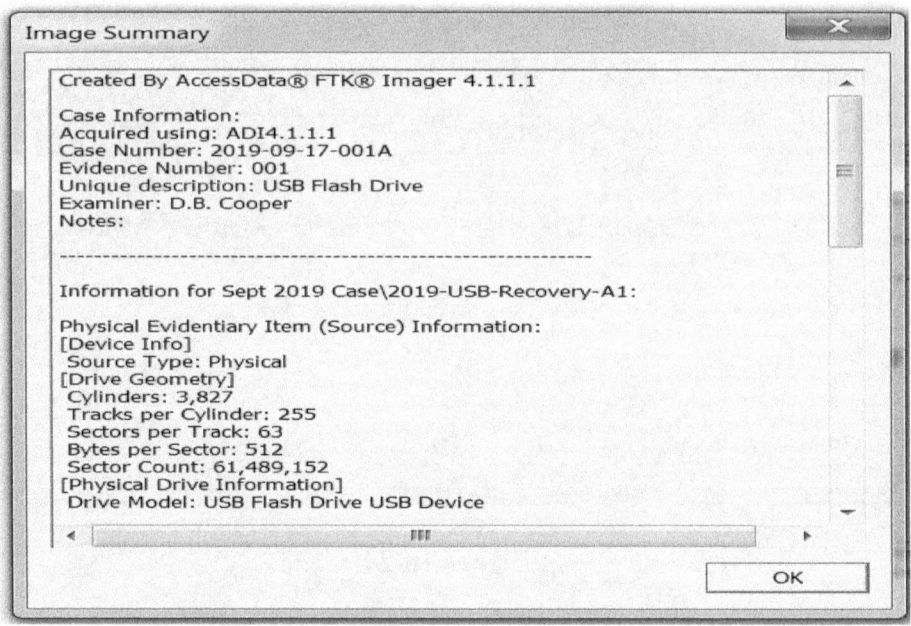

Figure 16-26

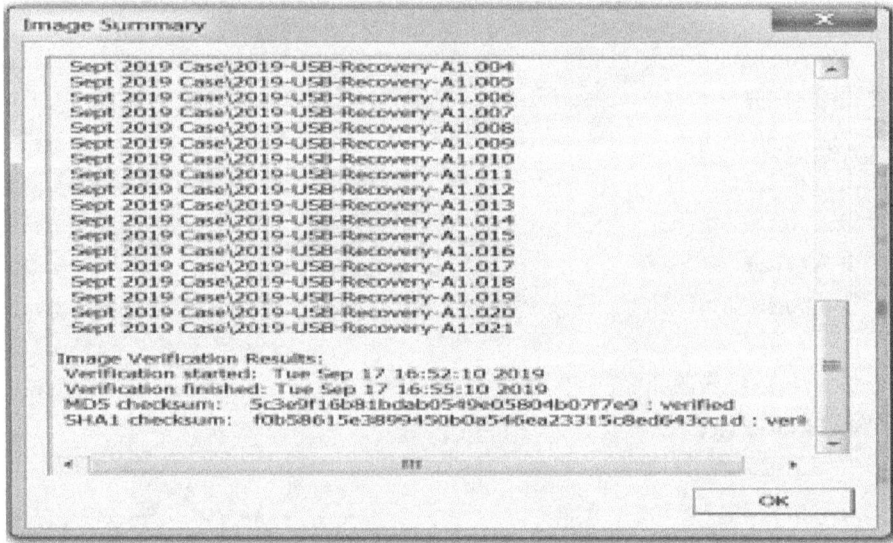

Figure 16-27

15. After the target image has been created, FTK Imager is no longer needed. Close the FTK Imager program.

16. Navigate to the folder where the new image is stored. Expand the folder. You will see each image segment and an associated .txt file. This file contains the same information as shown in the FTK Imager Image Summary. The text file is available so the examiner can include it in the examination report.

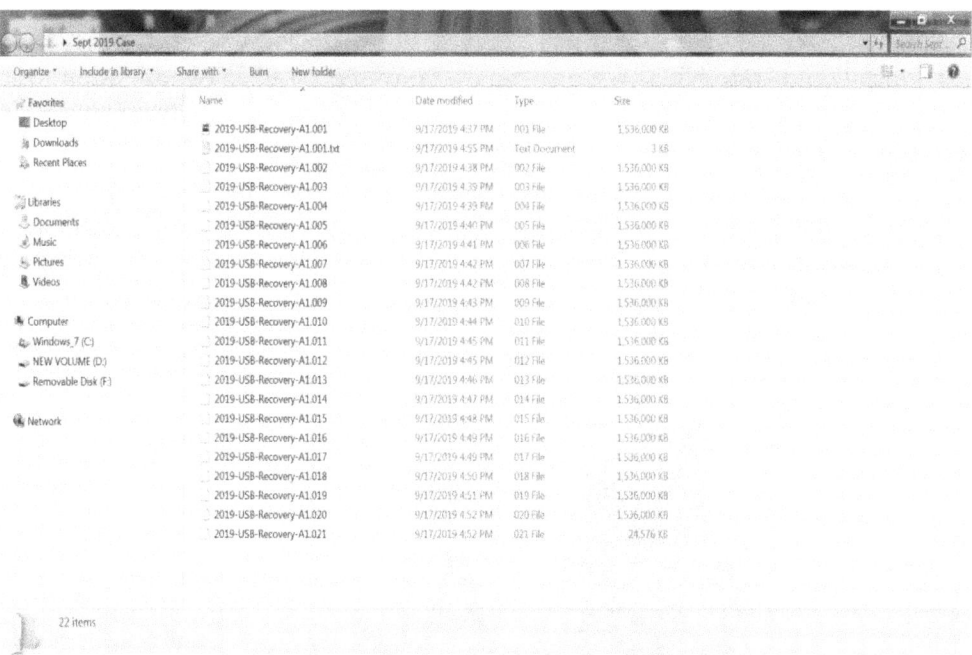

Figure 16-28

STUDENT SUMMARY:

1. What did you learn from this exercise?

2. You are preparing to create a bit-stream image of a 250 GB hard disk. Your forensics system has a 500 GB hard drive that contains all of your forensics tools, including the operating system. What must you consider before initiating FTK Imager?

Evaluators Review of Learners Performance

1   2   3   4   5

Forensics Exercise # 17
Introduction to Autopsy

OBJECTIVE:

To install and start using Autopsy, an open source forensic examination tool.

OVERVIEW:

To begin this exercise the Autopsy forensic program should have been introduced and demonstrated to you. If it has not already been downloaded to your system, perform a search of 'Autopsy download' and save it on your Desktop.

Figure 17-1

Install and Initialize Autopsy

STEPS

1. Click on the Autopsy link to begin the installation process.

Figure 17-2

2. The Install Wizard will appear. Select Next and the Select Destination Folder will appear. Accept the default location and click next. The ready to Install window will appear. The following installation window will appear.

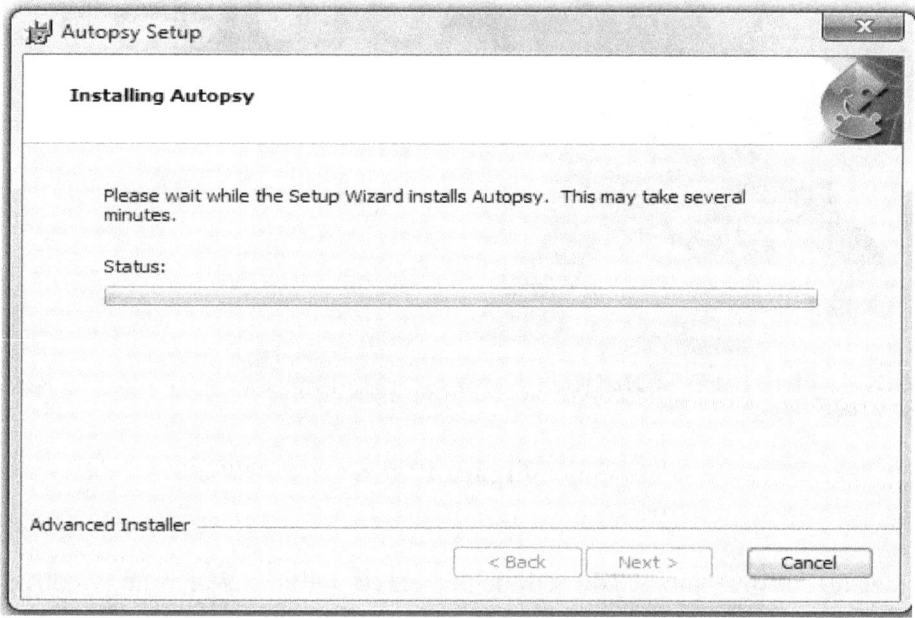

Figure 17-3

3. When the installation process is complete, click Finish. The Autopsy
   initialization icon will be loaded on your Desktop.

Figure 17-4

4. Click on the Autopsy icon. Autopsy will begin to load.

Figure 17-5

5. After Autopsy loads, you will be presented with the Welcome window. This
   window will allow the examiner to select three options, New Case, Open
   Recent Case, or Open Case. Select the New Case option.

Figure 17-6

6. The New Case Information window will now be displayed as shown in Figure 17-7 below. There are two steps associated with this phase, The Case Information and Optional Information steps.

Since this will be your first image file analysis using Autopsy, complete the Case Information by entering the following as shown below:

> Case Name: Bad Guy Case 1
> Base Directory: Browse to the Desktop to create your case image folder.
> Case Type: Single user

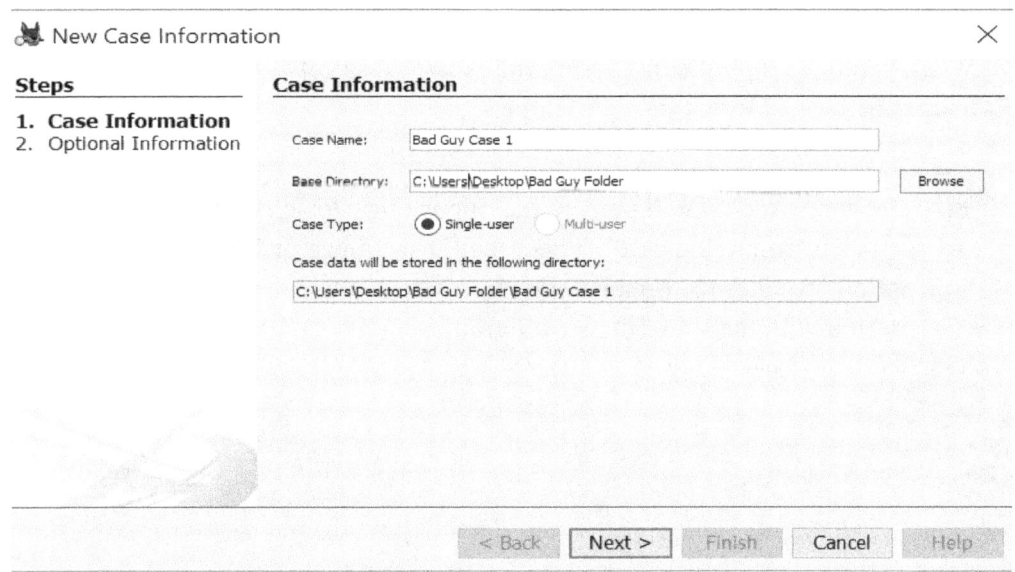

Figure 17-7

Once you have the above information populated into your New Case Information window, click the Next button. Complete the Optional Information step.

7. Input the following into the Optional Information window.

Case Number: Use the following format. Year-Month-Day-001A

This is one file naming convention used to maintain accuracy in case files. Some examiners work with several files per day and as a historical reference, knowing the date and the folder name associated with that case provides organizational control.

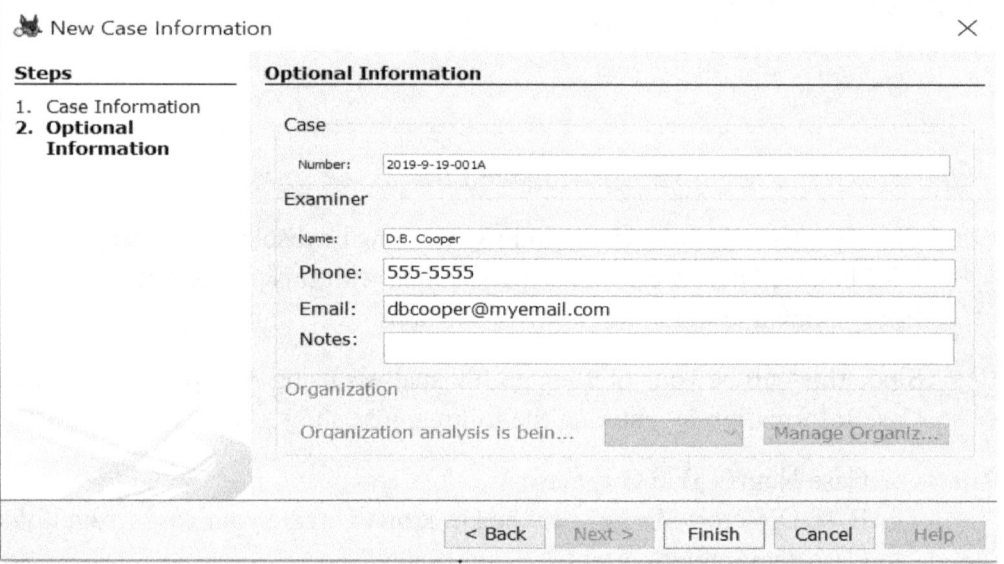

Figure 17-8

When you have input the necessary information, select 'Finish' to create the case image file.

8. The next window will present the opportunity to select the type of data source to add to the case. Select the 'Disk Image or VM File' option. This option provides the opportunity to browse to the desired disk image file you created with the FTK Imager program.

112

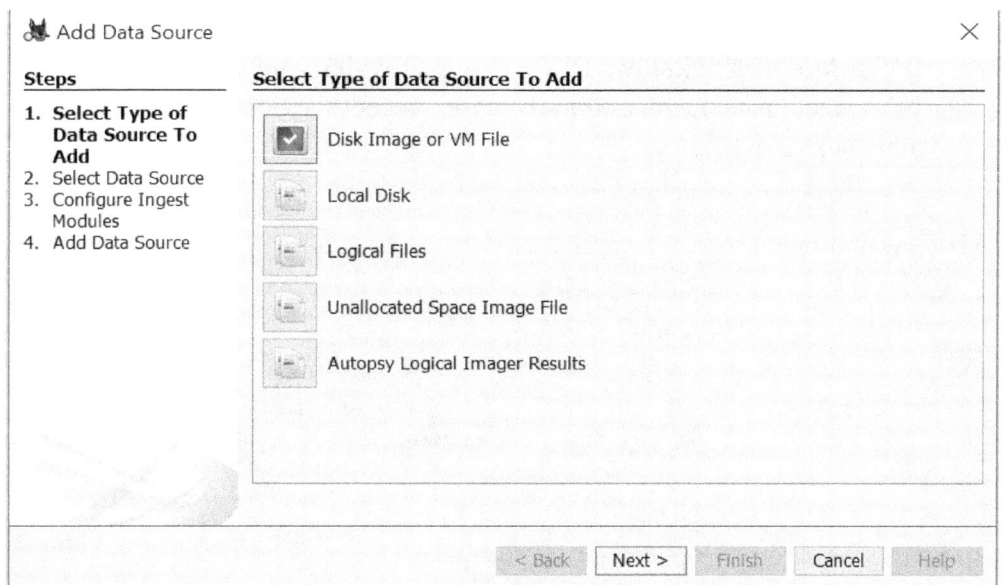

Figure 17-9

9. If your instructor previously provided you with a pre-created case image file, select the Browse option and navigate to where it is located. This example uses the 2005-20 case image file as an example. Your instructor may provide you with a different file. Select the time zone for your location, allow the default sector size and select 'Next'.

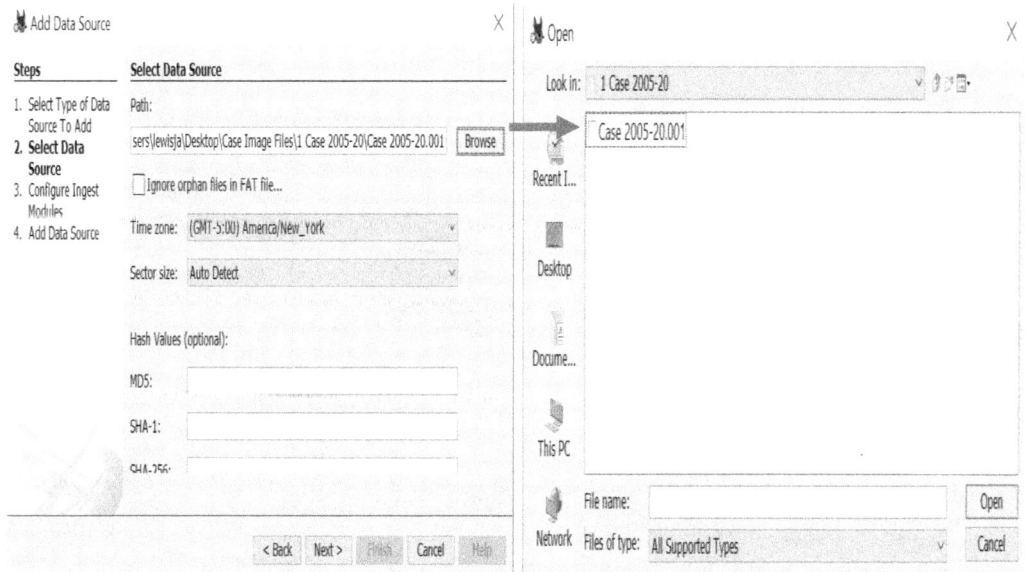

Figure 17-10

10. At this point you will be presented with the 'Add Data Source Configure Ingest Modules' window. This window provides you with multiple options to be indexed and categorized in the case. Accept the defaults as shown below and click 'Next'.

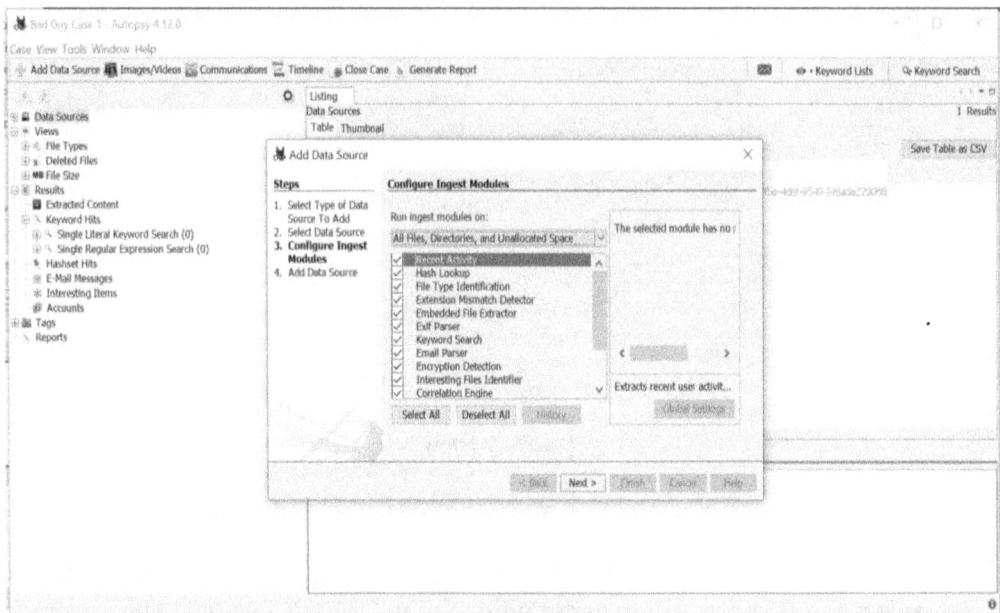

Figure 17-11

11. The source data file will now be added to the database in preparation for the image indexing operation. Click the Finish option and allow Autopsy time to index the data contained within the image.

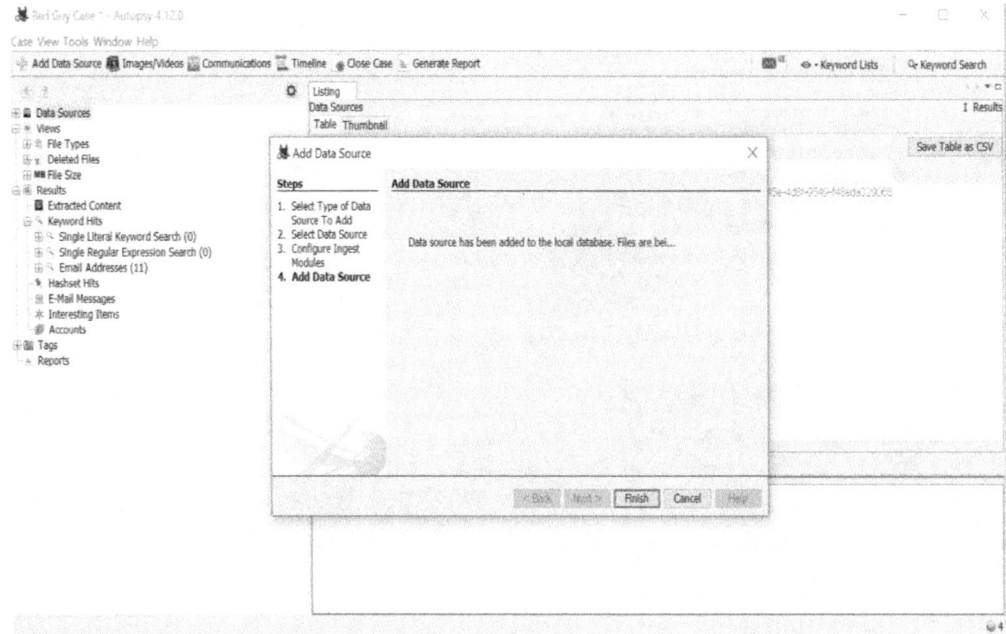

Figure 17-12

12. At this point, minimize Autopsy and using Windows explorer, navigate to the Bad Guy Case 1 folder and notice the following folders that were generated as a result of Autopsy indexing the case image file.

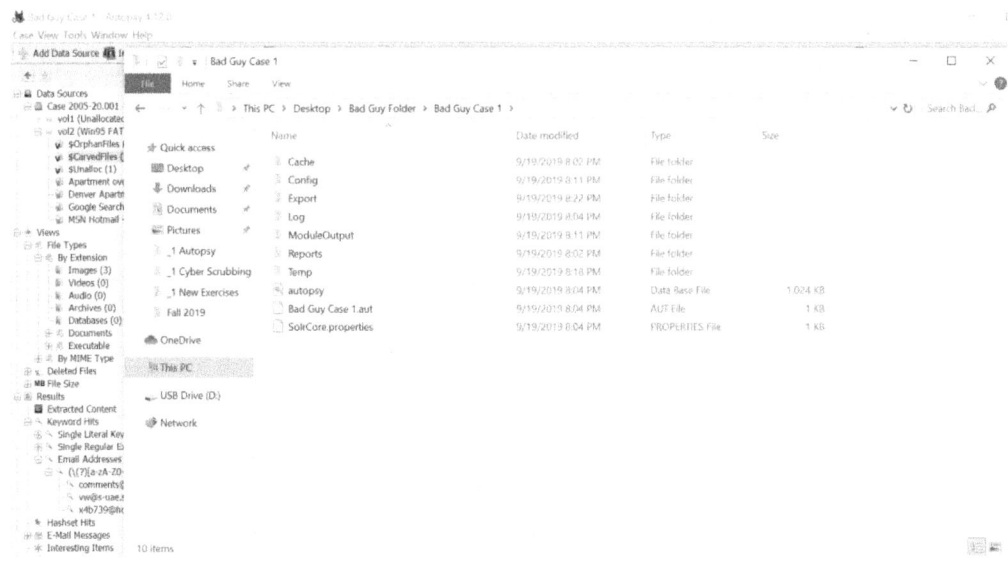

Figure 17-13

Does your folder match the one as shown in Figure 17-13?　　Yes　　No

If the folders do not match, notify your instructor.

13. Close Windows Explorer. You are now able to examine the case image file using forensically sound and industry recognized examination software.

The first step in a forensic examination is to secure the media device and protect it from unauthorized modification, which would be precarious in a legal situation and potentially ruinous of data or evidence. Simply booting a device will write files to it. Left over or unallocated data or files on a media often contain valuable information for either the employer or the law enforcement examiner.

The second step is to acquire an exact, bit-by-bit image of the media, including non-partition space. A correlating before and after hash value will validate the exact duplication.

The third step is, using forensically sound software, to index all recognizable bit patterns in the acquired image and present them for review, while maintaining a no-write examination to the image.

14. Using Autopsy, take a few minutes and navigate around the Bad Guy Case 1 indexed file. Browse several folders to become familiar with some of the categories and types of data and information that are contained within. Look at files, images and drive format information.

   a. What are your initial thoughts regarding potential discoveries that can be made by forensically examining a bit-steam image of an evidence drive?

   b. Can a file, remnant, or digital artifact be concealed from view under a forensically sound examination tool?

      Yes   No

      Explain why or why not! Be specific and factual as if you are presenting your understanding to both a technical and non-technical audience. Use a separate sheet of paper if necessary.

15. Sometimes the discovery of a long lost or forgotten object or artifact on a disk drive may seem mystical, especially when discovered by accident. Identify some items of interest within the image that you notice which may be interesting to you and briefly explain why some of the findings may have surprised or interested you.

Discovered Item	Your Impression Regarding its Discovery

16. Exit Autopsy and close the Bad Guy Case 1 folder.

OBJECTIVE:

To become more familiar with the concepts and techniques associated with performing a forensics examination by analyzing a media image to determine if any information of evidentiary value is contained within it, and to report your findings.

OVERVIEW:

This exercise will provide the student the opportunity to examine an existing case image file and analyze it for digital contraband or illegal files. The previous case image file was an introduction to installing and initializing Autopsy and the concepts and techniques of forensically examining a media image. This exercise will provide you with the opportunity to utilize tools and techniques learned in previous exercises for examination and recovery of data and information.

STEPS:

1. Acquire the case image file 2005-20 from your instructor.

2. Initialize Autopsy and select the 'Data Sources' menu option located in the left pane of Autopsy. You should see the Case 2005-20.001 imaged data file identified under the Listing tab.

Figure 18-1

117

3. Verify the source file path information located in the Data Storage Usage pane.

4. Expand the Views, File Types, By Extension option.

    a. How many Image files are identified in this case? _____

    b. Click on the file names under Images - Table. What do you see?

    c. What are the file extensions of these files? _____

    d. Look at each file and consider where this picture may have originated from or what type of information it may have been associated with, i.e. website, camera pic, thumbnail, etc.

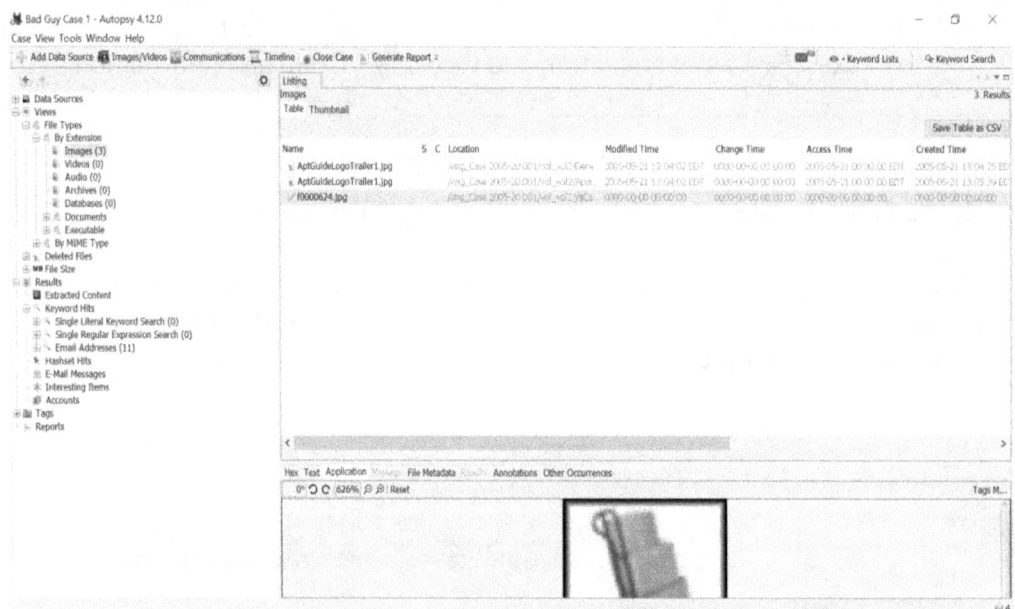

Figure 18-2

5. Next, navigate to and expand the Case 2005-20.001, select vol2 (Win95 FAT32) option. Under the 'Table' window, scroll down to where you see the file Grocery List.doc. In the bottom window pane you should observe what appears to be a grocery list.

    a. Did you locate this file?   Yes   No

    If you cannot locate this file, notify your instructor.

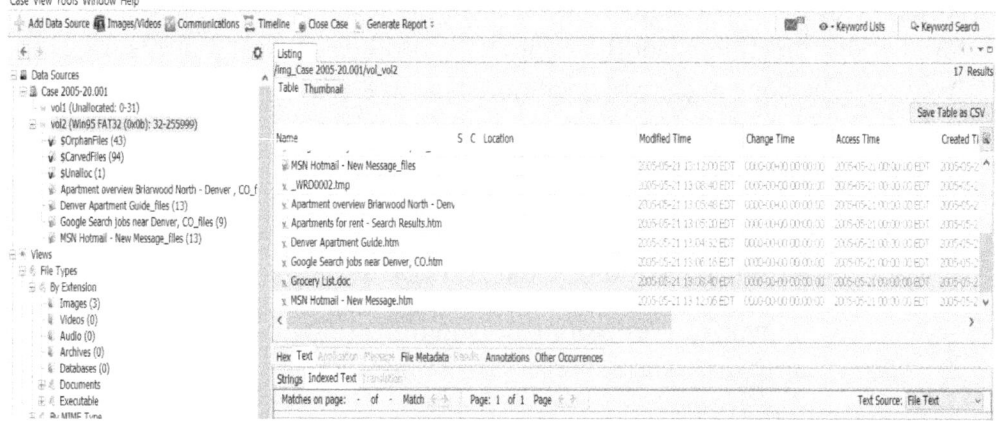

Figure 18-3

6. Minimize Autopsy and create a new folder on the Desktop titled 'Examiner Copied Documents'.

7. In the pane where the grocery list items are listed, right click; choose 'Select All', then copy.

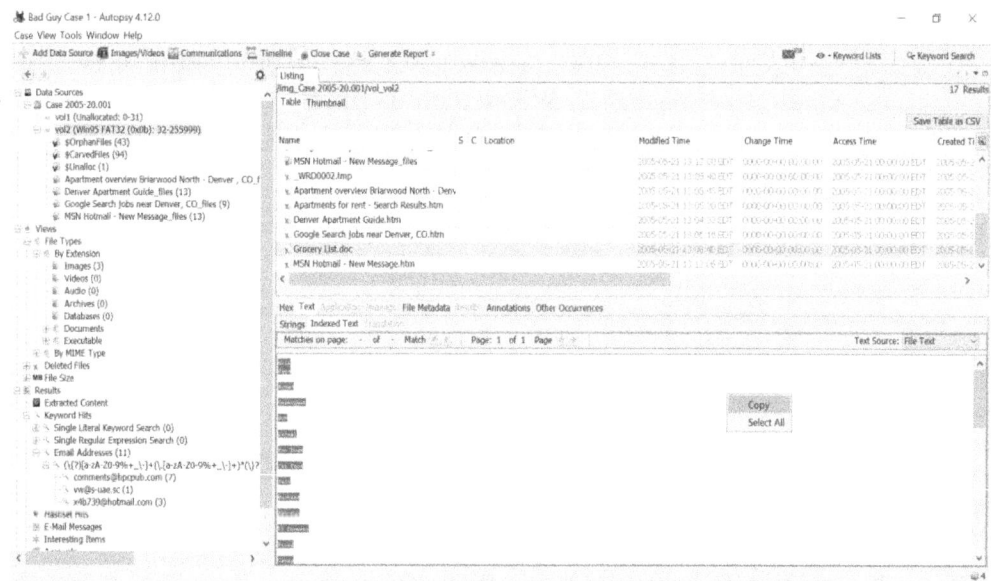

Figure 18-4

8. Open a Notepad file and paste the contents of copied information into it and save it as Exhibit 1 grocerylist into the Examiner Copied Documents folder.

The content of files you copy should be stored in your own created folder and not one created by the forensic analysis software. This is to maintain consistency and avoid confusion later when reviewing your results or providing this information for company or legal action.

Note! Copy and paste information from a file located inside of an image under forensic examination is not the same as exporting a copy of that file under Autopsy. The copy and paste operation of Step 8 is a Windows action while exporting that same file is a feature of the forensic examination software. Exporting files will be presented in a future step.

9. Examine the contents of the Notepad file.

    a. What type of information do you observe? Be specific!

    b. What, if any, brief conclusions can you draw when looking at this file?

    c. Using your own words, how would you explain this file to your employer? What is it? Where did it come from? Who put it there? Why was it put there? Give this careful consideration. Your perspective will be discussed in a future step.

10. Next, navigate to the $OrphanFiles.

    a. How many $OrphanFiles are identified? _____

    b. List the file types by extension.

        1. _____
        2. _____
        3. _____
        4. _____
        5. _____

11. Next, navigate to the $CarvedFiles and examine the files presented here.

    a. How many files are identified under $CarvedFiles? _____

    b. How many file types are identified? _____

    c. List the file extension types identified.

        1. _____
        2. _____
        3. _____
        4. _____
        5. _____
        6. _____
        7. _____

    d. Browse the files and identify what some of them contain.

        a. What type of information do you observe?

        b. What conclusions do you draw when looking at this file?

12. Next, navigate to the $Unalloc area.

    a. How many $Unalloc files are identified? _____

    b. What are some of the contents of the one $Unalloc file that you observe?

13. Navigate to Results – Keyword Hits – Email Addresses and expand them.

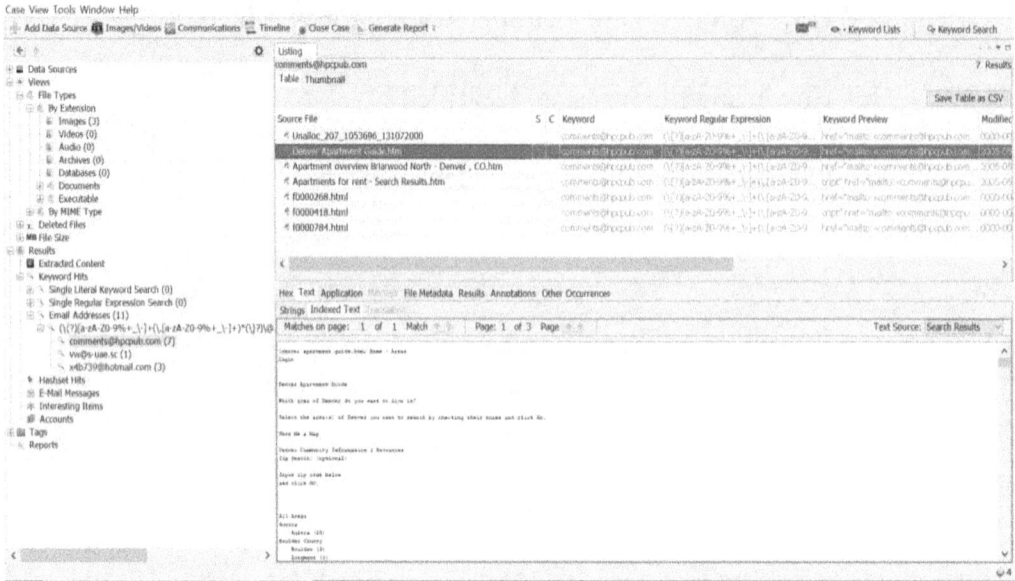

Figure 18-5

14. Expand the options under Email Addresses.

    a. What types of files do you observe and what do they contain?

15. Continue to examine the other files within this pane and state the following:

    a. How many additional files are there? _____

    b. What are the file names and types? _____

    _____

16. Select five different .gif files of your choice, right click on them and select Extract File(s). See Figure 18-6 on the next page.

Figure 18-7

17. Minimize Autopsy and navigate to the Case 2005-20 folder and open the Export folder.

Figure 18-8

You can now further examine the exported files. As stated in a previous step, exporting files is not the same as copy and paste their contents. The metadata that is associated with the actual file does not transport with the Windows copy function, whereas the forensic software 'Export' feature will make a hash verifiable duplicate of the file being exported.

18. Examine all other available information contained within this image file. Expand and examine Views, File Types, Extensions, Documents, Searches and any information available.

19. After you have reviewed all other categories of indexed data in this image file.

    a. What conclusions can you draw from examining these files? Describe your thoughts or any determinations regarding the use of this system based on the files and use patterns. Give this careful consideration!

20. Answer the following questions regarding this case image file.

    a. What type of text documents were identified?

    b. What type of person created these file?

    c. Where does this person live?

    d. What is this person's lifestyle?

    e. Was there any illegal activity identified?

    f. Is there any other information regarding this case image file that may be relevant?

21. Save your case image file and close Autopsy.

Instructor consultation regarding your first forensic examination of an image file.

The items discovered, such as the 'apparent' grocery list, apartment searches, emails, gif and other types of files might give the examiner an indication as to the potential use of the system under examination. It can lead the examiner to new search terms that will build an information profile that may focus the examination. However, the examiner cannot draw a conclusion as to the intentions of that user, that is the responsibility of the person or agency that employs the examiner, such as corporate HR or law enforcement.

Your instructor will caution that as a forensic examiner, you can explain what you discovered, where you discovered it and the metadata regarding that file, but you cannot interpret the intentions of the user or who put it there. A file titled 'grocerylist.txt' may or may not be a grocery list; it may be a smaller part of something much different from what you suspect. It could be a list of passwords misrepresented as a grocery list to conceal their true importance. One challenge in learning the profession of computer and digital forensics is not to present opinion as fact, or to take discoveries at face value. Something as innocent looking as the jpeg file of a lake could actually be a stenographic carrier file for a criminal act.

The computer examiner can state that a file titled 'Grocery List' was recovered, present the contents of that file and any metadata associated with it, but it is not within the responsibility for the computer examiner to interpret the intentions of the author of that file. To do so and be wrong could bring scrutiny on the examiner and the examiners intentions, as well as potential legal challenges.

STUDENT SUMMARY:

1. What did you learn from this exercise?

2. Think of and report three possible scenarios where data or information discovered in a forensics examination might not be what it actually appears.

    a. _____
       _____

    b. _____
       _____

    c. _____
       _____

Evaluators Review of Learners Performance

1   2   3   4   5

Forensics Exercise # 19
Introduction to Examining a Case Image File 2005-25 Using Autopsy

OBJECTIVE:

To become more familiar with the concepts and techniques associated with performing a forensics examination by analyzing a media image to determine if any information of evidentiary value is contained within it, and to report your findings.

OVERVIEW:

This exercise will provide the student the opportunity to examine an existing case image file and analyze it for digital contraband or illegal files. The previous case image file, 2005-25, was an introduction to using Autopsy and the concepts and techniques of forensically examining a media image. This exercise will provide you with the opportunity to utilize tools and techniques learned in previous exercises for examination and recovery of data and information. This exercise is expected to take much longer to examine and report as it contains much more information.

STEPS:

1. Acquire the case image file 2005-25 from your instructor.

2. Initialize Autopsy and import the 2005-25 case image file into it using the steps and techniques used in the previous exercise.

3 .Index the case image file 2005-25 using appropriate naming conventions.

4. Analyze the image and identify the following from this case image file:

    a. What types of files did you discover in this image?

    b. How did you open these files? Be very specific in how each file was opened.

    c. What are the contents of each of these files? Provide a screenshot if available.

You have been instructed that it is inappropriate to present opinion regarding intentions of the user, or generalized perceptions as to their motives, however, part of being an effective computer forensic examiner is to let the image guide you towards deeper discoveries contained therein. For example, discovery of emails confirming airline reservations may direct you to search registry information regarding searches for travel destinations. A password protected file that contains text regarding what appears to be a money laundering operation may direct the examiner to do a search for credit card or bank account numbering patterns. Credit cards that begin with 34 or 37 and are 15 characters long are the format for American Express. Credit cards that begin with 51 through 55 and are 16 characters long are the format for Master Card.

STUDENT SUMMARY:

1. What did you learn from this exercise?

Evaluators Review of Learners Performance

1   2   3   4   5

Exercise # 20
Locate Encrypted Files on Disk

THIS EXERCISE IS UNDER REVISION

Forensics Exercise # 21
Microsoft Word 2016 Password Recovery Using Passware

OBJECTIVE:

To understand how to recover a Microsoft Office 2016 password protected Word file using Passware.

OVERVIEW:

It is sometimes necessary to recover the password from protected files. Some forensic examiners utilize more than one type of password recovery tool or technique. These exercise procedures will step you through the process using the Passware recovery program. You can download the Passware recovery program from web site: http://www.freedownloadscenter.com. If this link is no longer available, perform a search and download.

STEPS:

1. Insert a sanitized thumb drive or small media device into the forensic examination system.

2. Using Microsoft Word 2016, create a text file that contains all the letters of the alphabet.

3. Select Tools – Options – Security on the pull down menu.

    A. In the box File Encryption Options for this document, Password to Open, enter a TWO-character password. Use only alphabetic characters!
    B. For the Password to Modify, enter another TWO-character alphabetic password.
    C. Click OK and save the file on the sanitized media device as a Microsoft Office 2016 document.
    D. Exit Microsoft Office

Evaluation versions of software often have limited functionality. This password recovery tool permits up to two characters to be recovered. For more advanced password recoveries, the software should be purchased and licensed. Practicing forensic examiners have fully functional tools.

4. Exchange media with another student.

5. Select Start – Programs – Passware – Office Key. The following window should appear.

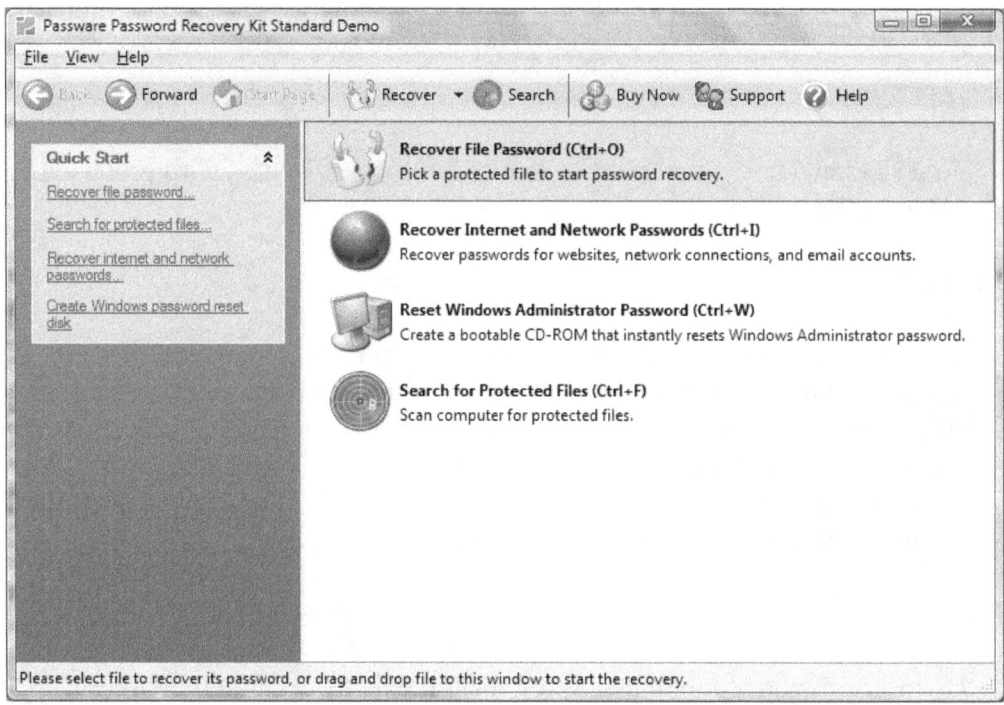

Figure 21-1

6. Click once on the Recover File Password (Ctrl+O) option to select it. The following window will appear as shown in Figure 21-2 below.

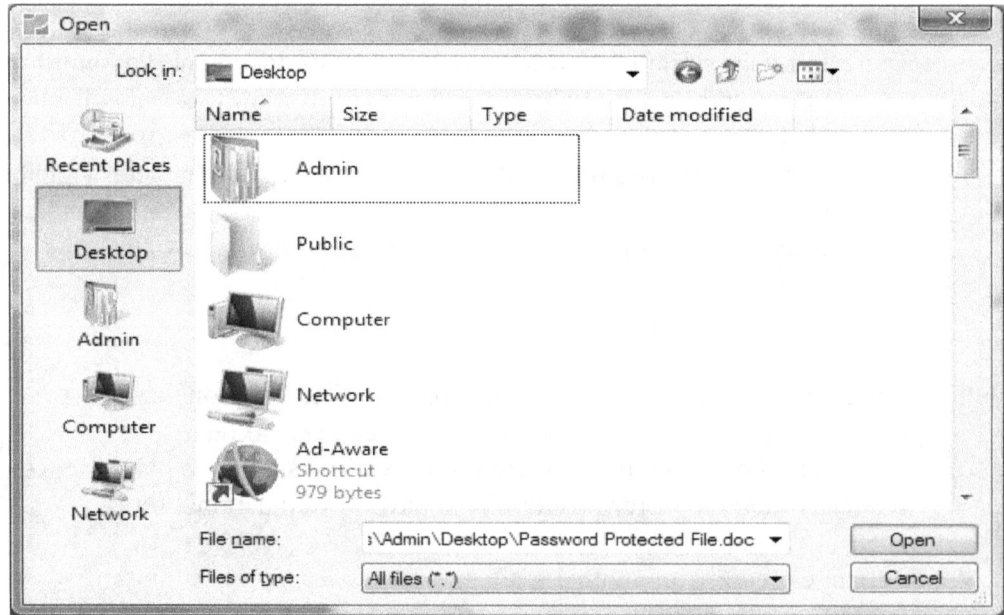

Figure 21-2

7. Navigate to the file you wish to identify the password on and click Open. You will be presented with three options as shown in Figure 21-3. The first password recovery option is Run Attack Wizard. Double click this option to select it.

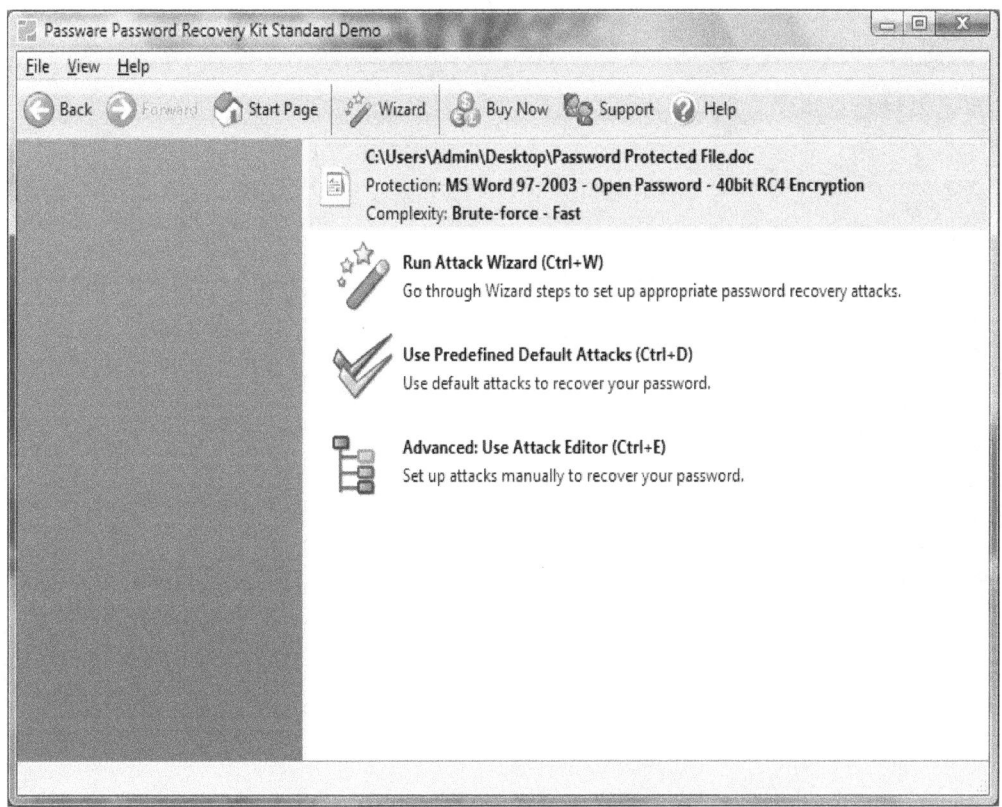

Figure 21-3

8. The next window to appear allows the examiner to select which type of action to be performed. Select the "I know nothing about the password" option and click next as shown in Figure 21-4 on the next page.

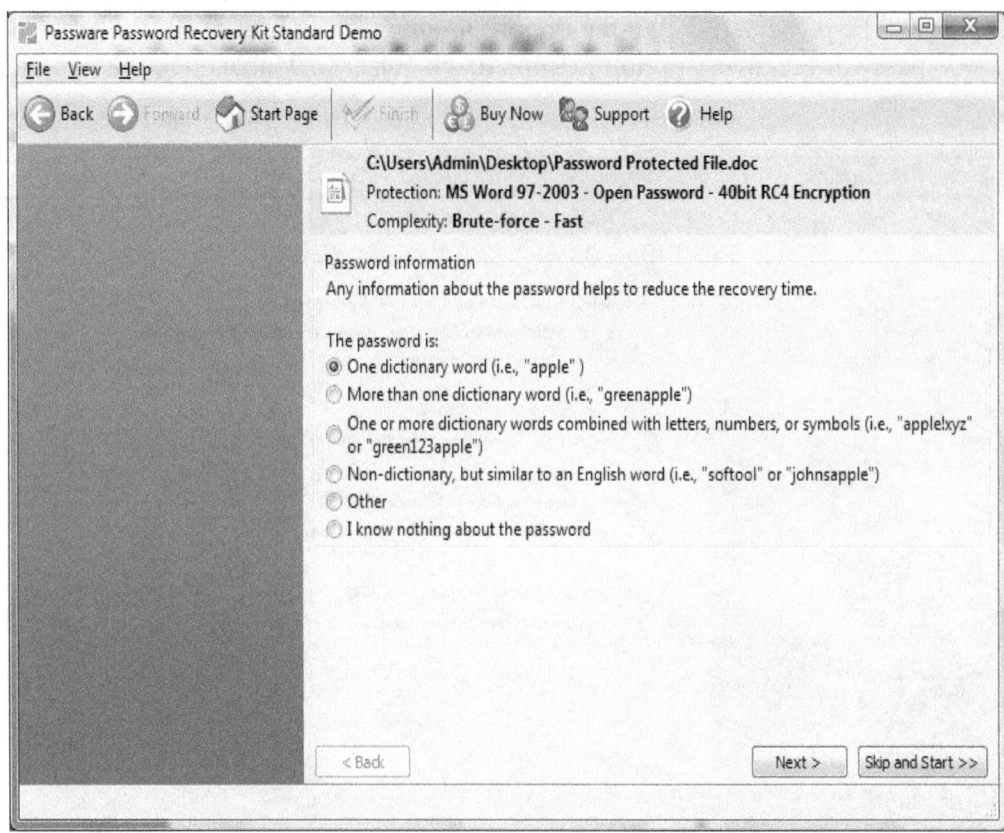

Figure 21-4

9. A new window will appear asking if the user/examiner desires for an online encryption process for this file. Select 'Yes' for this exercise as the hash value is the string that is sent and not the entire file as shown in Figure 21-5.

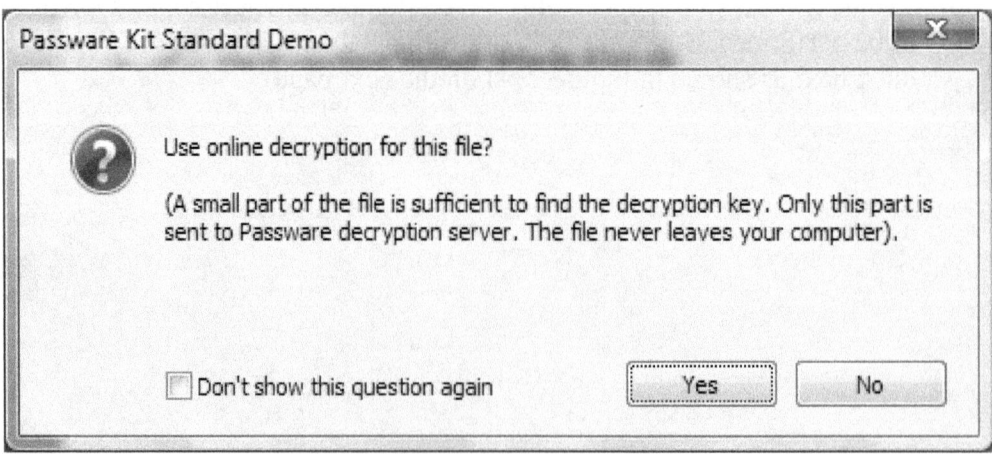

Figure 21-5

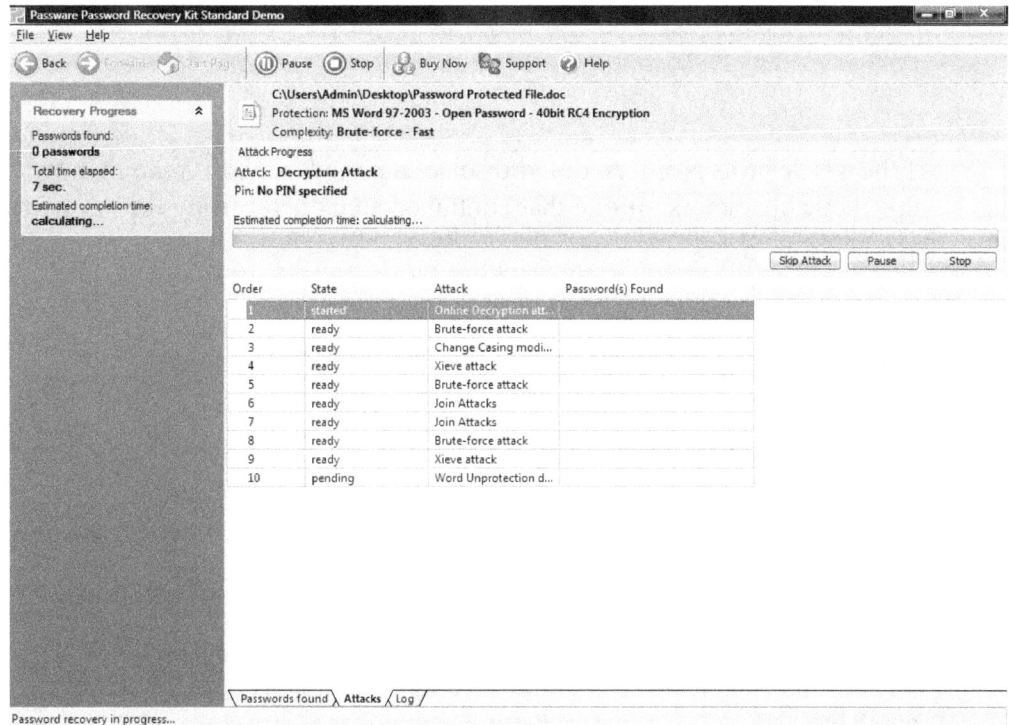

Figure 21-6

10. The attack parameters will be displayed. If the password is recovered, the following window will appear as shown in Figure 21-7.

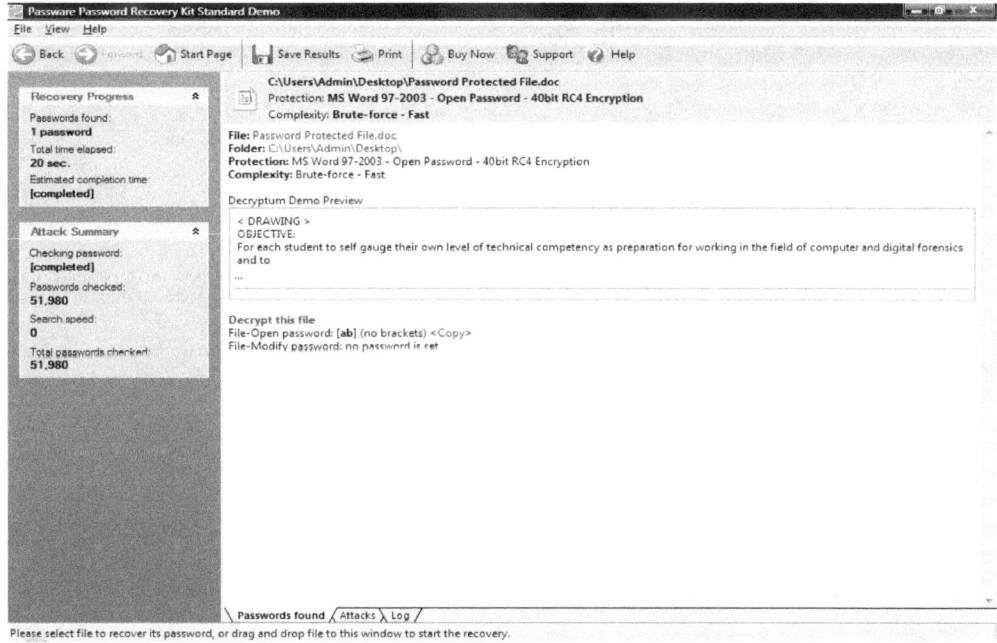

Figure 21-7

11. Was the password recovered?

        Yes   No

If the answer was No, then did you select a password with more than two alphabetic characters, or one that contained a character using the Alt button?

Did the recovered password permit the file to be opened?

12: Repeat this exercise but this time save the file as a Word 2007 file if available.

    A. Was the recovery successful?

        Yes   No

    Explain why or why not.

13. Return to the main start page and try each of the following attack methods for each of the versions of this same file:

    A. Use Predefined Default Attacks (Ctrl-D)

    B. The Advanced: Use Attack Editor (Ctrl+E)

14: Did each method recover the password for both files? Explain!

STUDENT SUMMARY:

1. What did you learn from this exercise?

2. The two character password recovery took how much time? _____

3. How much time would you expect it to take for a four character password recovery? _____

4. How much time would you expect it to take for a 12 character password recovery? _____

5. How much time would you expect it to take for a four character password recovery? _____

6. How much time would you expect it to take for a 25 character password recovery? _____

7. Does the speed of the password recovery system have any impact on the time it takes to perform a password recovery? Explain!

Evaluators Review of Learners Performance

1   2   3   4   5

Forensics Exercise # 22
Microsoft Excel 2016 Password Recovery Using Passware

OBJECTIVE:

To learn how to recover a password protected Microsoft Excel file using Passware.

OVERVIEW:

Many files in industry are password protected. Although the majority of password-protected files are encrypted using third party software, many users utilize the security option available in most Microsoft Office products. This exercise steps you thorough how to recover one of these files.

Part I – Excel File Recovery from a Student Provided File

STEPS:

1. Use the same media from the previous exercise create a Microsoft Excel spreadsheet file and input whatever information you desire into a couple of the cells.

2. Select Tools – Options – Security on the pull down menu.

   a. Save this file with name Excel1.
   b. In the File Encryption Options for this file, Password to Open, enter a TWO-character password.
   c. For the Password to Modify, enter another TWO-character password.
   d. Click OK and save the file to the media as a Microsoft Office 2003 document.
   e. Exit Microsoft Office

3. Exchange media with another student. If you are working independently, you may use the same media.

4. Repeat any necessary steps as provided in the previous exercise to recover the password from the Excel file.

5. Was the password identified? Once the passwords have been identified, attempt to open the Excel file. You will be prompted for the password. Enter the password as provided by the Passware program.

   A. Did the recovered password permit the file to be opened?

6. Open the Excel1 file however this time save it as an Excel 2016 file. Name this file Excel2.

7. Attempt to recover the password using the Password program.

    A. Was the password for the Excel 2016 file determined? Explain why or why not.

8. Double-click on the spreadsheet file attempting to open it. The password box will appear. Enter the recovered password into the password box and open the file.

    A. Was the recovery successful? Explain why or why not.

9. Open WinHex and view the file headers of both the Excel1 and Excel2 files.

    A. Record what the header for the Excel1 file looks like here by filling in the missing information in the shaded boxes.

Offset	0 1 2 3 4 5 6 7 8 9 A B C D E F
00000000	

    B. Record what the header for the Excel2 file looks like here by filling in the missing information in the shaded boxes.

Offset	0 1 2 3 4 5 6 7 8 9 A B C D E F
00000000	

10. Were their differences between the file headers? Explain why or why not!

Part II – Excel File Recovery from an Instructor Provided File

This portion of the exercise deals with password protected files with corrupted headers. You are to reconstruct the provided file, recover the password and determine the contents of the file. You instructor will provide you with a ZIP file titled RecoverThis.ZIP.

11. The RecoverThis.ZIP file contains the following files:

> i. FileX1.xlsx
> ii. FileX2.xls
> iii. FileX1.docx
> iv. FileX2.doc
> v. FileX1.pptx
> vi. FileX2.ppt

Notice the range of the extensions on each of these files. They cover Power Point™ Word™ and Excel™ file formats for both the Microsoft Office™ 2003 and 2007 Office Suites. These specific files have been password protected and their headers corrupted. You are to recover this text and report your findings. (Hint: Once the file is opened you may select the Find option of each file and enter random alphabetic characters. This will search the entire document).

12: Complete the following:

    a. What is the password for the FileX1.xlsx file? _____

    b. What is the recovered text for this file? _____

    c. What cell was this information located in? _____

    d. What is the password for the FileX2.xls file? _____

    e. What is the recovered text for this file? _____

    f. What cell was this information located in? _____

    g. What is the password for the FileX1.docx file? _____

    h. What is the recovered text for this file? _____

    i. What is the password for the FileX2.doc file? _____

    j. What is the recovered text for this file? _____

    k. What is the password for the FileX1.pptx file? _____

l. What is the recovered text for this file? _____

m. What is the password for the FileX2.ppt file? _____

n. What is the recovered text for this file? _____

STUDENT SUMMARY:

1. What did you learn from this exercise?

2. Explain how file reconstruction skills can be beneficial in a forensic examination of a hard drive or other media when the file is password protected.

Evaluators Review of Learners Performance

1   2   3   4   5

OBJECTIVE:

To create a fresh install of an operating system, personalize using it, and then perform a forensic examination of it for a better understanding of how data and information find their way on a system.

OVERVIEW:

This lab project covers the preparation and testing of a Windows 10 "Windows-To-Go" flash drive, which is a completely bootable full-blown version of Windows running from a 32GB USB version 3 Flash Drive. It should be noted, that for acceptable performance, the Flash Drive must be at least at the USB 3.0 standard, and the computer port to which it is plugged into, must support at least USB 3.0.

Part I: Initial Preparation of a USB Bootable Flash drive

Steps:

1. Obtain from your instructor the USB 3.0 Flash Drive, and a CD-Rom disk having the ISO image on it of Windows 10 version 1903.

2. Boot your student computer, and after logging on, right-click your desktop, and create a new folder titled Windows 10 ISO.

3. Put the Disc having the ISO on it into the CD-ROM, Open the CD-ROM, and copy the windows.iso file into the new folder that you created.

4. Open a Web Browser on your student machine and navigate to www.google.com. Enter in the following: Rufus Windows-To-Go. Scroll down until you find the entry called Rufus. The web url should be titled https://rufus.ie.

5. Double-click Rufus, and when that page opens, scroll on down until you see the Download section where it will show the latest version of Rufus. At the time of this lab creation, it was version 3.8.

Figure 23-1

6. Double-click the "Rufus 3.8" link (or whatever version is shown there), which will initiate the Download. Save this file to your Desktop.

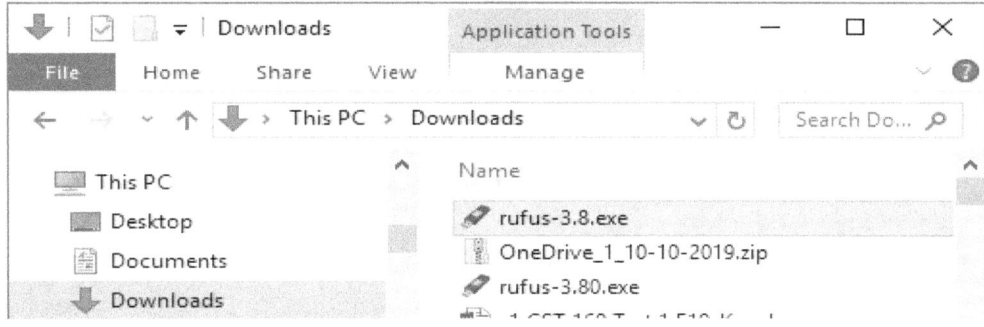

Figure 23-2

7. Copy rufus-3.8.exe to the Desktop.

Figure 23-3

8. Double-click the Rufus icon to start the program – note that it runs directly and does not require any installation. Click "Run" when prompted. You should be presented the screen below.

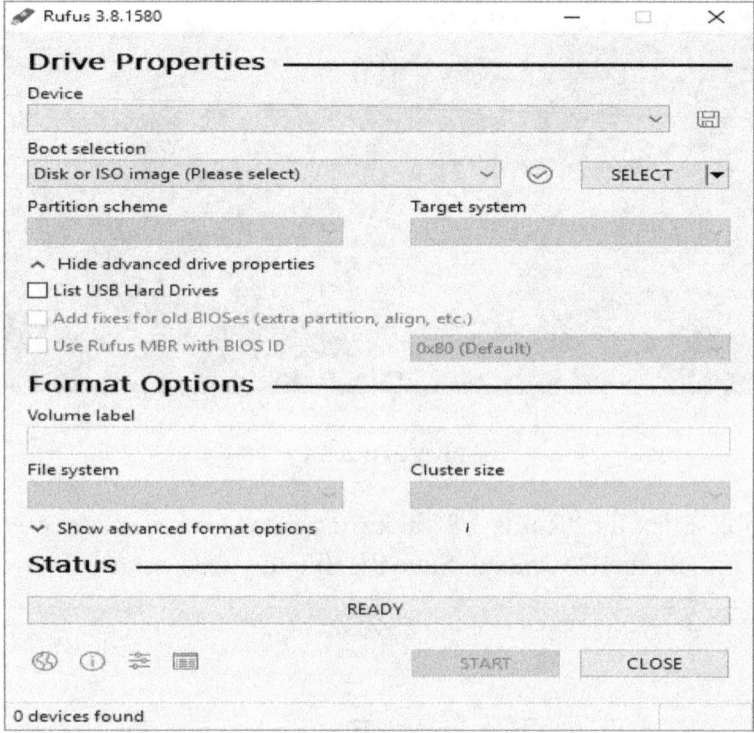

Figure 23-4

Next, configure Rufus by the following steps.

9. Insert your 32GB USB 3.0 Flash Drive into a USB 3.0 Port on your student system.

10. Initialize Rufus by double-clicking the Rufus icon on your desktop.

11. In the top box, under Device, you should see your 32GB flash drive listed.

12. Next, for the Boot Selection, leave it at Disk or ISO Image.

13. On the right of that selection, click directly on the Select button (do not use the arrow).

This step will bring you to an "Open" box, where on the left, you can click Desktop, and on the right side, you can double-click your Windows 10 ISO folder. You should see the ISO file as shown on the next page. Highlight it, and select Open at the bottom.

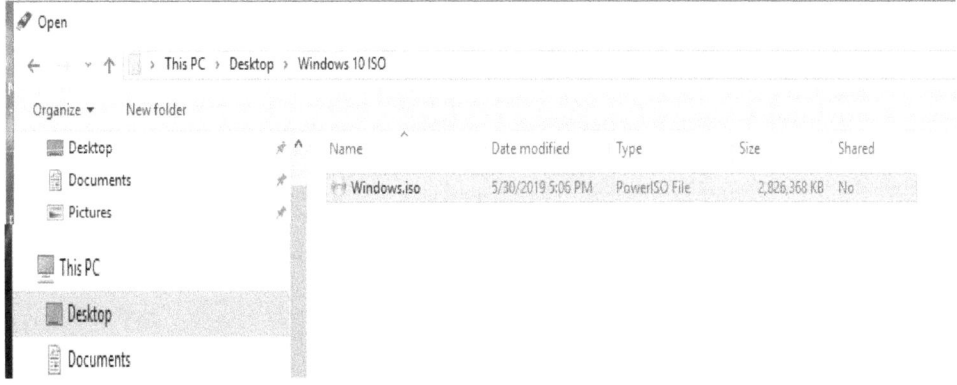

Figure 23-5

14. Next, under Image Option, use the Pull-Down and select Windows-To-Go.

15. Next, under Partition Scheme, use the Pull-Down and choose MBR.

16. For Target System, you will have no choice with the MBR selection – you will have to use "BIOS (sometimes referred to as 'Legacy) or UEFI". But you will have to disable "Secure Boot" if it has been configured in the computers BIOS! This selection is far more compatible if you are going to use your Windows to Go USB on both newer and older systems.

17. Expand the Advanced Options. You want to check the box for Rufus MBR with BIOS ID. This is not necessarily needed but it prevents rebooting back directly into the USB without prompting you to boot from either the USB or Hard Drive (like booting to a CD). With this option checked, you will be prompted each time to choose the USB. This does require you to be watching the screen during reboots (which during the initial configuration of your Windows to Go operating system Windows does a couple of times), but after the initial configuration during regular use of Windows you would be watching the screen anyway during booting and you probably will want to have that choice.

18. Under File System, select the NTFS option.

19. For Cluster Size, leave it at the default, 4096 Bytes

20. Select the Advanced Format Options, make sure Quick Format and Create Extended Label and Icon Files ARE checked – Do not check the box for Check the Device for Bad Blocks, or this step may take a significant amount of time.

21. Leave the default of One Pass as it is.

22. When you are all done, the setting should all look as below. Verify your configuration options as shown below.

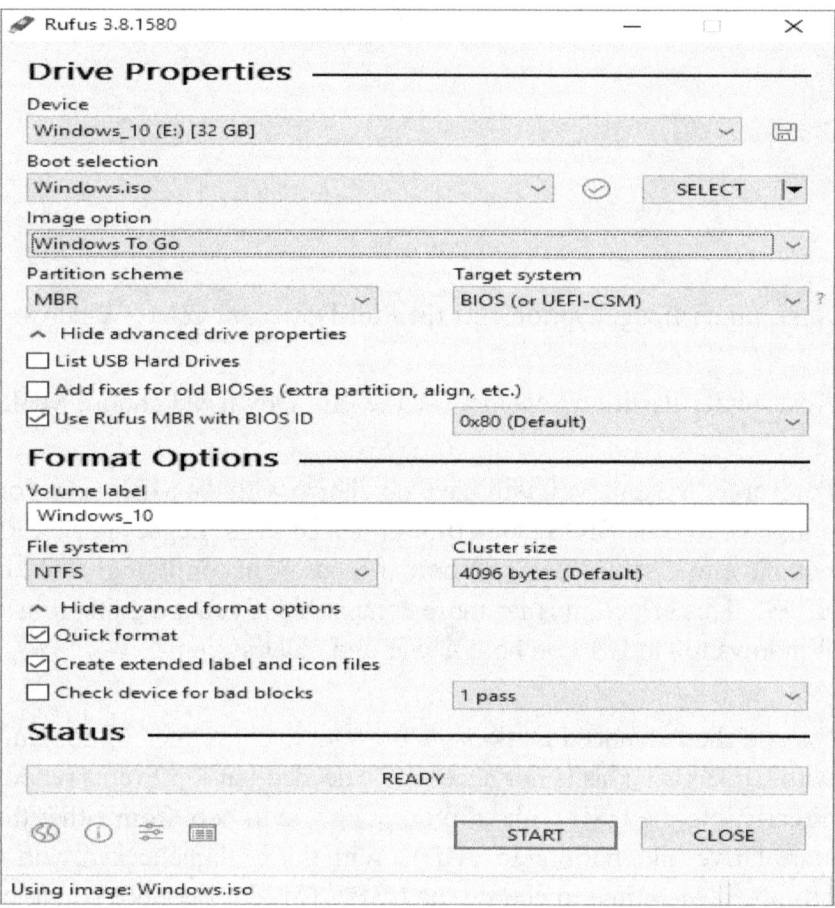

Figure 23-6

23. Next, click the Start button. On the screen that comes up, choose Windows 10 Pro. If you are using an empty drive, or one that you are not concerned about the data on it, select OK.

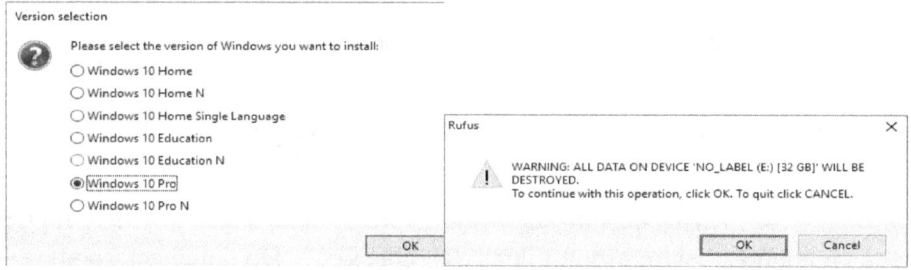

Figure 23-7

24. You will then see quite a number of operations occurring as shown below under STATUS. This step may take approximately 30 to 45 minutes.

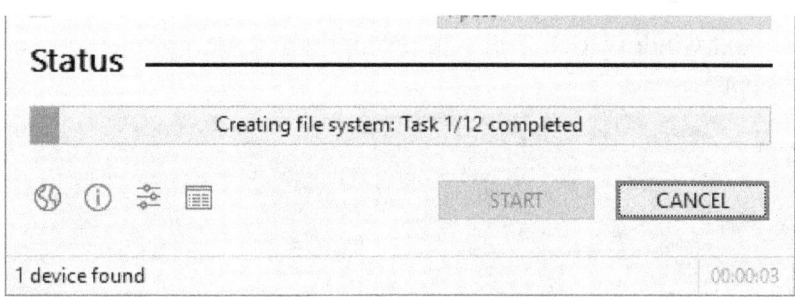

Figure 23-8

25. When you are done, close the Rufus program, which will first result in a message (below) reminding you about disabling SecureBoot in the BIOS if it is enabled. Just say OK to the message. If SecureBoot is enabled in the BIOS of the computer you are using the Flash Drive with, you must go in and disable it. All BIOS's can have this disabled, but the BIOS setting for this will be in different places depending on the brand of motherboard/computer.

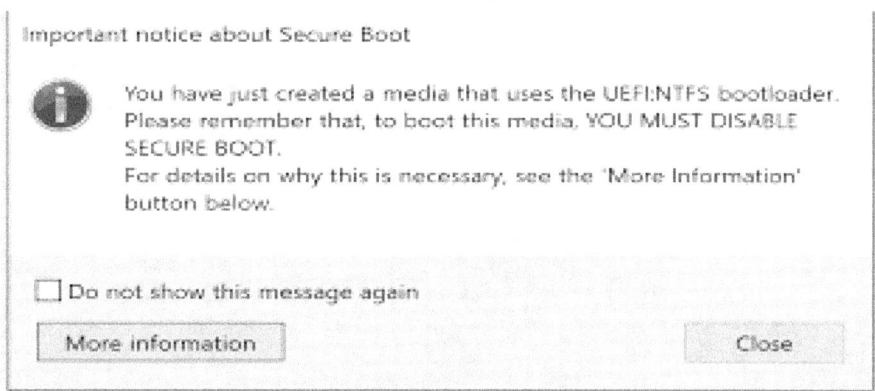

Figure 23-9

26. Your flash drive now is ready to use. To try it out, make sure it is connected to a USB 3.0 port, and during the initial startup, (you must do this QUICK), press the appropriate key for your system to bring up a boot menu. This also varies a lot on different computers. For Dell's it is "F12", for others it may be "F8" or a different "F" key, but it normally is one of these. You can usually Google the make of the computer/motherboard, and determine the proper key quite easily.

27. You will then get a prompt to hit a key for booting to the USB (rather than the computer's hard drive – make sure you hit a key. You will first see the Windows Logo, and Windows will go through the procedure to recognize devices, the hardware associated with that motherboard or computer. It will then reboot. Again, carefully observe the POST process, as you will have to choose again to get a boot menu, and again press a key to choose to boot from the USB.

28. You will sequence through a series of initialization screens where you will be prompted to select a region & language. For U.S. classes, select U.S. and English. The next screen will prompt for a 2nd keyboard, accept the U.S. default option. The next window to appear will prompt you to accept the license. Select 'Accept'.

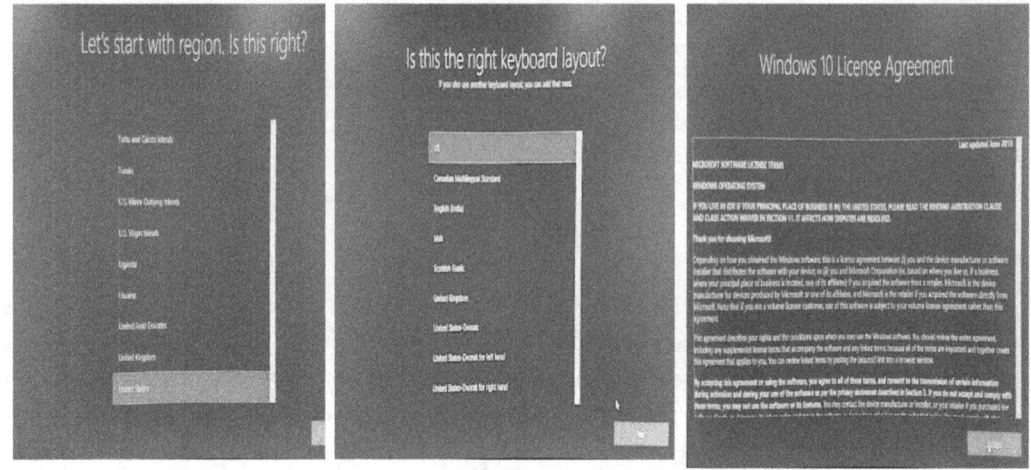

Figure 23-10

29. This next window to appear is much more important! For a college course or a corporate training program, select the 'Set Up for an Organization' option, not Personal Use!

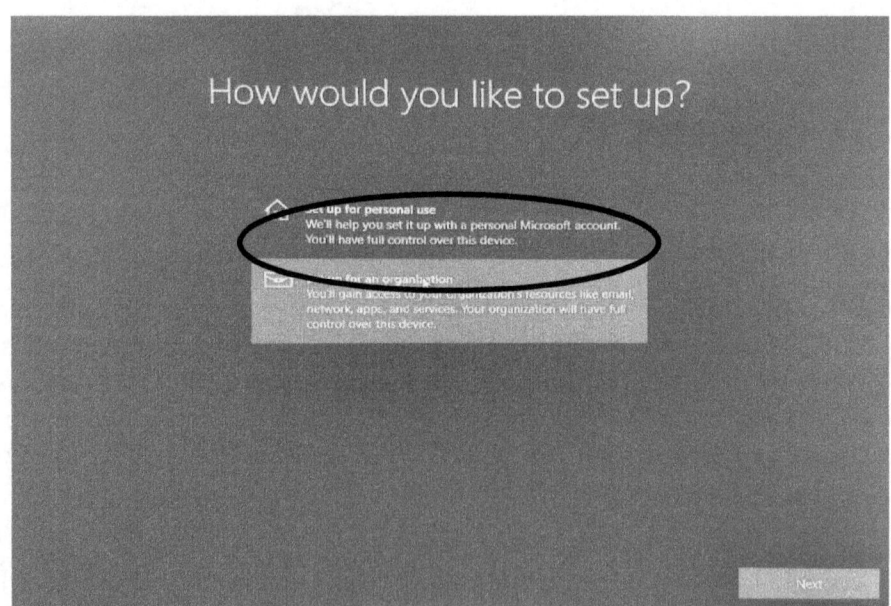

Figure 23-11

30. On the next screen, in the Lower Left corner, choose "Domain join instead"

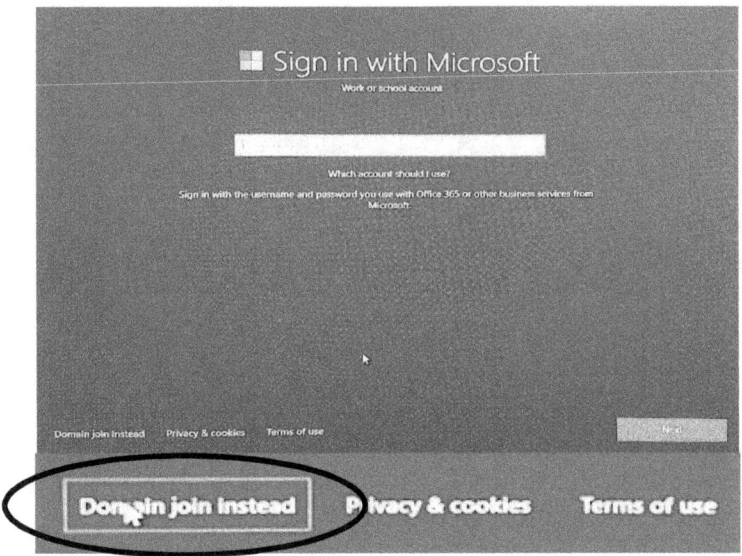

Figure 23-12

31. On the next, you can choose a User Name – for school projects, you probably will want to choose "student" – he will automatically be a member of the Administrators Group on the computer. On the next screen, choose the password "forensics".

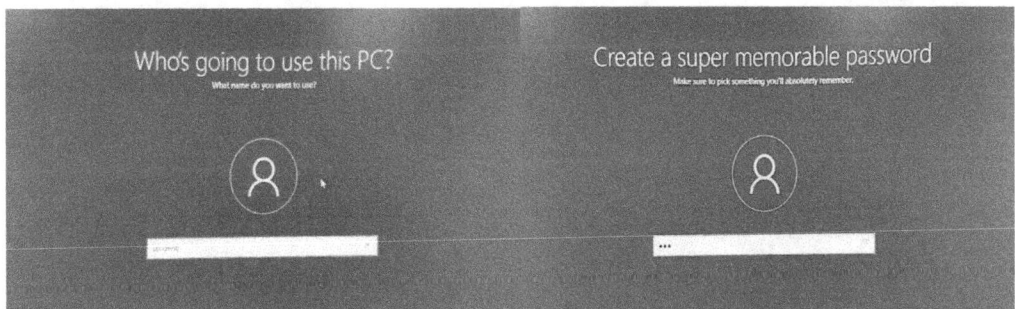

Figure 23-13

32. On the next screen, you will confirm your password, and on the following three screens, you will be prompted for "Password Hints". For use in your forensics program in all three screens, just choose the default question – whatever comes up – then answer it with a password hint that corresponds to the password 'forensics'.

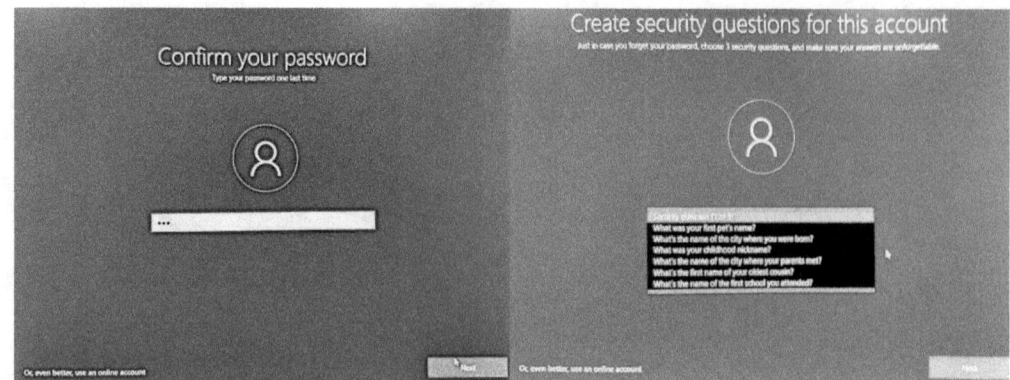

Figure 23-14

33. On the next screen, select No! We do not want Microsoft to start Personalizing our Experiences and Settings on a Recovery, Repair, or Forensics tool. In addition, we do not want Cortana collecting information from our computer and feeding it back to Microsoft. This may be an acceptable practice for end users, depending on corporate policy, but this is inappropriate for a forensics environment. Make sure you choose Decline for this option.

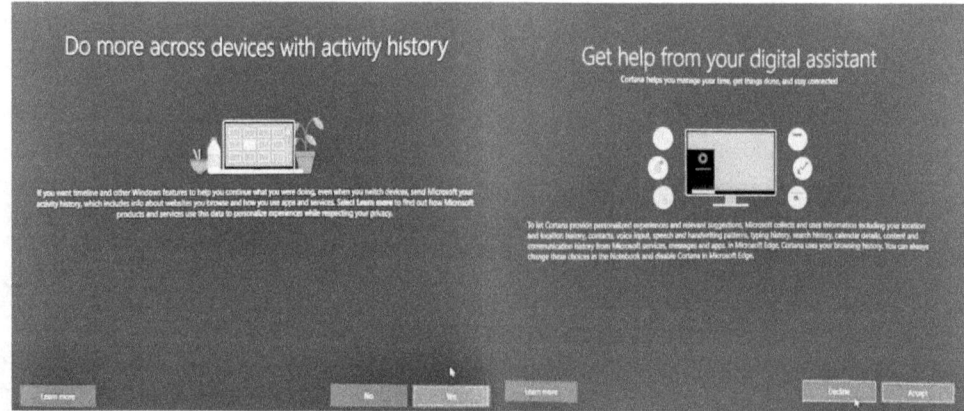

Figure 23-15

34. On the next screen change all Settings to "NO"! and click the Accept button. Virtually all of these settings have to do with sending or receiving some type of information to or from Microsoft.

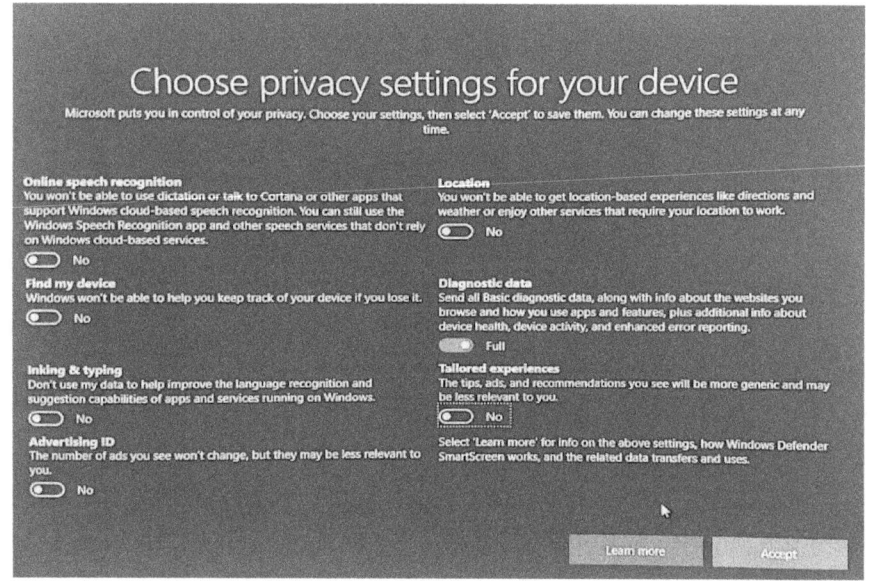

Figure 23-16

35. At this point you are ready to reboot into a complete Windows-To-Go system right from a USB 3.0 Flash Drive in a USB 3.0 Port. This reboot will be much faster than a hard disk, but not quite as fast as a Solid State Hard Drive! Remember to hit the key for a Boot Menu for your particular system, choose USB, and when prompted a 2nd time, choose USB again. You should now come to a full Windows 10 Desktop!!!!

Note regarding Windows Activation: This being a new Windows initialization, the boot process discovered all new hardware, thus, it will try to be activated. For a Recovery, Repair, Forensics use as a forensics target media, activation would be a problem as this Flash Drive could possibly be used with many different computers, all having different hardware, each requiring a separate activation! Therefore, we will not activate it which will cause a Personalization concern for which Windows will give you an error message for.

However, as a technician, it would be beneficial to have the regular Desktop icons on the Desktop. So verify that the original Windows 10 ISO CD-ROM is still installed and search for a folder named 'Personalization'. Copy this folder to your desktop and double-click it, which will open it and bring you the screen shown in Figure 23-17.

149

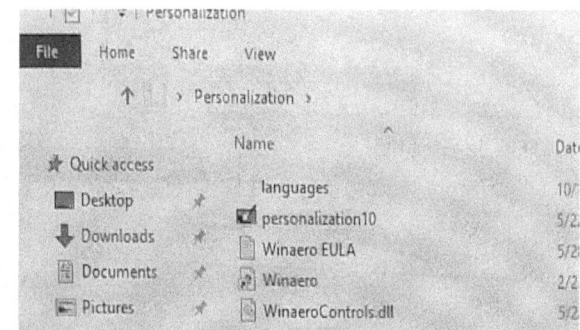

Figure 23-18

36. Click Personalization 10 and accept the license, then the next screen should look as below, left. Click at the upper left, "Change Desktop Icons" which will bring up the screen, below right. Put checks in all the boxes and click OK at the bottom.

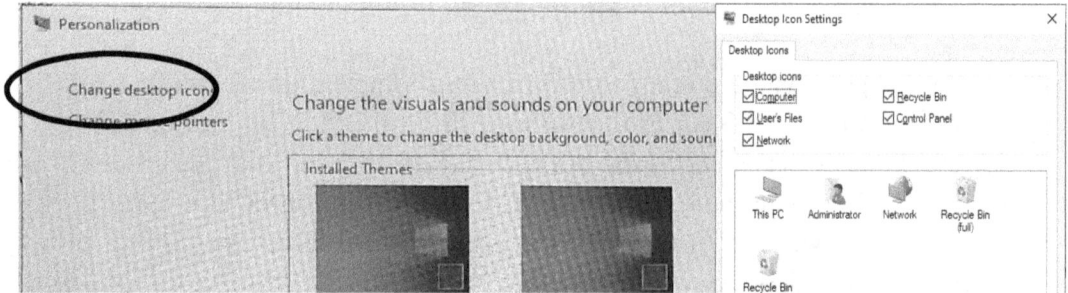

Figure 23-19

37. The USB version of the Windows desktop should look as below. You now have a completely installed running version of Windows 10 version 1903 booting and running directly from a Flash Drive.

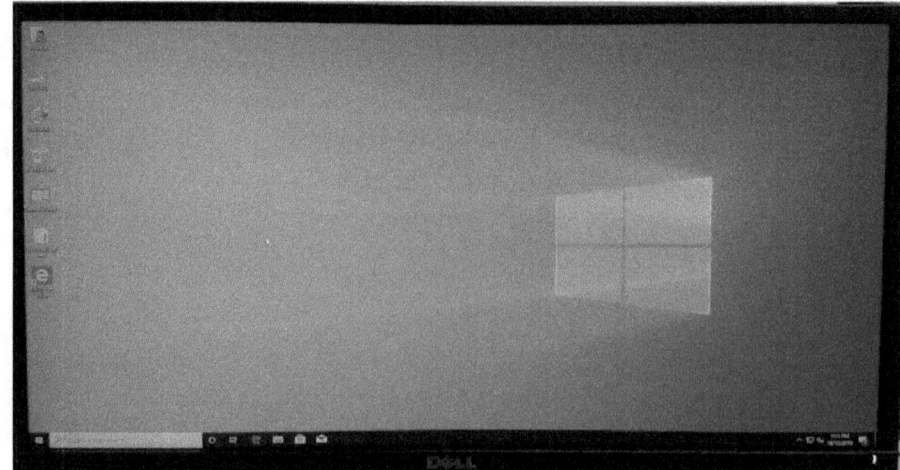

Figure 23-20

150

Part II: Create a Personalized Working Image for Forensic Analysis

38. After you have booted your newly created Windows 10 flash drive. Ensure it is connected to the Internet. If it is not, then take the appropriate steps to connect to it. This may entail configuring IP addressing information. If you are unsure how to do this, ask your instructor.

39. Once you have Internet connectivity, perform the following:

    - Google searches on items of your interest

    - Visit travel agency websites and navigate to areas of your interest

    - Navigate to airline reservation sites and select destinations of your interest.

    - Create Word and Notepad text files. Input various items such as grocery lists, computer parts, list of travel items, and other items of interest

    - Select other items of interest in your Internet searches

    - Create a new user account with a name of your choice. Use a password of two characters

    - Navigate around the operating system, view account setting, system tools, etc.

    - Ask your instructor for any additional guidance or suggestions regarding how to personalize this bootable device in preparation for a forensic examination.

    Note: You should not use this bootable flash drive for actual personal use such as banking, email or other account information. This bootable flash drive will be imaged and examined.

40. Once you feel you have created a few user experiences on this system, properly shut down the operating system and eject the flash drive.

STUDENT SUMMARY:

1. What did you learn from this exercise?

2. Explain how this fully functional operating system will become a treasure trove of information once a user has utilized it. Explain how the registry, cookie folders, download folder, user account and how the user will personalize password information.

3. Considering question # 2 above, explain how a user use profile may be a component of a much larger or more significant investigation or examination, and without prejudging the user's intentions or expressing your own personal opinion, explain how what you find may lead you to search in other areas of the image. For example, thumbnails of exotic travel destinations may be linked to ??? in the registry. Be prepared to discuss this student summary with your instructor.

Evaluators Review of Learners Performance

1   2   3   4   5

Forensics Exercise # 24
Forensically Examine a Personalized Working Image

OBJECTIVE:

To examine an operating system that you created and used for a more personalized understanding of how and what types of data are contained in a Windows operating system.

OVERVIEW:

This exercise will have the student acquire a bit-stream image of a personalized operating system using FTK imager and Autopsy forensic examination software, then report their findings.

STEPS:

1. Switch USB devices with another student. (Unless your instructor advises otherwise)

2. If you have a USB write blocker, insert it into your student forensics system.

3. Initialize FTK Imager and using steps previously learned, create an image of the Windows 10 bootable USB device. Use an appropriate naming convention and record your information here:

   Name of the Case Image File: _____

   Examiners Name: _____

   Software used to create the Image File: _____

   Version of the software used to create the Image File: _____

   Date the Case Image File was Created: _____

   Time Zone of the Created Image File: _____

   Device Make: _____

   Device Serial Number: _____

   MD5 Before Hash Value: _____

   MD5 After Hash Value: _____

   Drive Capacity: _____

4. After you have created the image file, remove the USB device and return it to the student you exchanged drives with.

5. Initialize Autopsy and using previously learned naming and configuration conventions, import the newly created image file and begin a full indexing operation.

6. Analyze the image and identify the following from this case image file:

    a. What types of files did you discover in this image?

    b. How did you open these files? Be very specific in how each file was opened.

    c. What are the contents of each of these files? Provide a screenshot if available.

    d. Identify the following:

        1. Types of documents, contents, passwords for each file.

        2. Pictures, types of pictures, locations of pictures (Note: Review background information of the pictures to potentially identify a probable location. Consider foliage, buildings, signs, vehicles, license plates, water color or hue, dress and apparel of people in the pictures, etc.

        3. Registry entries, Internet searches, websites visited, files downloaded.

As a reminder, you have been instructed that it is inappropriate to present opinion regarding intentions of the user, or generalized perceptions as to their motives, however, part of being an effective computer forensic examiner is to let the image guide you towards deeper discoveries contained therein.

STUDENT SUMMARY:

1. What did you learn from this exercise?

2. What various types of information did you discover? Consider those items as identified in step # 6 of this exercise.

Evaluators Review of Learners Performance

1   2   3   4   5

Forensics Exercise # 25
Anti-Forensics Videos – Drive Shredding

OBJECTIVE:

To become familiar with the techniques utilized by both corporate and government organizations and agencies regarding the discarding and destruction of potentially sensitive information.

OVERVIEW:

It is possible that even after a disk has been formatted that data and information can still be retrieved from it, especially if the format operation was a 'Quick Format'. Data that are no longer desired or media that is no longer in operational use should be handled per company or agency policy. Data that may be of no use to your organization may be of significant benefit to a competitor or cyber-criminal. When data is no longer viable to your organization because it is outdated, it sometimes referred to as data rot.

Storage devices become candidate for physical destruction when they become either defective, or the data on them is too sensitive to risk being inadvertently discovered by an unauthorized person. There are various methods used for the physical destruction of a disk drive, including, shredding, crushing, melting, incinerating and drilling.

Figure 25-1

Steps:

1. Navigate to Youtube and perform a search on disk drive shredder. You will be presented with several videos showing how storage devices are destroyed. View a couple of these videos to gain a better understanding as to the process of physical destruction of storage devices.

2. Identify the websites you visited by title of the video and company information if provided:

Title of Video	Company Name if Available

3. After viewing the videos, perform a search online and answer the questions below:

   a. What is e-scrap?

   b. How is e-scrap discarded?

   c. Identify one make, model and manufacturer of a commercially available disk drive shredder.

   d. Identify the cost of the disk drive shredder in step c. above.

   e. What is bulk erasing of a hard disk or tape drive?

   f. Identify two types of bulk erasers. Identify by make, model and any other specifications available such as gauss or oersteds.

   g. Identify the price of at least one degausser model.

STUDENT SUMMARY:

1. What did you learn from this exercise?

Evaluators Review of Learners Performance

1   2   3   4   5

Forensics Exercise # 26
Anti-Forensics - Cyber Scrubbing

OBJECTIVE:

To become familiar with the techniques utilized by both corporate and government organizations and agencies regarding the cyber-scrubbing of existing disk and other magnetic storage devices to eliminate potentially sensitive information.

OVERVIEW:

This exercise will have the student utilize some readily available tools to cyber-scrub a hard disk or SSD. Cyber-scrubbing is an important aspect of an organizations security policy. The student should become familiar with data erasing standards, including DoD 5220.22.

The student should understand that deleted files remain on the computer, including passwords, emails, all types of documents including encrypted files. These types of information can provide a user profile that can be sensitive to an unauthorized individual. In a corporate or governmental organization, the user is not the only person authorized to access their computer. Computer technicians and network personnel also have access to their systems, and thus, the data contained on them.

Part I – DoD Standards and Eraser On-Demand

STEPS:

1. Perform a search and identify the steps known as the DoD 5220.22-M, or the DoD 3-pass method. Fill in the description for each pass

Pass 1: _____   _____

Pass 2: _____

Pass 3: _____

Then, _____ the final overwrite pass.

2. Acquire a copy of the cyber scrubbing tools identified below. You may download or your instructor may provide you with a copy.

      A. Eraser Standalone [On-Demand] program
      B. BleachBit
      C. CCleaner

3. Make several copies of any file you choose. Place them on the Desktop for quick availability.

4. Initialize the Eraser On-Demand cyber scrubbing program.

    Note: This version of Eraser does not require use of the .net framework while the 6.2 version does. It is not appropriate to install programs that require support or interaction with outside services on a forensics examination system.

5. Drag and drop one of the copied files into the Eraser On-Demand program. Your Eraser program GUI should look something like this.

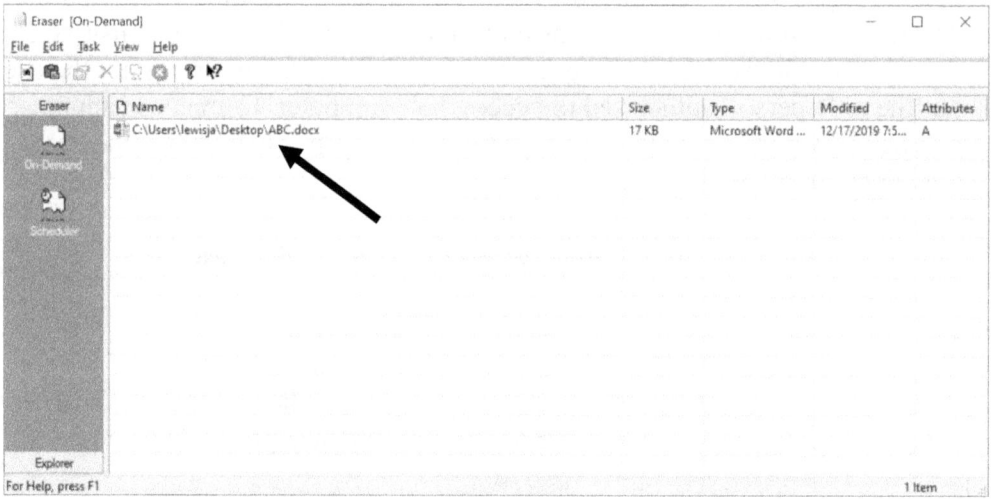

Figure 26-1

    Note: It is important that the correct path information is displayed, and authorized user rights are granted to perform this operation. Erasing operations are unrecoverable.

6. Select the 'Task' pull down menu, then 'Run All'. You will then be presented with a pop-up window that is asking you to confirm you want to destroy the selected data. Select the 'Yes' option. See Figure 26-2.

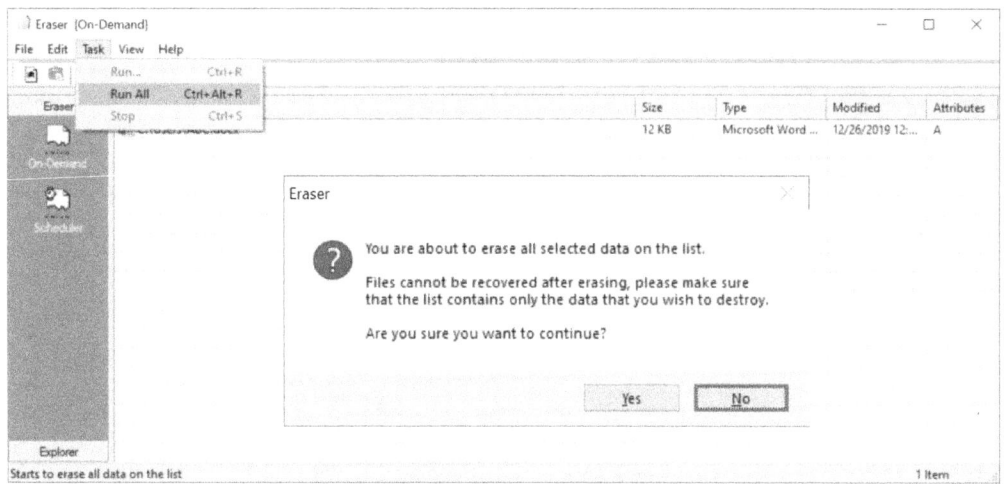

Figure 26-3

7. After the data has been erased, an Erasing Report window will appear identifying successfully completion of the erase operation.

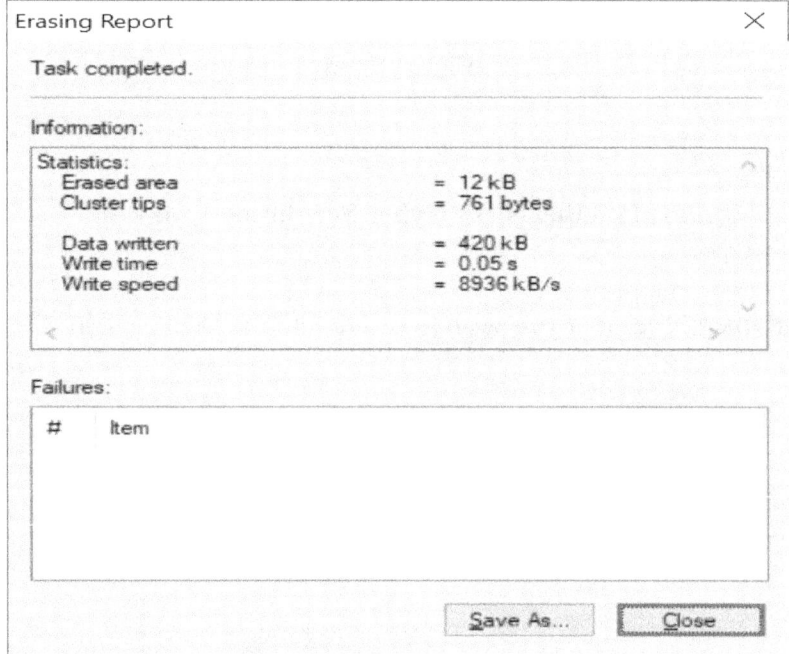

Figure 26-4

8. Many organizations now restrict file write and storage access to various locations on the company's computer. If an erase function is applied to a file in a restricted location, the Eraser On-Demand program will be prevented from completing the operation and an Access is Denied fail message will result as shown in Figure 26-5.

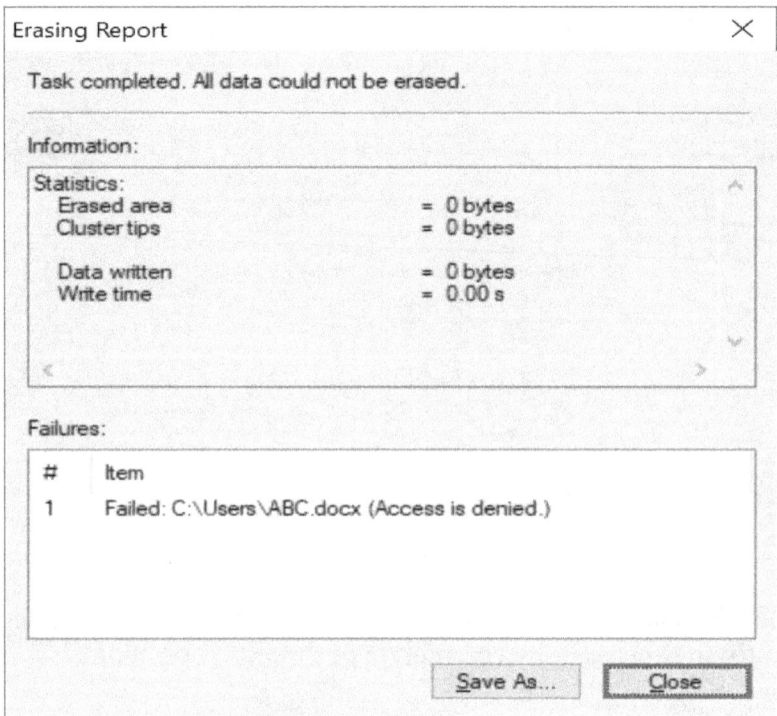

Figure 26-5

Part II – BleachBit Cyber Scrubbing Program

9. Put several files that you wish to delete into the Recycle Bin.

Figure 26-6

10. Initialize the BleachBit cyber scrubbing tool. Notice the multiple options located in the left pane of the BleachBit window.

11. Make sure the Recycle Bin option is checked. Under the Windows Explorer option check the Cookies and History options.

12. Click on the 'Clean' icon located on the top taskbar. You will be presented with the following message.

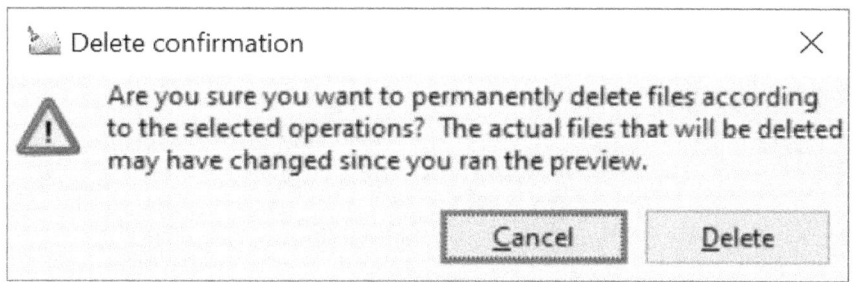

Figure 26-7

13. Select the 'Delete' option. BleachBit will now run the selected operations and a completion process report will appear.

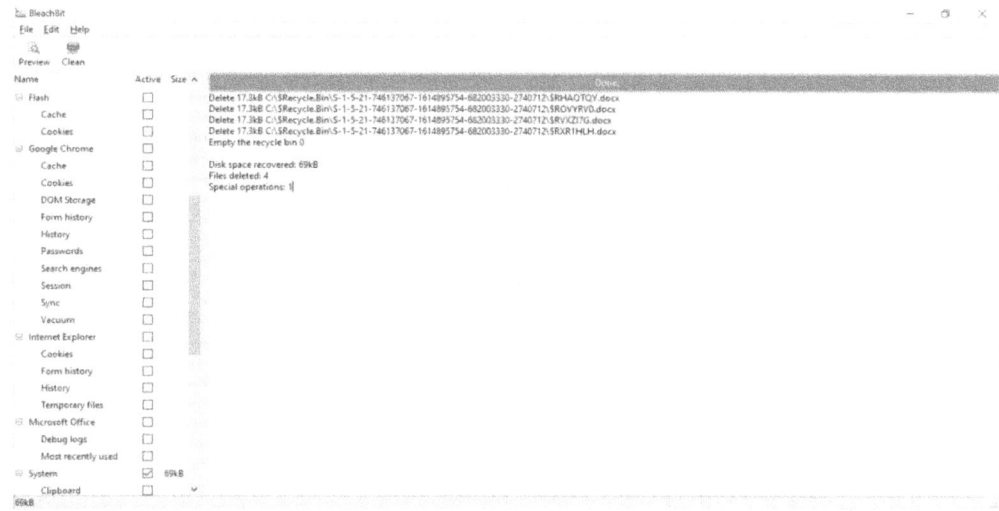

Figure 26-8

14. Notice the individual delete lines of information. Does any of the information look familiar?

    a.   What does the S-X-X-X information represent?

    b.   The file extensions of the deleted files will match what was in the Recycle Bin. What is reported as the number of files deleted and the amount of disk space recovered?

15. Select the Deep Scan, System, Windows Explorer options for cleaning.

16. Select the Preview option on the toolbar. See Figure 26-9 below.

Figure 26-9

17. Select the Clean option. The cyber scrubbing operation will begin. A time line will appear that indicates how much time remains for the disk wiping operation to complete.

18. Your instructor will designate an amount of time for you to become familiar with the BleachBit program. During this time become familiar with cleaning the following:

    a. url history of various web browsers.
    b. Passwords stored per various web browsers.
    c. Windows Explorer mru, run and search history.
    d. System Free disk space.

19. Consider that all options are checked within the BleachBit program. What would be the consequences of a forensics examination after such an operation has been performed on a system?

20. Identify a minimum of three indicators that a cyber-scrubbing operation has been performed on a target computer.

a. _____

b. _____

c. _____

21. Identify two reasons that might require the cyber-scrubbing of a company computer.

a. _____

b. _____

22. Identify two reasons that might require the cyber-scrubbing of a home or personal computer.

a. _____

b. _____

Part III – CCleaner

23. Install and initialize the CCleaner program on your student workstation.

24. The program window will appear as shown below. Notice the Easy Clean option is selected by default.

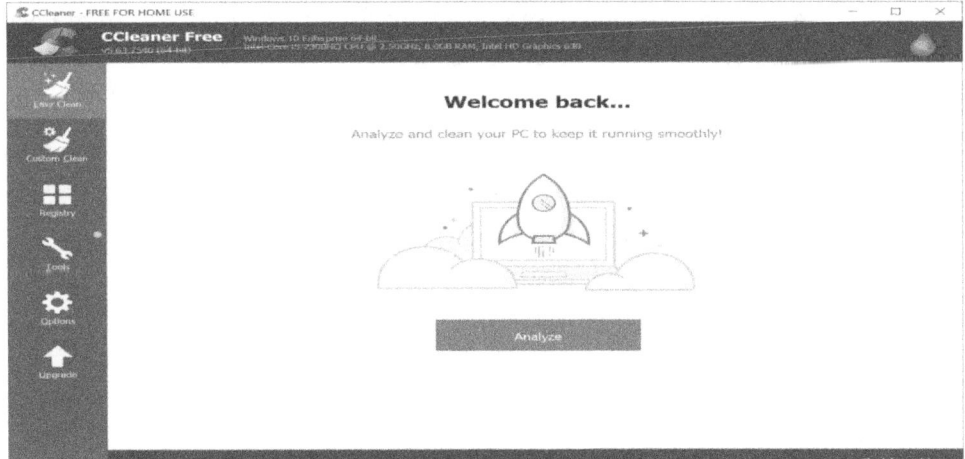

Figure 26-10

25. Select the Analyze button located in the center of the window. CCleaner will scan the drive and identify unnecessary items that can be discarded, including Recycle Bin, Temporary System, Internet and Application files, and tracking cookies associated with each of the available Internet browsers.

26. Select the Clean All option. CCleaner will now remove all the identified and selected items.

27. After you have cleaned your system, close CCLeaner and navigate to three different websites.

28. Open CCLeander again and run the Easy Clean operation.

    a. How many trackers were identified?

    b. How many MB of 'Junk' were identified?

    c. Clean out these new discoveries.

29. Your instructor will designate an amount of time for you to become familiar with the CCleaner program. During this time become familiar with cleaning the following:

    a. url history of various web browsers.
    b. Passwords stored per various web browsers.
    c. Windows Explorer mru, run and search history.
    d. System Free disk space.

30. Experiment with several of these options making note of how these data areas may correlate to where a forensics examiner may search.

    a. Assuming the user performed a cleaning of their system, where else might the forensics examiner look for data or information relevant to their examination or investigation?

STUDENT SUMMARY:

    1. What did you learn from this exercise?

    2. Identify two additional cyber-scrubbing tools that are available, either free or for purchase. Identify the name, where to acquire them, and either free or cost.

Cyber Scrubbing Tool	Where to Acquire	Free or Purchase

Evaluators Review of Learners Performance

1   2   3   4   5

Forensics Exercise # 27
Anti-Forensics - Encryption

OBJECTIVE:

To become more familiar with various encryption options available for client systems. This exercise will have the student identify several end user encryption tools and become familiar with their common characteristics.

OVERVIEW:

There are numerous encryption tools available, both free and for purchase. Users of encryption programs from unknown sources must exercise caution when downloading as not all developers of encryption software have benevolent intentions. This exercise will have the student identify several popular encryption tools, and demonstrate their use.

Part I – WinZip Compression and Encryption Software

STEPS:

1. Download a copy of WinZip and install it on your student system. Newer versions of WinZip use an installer and have a limited time trial.

2. What did Once it has been installed, initialize WinZip and select the 'Use Evaluation Version' option.

3. What did Notice the Actions pane on the right side of the GUI. Select the Encrypt option slider bar to On.

Figure 27-1

4. Select a file from the Desktop and make a copy of it. You will not want to experiment with a file of value.

5. Drag this copied file into the WinZip GUI. An 'Add Complete' window will appear.

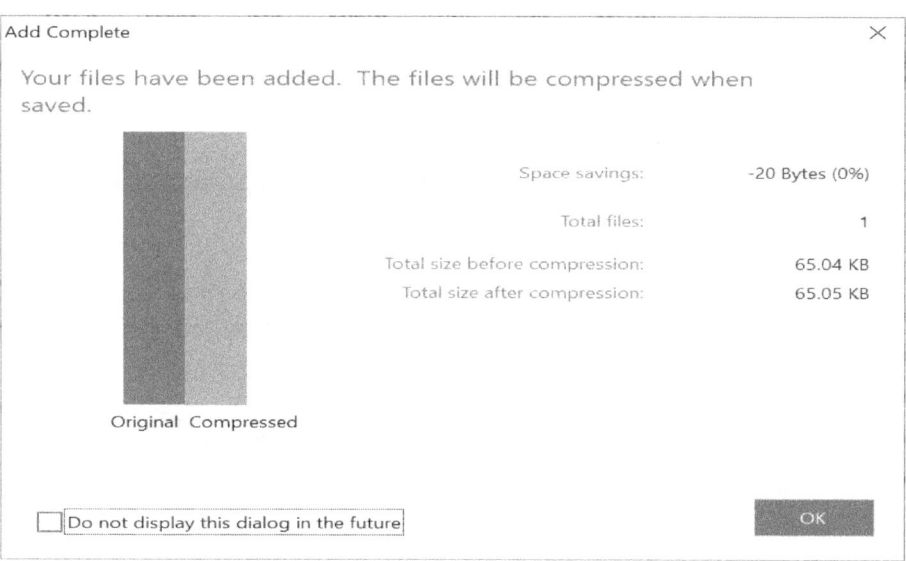

Figure 27-2

6. Notice the Space savings amount for the compression of this file. How much space savings will result in the compression of the file you selected? _____

7. Select 'Ok'.

8. Your WinZip GUI will now display the name of your file to be compressed. Select 'File', then 'Save' and navigate to the Desktop for the location to save the file. Select an appropriate file name and then 'Save'.

9. Close WinZip.

10. Open WinZip again and make sure there is no file selected to be compressed. Notice the Actions pane on the right side of the GUI. Select the Encrypt option slider bar to On.

11. Drag the same uncompressed source file from step # 5 into the WinZip file compression window. A WinZip Caution window should appear advising of the option to review additional information regarding encryption cautions. If you feel it necessary, select the F1 key to navigate to more information regarding encryption. If you do not feel the need, select 'Ok'.

12. An Encrypt window with a password file will appear. Enter an eight character password, confirm it in the Re-enter field and select 'Ok'. Your selected file will now be compressed and encrypted and the Add Complete window will present the compression information. Save the file and exit WinZip.

13. Try to open the compressed and encrypted file. Were you successful?

    If you had difficulty with this step, notify your instructor.

Part II – WinZip Compression and Encryption Software

14. Perform an online search and identify three popular and free file encryption programs. Identify the name, manufacture, features and location to download each.

Name of Encryption Software	Manufacturer	Features	Download Site

Table 27- 1

15. In your own words, describe the Bitlocker feature available on specific versions of the Windows operating system. Identify which specific versions and how to activate it.

16. Perform an online search and identify three popular and purchase file encryption programs. Identify the name, manufacture, features, price and location to download each.

Name of Encryption Software	Manufacturer	Features	Download Site	Price of Software

Table 27-2

17. Perform an online search and identify three popular and purchase flash drive encryption programs. Identify the name, manufacture, features, price and location to download each.

Name of Encryption Software	Manufacturer	Features	Download Site	Price of Software

Table 27-3

18. Perform a search and identify an online hash table, also known as a rainbow table, and how to use it to identify a password. Identify the online address, how many characters the hash tables contain (8, 9, 10, etc), and how to use the tables.

19. Perform an online search and identify three popular and purchase disk drive encryption programs. Identify the name, manufacture, features, price and location to download each.

Name of Encryption Software	Manufacturer	Features	Download Site	Price of Software

Table 27-4

20. Answer the following questions:

a. What is AES encryption?

b. What is DES encryption?

c. How significant is 128-bit versus 256-bit encryption? Be specific in your answer.

STUDENT SUMMARY:

1. What did you learn from this exercise?

2. Consider the challenge presented to a computer forensic examiner if a Microsoft file was encrypted by Word or Excel encryption, then compressed and encrypted by WinZip or another similar program.

    a. What steps must the forensic examiner take to recover the text file? Be specific!

3. Consider the challenge presented to a computer forensic examiner if a Microsoft file was encrypted by Word or Excel encryption, the file header corrupted under WinHex, then compressed and encrypted by WinZip or another similar program, and the file header corrupted.

    a. What steps must the forensic examiner take to recover the text file? Be specific!

    b. As a computer forensic examiner, how would you detect such actions?

Evaluators Review of Learners Performance

1   2   3   4   5

Forensics Exercise # 28
Anti-Forensics - Steganography

OBJECTIVE:

To demonstrate how steganography software is used to conceal documents and pictures from detection and recovery, and to gain experience attempting to detect whether a jpg file was altered by use of a Stenography program.

OVERVIEW:

Steganography tools can conceal text documents, e-mail messages, pictures and spreadsheets, all of which may be hidden inside a jpeg or mp3 file. Discovery of stenographic tools on a drive should direct the examiner to consider that there may be stenographic images on the drive. There are numerous tools used to detect stenographic files.

Steganography is the art of covered or hidden writing and it is used in computer technology as a means of covert communication to conceal information from a third party. Some steganography applications work by embedding the message to be concealed into a carrier file, then breaking it into multiple pieces. This is known as file splitting.

Figure 28-1

Steganography is easily learned with automated tools and is a concern when working with intellectual property and possible terrorism. In this exercise you will learn some of the techniques used to create stenographic images.

174

Part I – Steganography – Embedding a File within a File

STEPS

1. Create a .txt file that contains the following text.

   This is a hidden file to demonstrate how hiding it in a picture file
   can be accomplished.

   Save this file with the name hidden.txt.

2. Perform a search for and download and install any steganographic program
   you desire. There are multiple versions available. This exercise uses the sg.exe
   version 1.81 application. A good site to check at the time of this printing is
   http://www.soft32.com. Once sg.exe (or your choice of stego programs) has
   been downloaded and installed, initialize it.

Figure 28-2

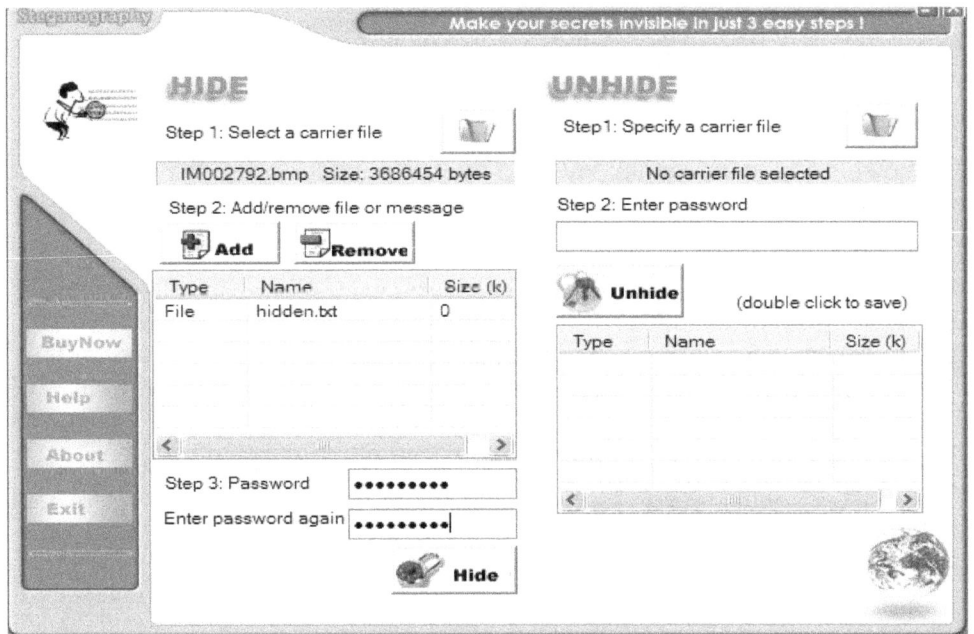

Figure 28-3

3. Next, select a .jpg or .bmp file as your carrier file by navigating to it using the 'Select a carrier file' option under the 'Hide' column. The image file selected for this example is shown in the window immediately below the Select a carrier file option.

4. Select the Add button below Add/remove file or message option. You should be presented with the following image.

Figure 28-4

5. At this point select the File button and select Next. You will be prompted to enter a password to hide and encrypt this hidden file inside of the carrier file.

6. Click Hide and you will be prompted for the name and save location for the newly created file.

7. Minimize or close the Steganography program and double click on the newly created stenographic file to open it. It should look the same as it did before the text file was hidden in it. Close the file.

8. Go to the Unhide section of this application and select the carrier file. This is the file you just created using the Steganography program. Enter the password you provided in the Hide section and click the Unhide button. You will be prompted for a location of where to save the recovered hidden.txt file.

9: To verify the contents of the hidden.txt file are encrypted, initialize the WinHex application and select File, then Open. Select the newly created carrier file and load it into the WinHex viewer. The display should be incomprehensible.

10. Next, select View from the pull down menu and click on Text. Your display should still show data that is incomprehensible.

11. To further validate that the hidden.txt file is encrypted within the new
    stego file, select Search from the pull down menu and click on Find Text. In
    the "The following text string will be searched" window enter the word
    hidden and click OK. You should receive a message informing you that the
    search string was not found.

Part II – Steganography – Detecting a File within a File

This exercise involves using Stegdetect for detecting stenographic programs. The
computer examiner realizes that there are multiple application tools of this type
and they should be familiar with a variety of them. The forensic examiner should
take notice anytime a steganography program is identified. Although the detection
of stenographic files is frequently left to automated scanning and analysis tools,
once identified, extracting the hidden content from the message proves much
more difficult.

When a file is steganography embedded into another file, the structure of that file,
also known as the carrier or host file, is altered. This alteration generally results
in the leaving of a known signature, or a unique hexadecimal pattern within that
file. Some automated stenographic detection tools search for and report these
identifiable patterns. There are two general approaches to creating a
stenographical altered image file. The files may either append or embed the
hidden file or information into the carrier file. Appending to the carrier file can
be detected by scanning the carrier beyond the end-of-file marker for hidden
information. Embedding hidden information within the file would involve
rearranging the least significant bit of a carrier file to accommodate acceptance
and inclusion of the new information.

Automated stenographic detection tools scan files looking for evidence of these
alterations. When an alteration is detected or suspect for a particular file, it is
reported as such. There is a variety of stenographic detection tools available on
the market and the computer examiner should determine which tool is best for
their analysis. Since stenographic detection is a relatively new concept in the
open market, software analysis tools and processes are being constantly refined
and some tools will provide false positive reports. A false positive is the report of
a file that contains stenographic information in it when it actually does not.

One indicator that should direct the examiner to search for stenographic files
would be the discovery of stenographic tools on the evidence drive. Once
discovered, stenographic detection can commence for the rest of the drive. This is
accomplished by detection software analyzes image files for stenographic content
by searching for these identifiable hexadecimal signatures as previously
discussed. Some commercially available stenographic detection software may be

very expensive to purchase but well worth the investment in circumstances where highly sensitive or confidential intellectual property is to be maintained.

For demonstration and training purposes, one particular stego detection package can be found at http://www.spy-hunter.com/stegspydownload.htm.

12. Using the StegSpy or a similar program, select the carrier file that you embedded the hidden.txt file in. Import this into your StegSpy detection software.

   a. Was the file detected as a stenographic file?

13. Select another picture file that you know does not contain a hidden file within it and perform the same operation.

   a. What are the results of this operation?

StegSpy Stenographic Detection Software

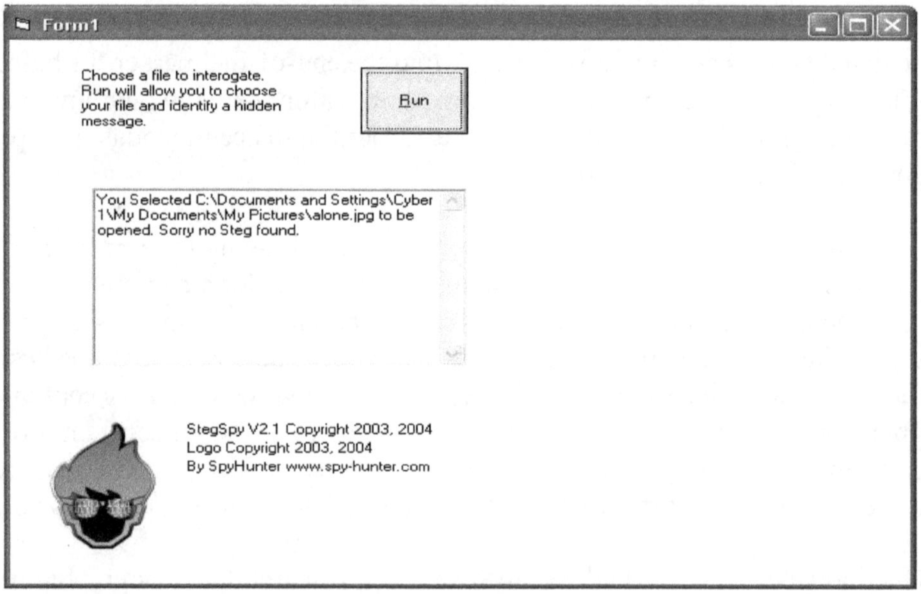

Figure 28-5

STUDENT SUMMARY:

1. What did you learn from this exercise?

2. You are working for a law firm and have been asked to give a brief presentation on steganography. You have been instructed to explain:

   a. What steganography is!

   b. Why may it be a concern to computer forensic examiners and law enforcement.

3. Perform a search and identify three steganography tools.

   a. _____

   b. _____

   c. _____

4. Perform a search and identify three steganography detection tools.

   d. _____

   e. _____

   f. _____

Evaluators Review of Learners Performance

1   2   3   4   5

Exercise # 29
Forensic Write Blockers

OBJECTIVE:

To connect a write blocker to a system and demonstrate its functionality in a live image acquisition.

OVERVIEW:

A forensic write-blocker is a specialized type of device made specifically for being able to read from a disk drive while restricting any possibility of writing to it. Permitting read-only access to data storage devices without compromising the integrity of the data is fundamental in any forensic examination. A write blocker, is necessary to guarantee the protection of the data chain of custody.

The National Institute of Standards and Technology mandates three general write blocking requirements. Those requirements are that the write blocker;

      a. Must not allow a protected drive to be changed
      b. Must allow the acquisition of any information from or about any drive
      c. Shall not prevent any operation to the drive that are not protected.

There are both hardware and software write blockers, with hardware ones being the most common and trusted. Hardware write blockers physically prevent write operations while software ones filter write commands sent to the drive through the interface.

Write blockers must have the same type of interface that the media to be examined has. If a disk drive has a SATA interface, the write blocker will have a SATA interface. If the disk drive has only a USB interface, the write blocker will have a USB interface.

This course utilizes two types of write blockers, a hard disk Tableau with SATA and IDE interface, and a similar one for small storage devices such as memory cards or compact flash.

Steps:

1. Your instructor should have demonstrated how to connect a write blocker to your student forensics system. If this step has not been performed, notify your instructor.

2. Review the accessories that come with the write blocker used in your particular course. These accessories should include a power connector, USB cable, SATA and IDE cables, and disk drive power connectors for each hard drive interface type.

3. Connect the write blocker to the student forensic workstation. Have your instructor verify proper connectivity before using the device.

4. Connect the write blocker and associated power connector to a small capacity target hard disk drive.

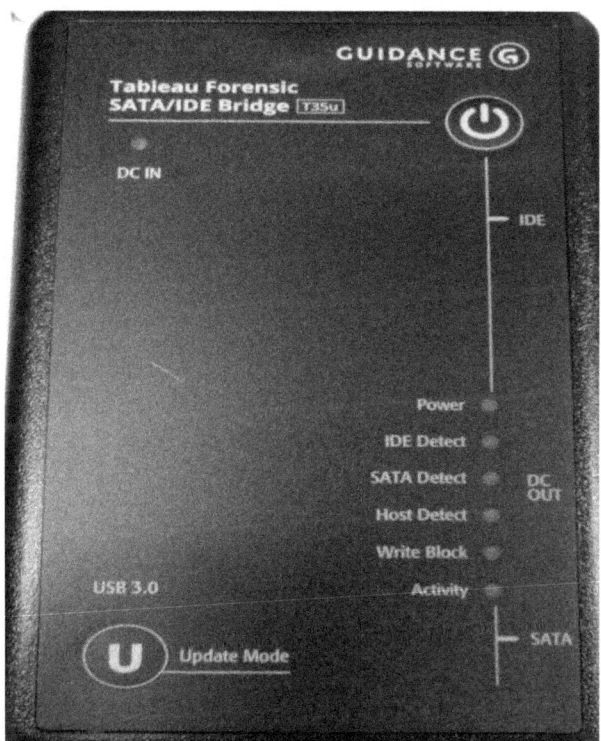

Figure 29-1

5. Initialize FTK Imager and using steps previously demonstrated; create a bit-stream image of the storage device.

6. Once the bit-stream image file has completed, close FTK Imager and disconnect the write blocker. Have your instructor verify these actions.

7. Connect the small media write blocker to the student forensic workstation.

Figure 29-2

8. Connect a small media storage card such as a MicroSD or Compact Flash card to the write blocker.

9. Initialize FTK Imager and using steps previously demonstrated; create a bit-stream image of the storage device.

10. Once the bit-stream image file has completed, close FTK Imager and disconnect the write blocker. Have your instructor verify these actions.

11. Perform a search and identify two types of hardware write blockers. Identify the model, manufacture, interfaces and price.

Model	Manufacturer	Interfaces	Price

Table 29-1

12. Perform a search and identify two types of software write blockers. Identify the model, manufacture, specifications (OS support) and price.

Model	Manufacturer	Specifications	Price

Table 29-2

13. Perform a search and identify two complete forensic write blocker kits that contain multiple write blockers. Identify the model, manufacture, interfaces and price. Note: Forensic write blocker kits are significantly more expensive as kits than individual ones.

Model	Manufacturer	Interfaces	Price

Table 29-3

STUDENT SUMMARY:

1. What did you learn from this exercise?

2. Some forensic examiners do not initially purchase all manner of available write blockers. Many will purchase the necessary interfaces as needed, thus passing the costs to the client. Consider that you are a computer examiner and will initially equip your forensic workstation with a minimal number of write blockers.

   a. What types of interfaces will you start with?

   b. Why did you choose these interfaces?

Evaluators Review of Learners Performance

1   2   3   4   5

Perform Forensics Exercise # 30
United States Department of Justice Best Practices for Seizing
Electronic Evidence

OBJECTIVE:

To introduce the learner to the environment, steps and thought process of how law enforcement deals with securing and investigating electronic crime scenes.

OVERVIEW:

The steps identified in this procedure follow recommended guidelines for electronic crime scene first responders. The material covered in the NIJ guide is directed at law enforcement officials. For corporate examiners, understanding these processes and procedures is vital to understanding how to comply with the law enforcement aspect.

You, as a computer forensic examiner, will almost certainly interact with law enforcement personnel at some points in your career. You need to be prepared to handle and document your actions in a appropriate for the handling of evidence media. Computer disk drives contain untold stories; you do not want to be the reason illegal activity cannot be prosecuted, or the reason exculpatory evidence is destroyed. As a corporate computer examiner, you must also realize that you are not law enforcement and processing a crime scene is to be done by authorized personnel.

STEPS:

1. Perform a Google Search for Best Practices for Seizing Electronic Evidence, Version 4.2, A Pocket Guide for First Responders.

Figure 30-1

2. What is the title of the document identified at this web site?

_____

_____

3. Who produces the document?

_____

_____

4. What is the purpose of this document?

_____

_____

5. What are the letters **NIJ** an abbreviation for?

_____

6. Search the Best Practices Guide and fill in the missing information from the identified topics.

Officer Safety

The _____ of the _____ is paramount in the investigation of any crime.

Authority for Seizing Evidence

The Plain View exception to the warrant requirement only gives the legal authority to _____ a computer, hardware, software and electronic media, but does _____ give the legal authority to conduct a _____ of this same listed electronic media.

Consent

When obtaining _____, be sure that your document has language specific to both to the _____ and the future forensic _____ of the computer hardware, software, electronic media and data by a trained _____ _____/_____.

Search Warrant

Search warrants allow for the _____ and _____ of electronic evidence as _____ under the _____.

Specify Evidence Sought

Specifically describe the evidence you have _____ _____ to search for and any evidence of _____ of that computer.

Special Master

Special legal considerations should be given to investigations involving _____, _____, _____, _____, _____, etc.

7. What document is presented on page 7 of the Best Practices Guide?

8. Describe the purpose of this document. Be specific in your explanation!

9. On page eight is a listing of nine general principles to follow when responding to any crime scene in which computers and electronic technology may be involved. Provide a brief summary of five of these principles.

    a. _____

       _____

    b. _____

       _____

    c. _____

       _____

    d. _____

       _____

    e. _____

       _____

10. Review pages nine through twelve of this guide and answer the following questions:

a. Should you ever try to determine IP address and other volatile information when seizing a computer that is on and connected to a network? Explain why or why not!

b. If the computer is off, turn it on to make sure you have the correct one?

        True   False

Explain why or why not!

c. Electronic devices that receive a wireless signal should be placed in a _____! Explain your answer!

d. Unplug the computer from the _____!

e. If a portable computer does not shut down when you remove the power, what should you do? Explain your answer!

f. Keep all computers and electronic storage media away from _____, _____ _____ and other potentially damaging elements.

g. Why is the law enforcement official instructed to collect all manuals, documentation and notes?

h. If a law enforcement official is tasked with seizing a company server, what actions should they take that are different than when seizing a home computer?

i. Consideration should be given to checking if _____ is present on live computers.

11. Pages 16 - 18 identify special considerations in seizing mobile devices and the potential categories of crimes that may be associated with them. Review and identify each of these categories.

     i. _____
     ii. _____
     iii. _____
     iv. _____
     v. _____
     vi. _____
     vii. _____
     viii. _____
     ix. _____
     x. _____
     xi. _____

12. Pages 19 – 20 identify General Investigative Questions. How many are listed? _____

13. Pages 20 – 22 identify Electronic Crime Scene Specific Questions. Review and identify the categories.

     i. _____
     ii. _____
     iii. _____
     iv. _____

STUDENT SUMMARY:

1. What did you learn from this exercise?

Evaluators Review of Learners Performance

1   2   3   4   5

Forensics Exercise # 31
Managing Swap Files

OBJECTIVE

To better understand the forensic significance of swap files and how they are managed by the user and the operating system.

This particular exercise is optional and at the discretion of the instructor.

This exercise demonstrates using the Windows 10 operating system. Other versions have slightly different steps for accomplishing these same objectives.

You have already viewed the pagefile.sys and hiberfil.sys geometry while using SequoiaView. In this exercise you will adjust the size and operation of it.

STEPS:

1. Right-click on This PC and open Properties.

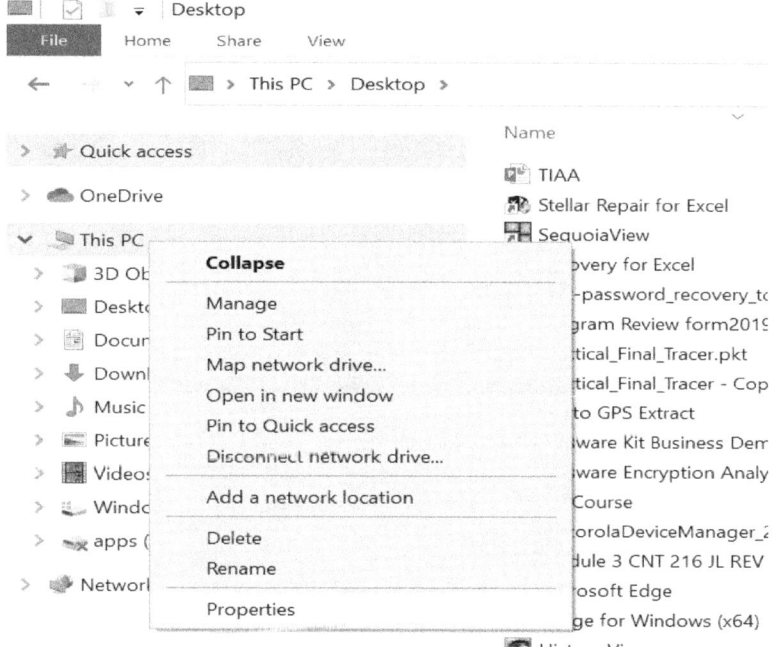

Figure 31-1

2. When the System control window appears, select Advanced System Properties.

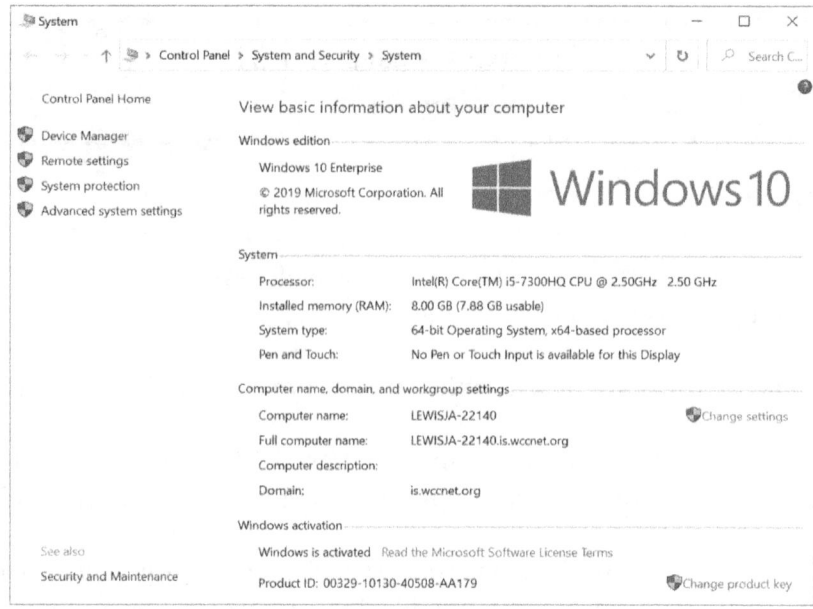

Figure 31-2

3. Then select the Advanced System Settings option. The System Properties window will display.

4. Select the Advanced tab, then the Settings option under the Performance category. The Performance Options window will be displayed.

5. Select the Advanced tab. Under the Virtual memory option, select the 'Change' option. The following window will appear.

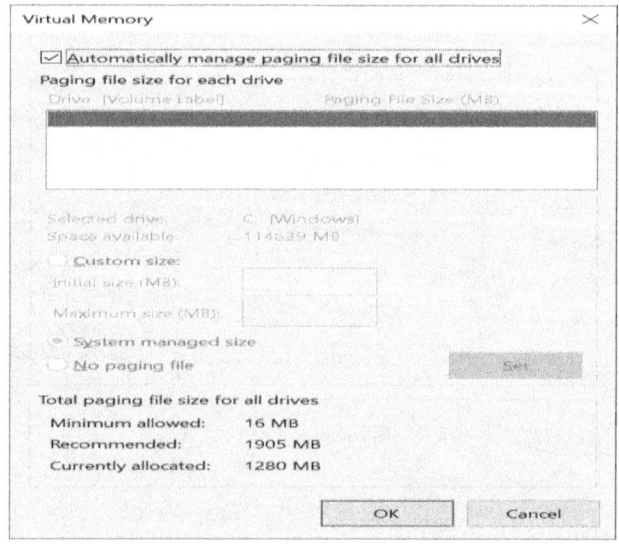

Figure 31-3

6. At this point the user can adjust the size of, or even eliminate the pagefile.sys file.

7. The paging (swap) file has forensic significance for the computer examiner in that if it is disabled by the user, much less potential artifact data may be recovered. Some users are aware of this and disable this feature in order to minimize the chances of unknown pieces of information (artifacts) from being discovered should the disk drive be examined. Although not officially categorized as such, this is an anti-forensics technique.

STUDENT SUMMARY:

1. What did you learn from this exercise?

2. Identify how adjusting the paging file on your forensic acquisition and analysis system could improve its performance when working with extremely large case image files.

3. Explain how valuable the paging file could be in a computer forensics examination. Consider and state an example of how it could provide valuable information.

4. Initialize the SequoiaView software tool and identify the size of the paging file on your student system. The size of the paging file on my student system is _____.

Evaluators Review of Learners Performance

1   2   3   4   5

Forensics Exercise # 32
Protection of Evidence

OBJECTIVE:

To understand handling and storage procedures for protection of data and devices.

OVERVIEW:

Anti-static bags, mats, ground clips, and technician ESD protection are aspects of handling electronic systems and devices. It is critical that the forensic specialist adhere to appropriate handling procedures. Your forensics laboratory should include plastic containers for media, anti-static bags, labels, secure storage areas, faraday bags, chain of custody documentation and receipt forms. Environmental conditions must be maintained for electronic storage devices as specified by the manufacturer. Temperature and humidity parameters vary by manufacturer, however, due to the commonality of the technology they are relatively close.

Each stored device should have the container it is housed in labeled appropriately. Placing an adhesive backed blank label and marking with a permanent marker is usually sufficient. The stored device must then be maintained in a secure and monitored location.

STEPS:

1. Identify the typical environmental specifications for the following devices. Consider storage and use temperature, shock and vibration specifications, and humidity. Note: Some of this information may be found on a technical data or specification sheet.

Device	Manufacturer	Storage and Use Specifications	Info Acquired From
128 GB Thumb Drive			
500 GB Solid State Drive			
1 TB Hard Drive			
4.7 GB DVD			

Table 32-1

2. Identify a manufacturer of anti-static bags used for storing or transporting sensitive electronic devices. Identify where they can be purchased, how much they cost and any other technical specifications that may be associated with them.

Manufacturer	Cost per Bag or Quantity	Where to Purchase	Specifications

Table 32-2

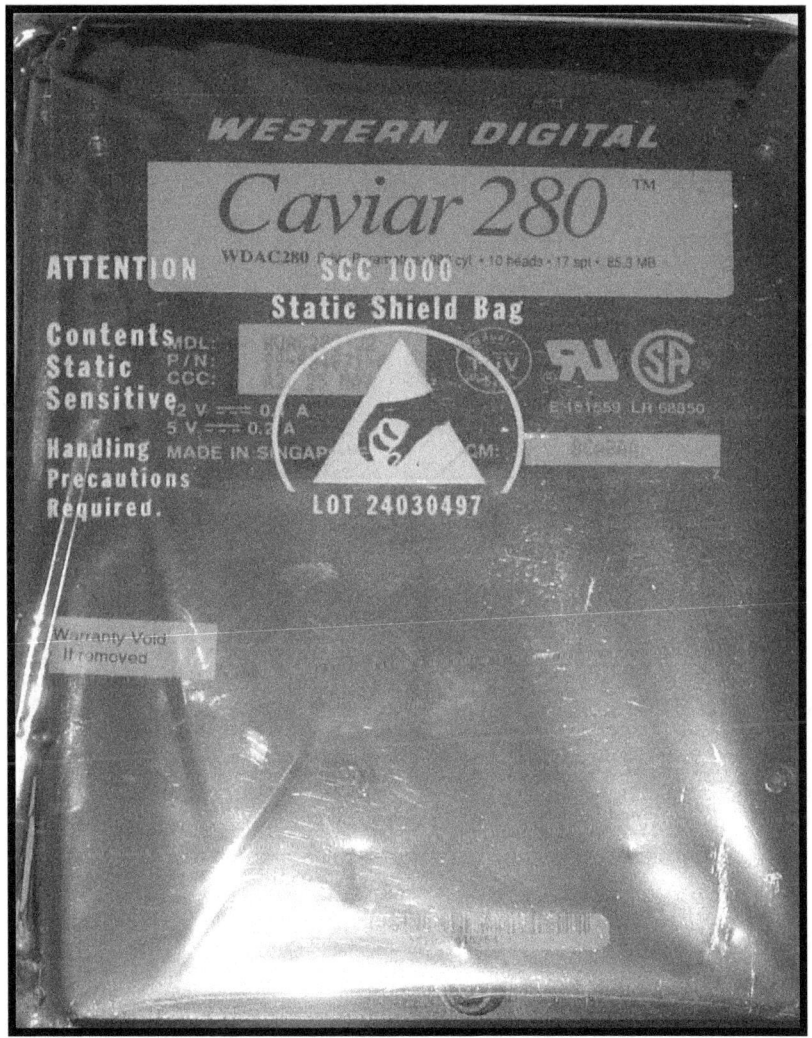

Figure 32-1

193

3. Acquire the hard drive from a target system. Your instructor should direct you to which system to acquire the drive from.

4. Document the steps, in order, that must be taken to secure this hard drive for transportation and storage. Include the steps of photographing, chain-of-custody, receipt, drawings and notes.

    1. _____

    2. _____

    3. _____

    4. _____

    5. _____

    6. _____

    7. _____

    8. _____

    9. _____

    10. _____

    11. _____

    12. _____

    13. _____

    14. _____

    15. _____

STUDENT SUMMARY:

1. What did you learn from this exercise?

2. What are the risks of leaving a disk drive in your automobile on a very hot day?

3. What are the risks of leaving a disk drive in your automobile on a very cold day?

4. It is 4:00 PM and the middle of July. You have just been handed a disk drive with a request to examine it for evidence of illegal activity. You asked the person who handed you the disk drive "Where has this drive been? It feels like it came out of an oven!" The reply was "It was in my vehicle since 8:00 AM this morning. You are in Phoenix when this happens. What should you immediately do with this device? Circle the most reasonable response.

    A. Take the drive inside the forensics lab and insert it into an examination system.

    B. Place the drive in a refrigeration unit until it cools off.

    C. Place the drive back into the automobile and leave it there for 4 hours until it cools off later in the day.

    D. Place the drive in a temperature controlled environment until it acclimates to ambient room temperature as defined by the drive manufacturer specifications.

Evaluators Review of Learners Performance

1   2   3   4   5

Forensics Exercise # 33
Creating Scripts for Volatile Memory Captures

OBJECTIVE:

To create a data capture script that can be used to acquired volatile information in a forensics examination.

OVERVIEW:

Computer forensic examinations are not limited to data on disk. They often require examination of the volatile contents of memory. There are several different locations that volatile data and information may be contained within a functioning system. While some of this information may not be of importance to the examiner, some of it may be.

All too often the beginning student of computer forensics lacks familiarity with the command line tools available in various operating systems. This exercise attempts to bridge the gap between users that are familiar with the GUI based operating systems and the command line tools sometimes used during a system capture or seizure.

STEPS

1. Make sure your computer is on and has a valid network connection.

2. Open a command prompt and issue the following command;

   Netstat /?

Complete the following information for this command:

Purpose of the Netstat command: _____

_____

Provide a brief description of each switch option for this command:

   -a _____

   _____

   -b _____

   _____

-e _____
_____

-f _____
_____

-n _____
_____

-o _____
_____

-p _____
_____

-r _____
_____

-s _____
_____

-t _____
_____

interval_____
_____

3. Initialize your Internet browser and verify the home page is displayed.

4. Using the browser navigate to three web sites.

5. Once you have finished navigating to several web sites issue the following command.

    Netstat -a

You should see the command window fill with connection information that looks like this;

Active Connections
  Proto   **Local Address**   **Foreign Address**   **State**

Each field identifies some aspect of the state of network connectivity of your system. The Proto field indicates the type of protocol for each identified connection, usually TCP or UDP.

The Local Address is the local IP address of your PC on the network. You may see multiple examples of address 127.0.0.1 and other IP addresses. The 127.0.0.1 is what is known as the loop back address of your computer.

The Foreign Address is the address of a remote or foreign host, including port number or service such as HTTP for any web sites that you have recently visited.

The State column indicates the state of a particular port on your system and whether it is listening or established with another host.

6. Commands vary among operating systems and each may provide revealing information about the system while it is functioning. Experiment with the following commands:

ipconfig /all	systeminfo	tasklist
nbtstat –s	route print	arp -a

Briefly summarize the type of information provided by each of these commands:

Ipconfig /all

systeminfo

tasklist

nbtstat –s

route print

arp -a

What do each of these commands have in common? (Answer: They all display volatile system information that will be lost when the system is shut down or loses power).

Prior to turning off a computer system, the computer examiner may need to capture the volatile information contained in the systems RAM. Information such as current IP address, contents of RAM, ARP tables and current network connection status is not available once the system has been turned off. The competent computer examiner must be familiar with the commands and techniques used to obtain such information on site.

7. Open a command prompt from your Windows based operating system by selecting Start, Run, and then enter cmd into the run dialog box. A command window should appear that is similar to this one.

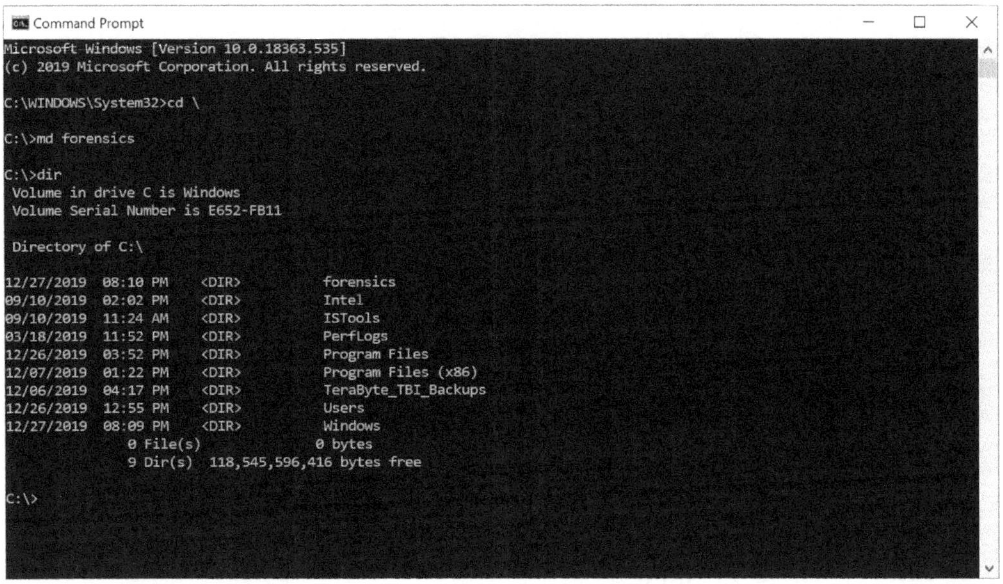

Figure 33-1

8. Enter the "DIR" command to list the files or directories. The list of files will vary from system to system.

9. Enter the "TREE" command. You should observe a tree structure identifying the folder structure of the disk. Your screen may begin scrolling with the disk folder structure?

10. Enter the "TREE | MORE" command.

    a. Was the scrolling limited to the Windows command screen size?

    b. Press the space bar to continue scrolling the results of the TREE | MORE command.

11. Enter the "TREE / '?'" command.

    a. What additional information does this switch option provide?

12. Enter the "TREE / F" command.

      a. What additional information was provided as a result of this command?

13. Explain the purpose of the | (pipe) and the MORE command?

14. This step has you create and search for a file on the hard disk using only the command line.

      a. Create a file with the name TEST1.TXT
      b. Place all letters of the alphabet in this file.
      c. Save this file in the Windows directory
      d. Open the command line window and navigate to the root directory
      e. Issue the following command:

            dir test1.txt /s

      Did you find the file? _____

      f. You are to use the appropriate command to display your computers IP Address and Subnet Mask information.

          1. What is your computers IP address?

              _____

          2. What is your computers Subnet Mask?

              _____

      g. Display the arp to ip address mapping on your computer.

          1. How many arp entries do you observe? _____

          2. Record some of those entries here?
              ARP _____ IP _____
              ARP _____ IP _____
              ARP _____ IP _____

      h. Create a folder on a removable thumb drive and title it Volatile.

      i. Perform an Internet search for and download the following tools if available and store them into the recently created Volatile folder. A search for the phrase PSTOOLS should be able to locate all of these

- Fport
- Handle
- Ipconfig
- Listdlls
- Nbtstat
- Netstat
- NTlast
- PSInfo
- PSLoggedon
- PSLoglist

Perform an Internet search for these additional software tools:
- Dumpel

15. Create the following batch file and store it into the Volatile folder. Name the batch file Volatile.bat

```
@echo off
cls
echo. This Batchfile will collect volatile information
echo. from the selected computer and store it where specified on %1

REM Verify filename is specified
IF "%1"=="" GOTO Syntax
IF "%1"=="/?" GOTO Syntax

:Start
REM Capture system current time and send to %1
echo. ********************************** > %1
echo. Current time on %COMPUTERNAME% >> %1
time /t >> %1
echo. ********************************** >> %1

REM Capture system current Date and send to %1
echo. ********************************** >> %1
echo. Current Date on %COMPUTERNAME% >> %1
date /t >> %1
echo. ********************************** >> %1
REM Capture system IP address and send to %1
echo. ********************************** >> %1
echo. ********************************** >> %1

echo. Current IP Information on %COMPUTERNAME% >> %1
echo. >> %1
```

```
ipconfig /all >> %1
echo. ********************************* >> %1


REM Capture current connections information
echo. ********************************* >> %1
echo. Current IP Connections info for %COMPUTERNAME% >> %1
echo. >> %1
netstat -an >> %1
echo. ********************************* >> %1


REM Capture NetBIOS over TCP/IP (NetBT) protocol statistics
echo. ************************************ >> %1
echo. Displays NetBIOS over TCP/IP (NetBT) protocol statistics for Machine
%COMPUTERNAME% >> %1
nbtstat -c >> %1
echo. ********************************* >> %1


REM Capture Task Information for active programs
echo. ************************************* >> %1
echo. Task List Information for %COMPUTERNAME% >> %1
tasklist
tasklist /m
tasklist /apps /FI "STATUS eq running"
echo. ********************************* >> %1


REM Capture Current Environment Information for %COMPUTERNAME%
echo. ********************************* >> %1
echo. Current Environment Information for %COMPUTERNAME%  >> %1
echo. >> %1
SET >> %1
echo. ********************************* >> %1


REM Capture System type of installation, kernel build, registered organization and owner
REM number of processors and their type, amount of physical memory, the install date of
the system,
REM and expiration date if a trial version.
echo. ********************************* >> %1
echo. Current System Type on %COMPUTERNAME%  >> %1
echo. >> %1
psinfo >> %1
echo. ********************************* >> %1


REM Capture Current open TCP/IP and UDP ports and maps them to the owning
application for %COMPUTERNAME%
echo. ********************************* >> %1
echo. Current Open TCP/IP and UDP Ports for %COMPUTERNAME%  >> %1
echo. >> %1
fport >> %1
echo. ********************************* >> %1
```

```
REM Capture Current PIDs for %COMPUTERNAME%
echo. ********************************* >> %1
echo. Current for Process ID's %COMPUTERNAME% >> %1
echo. >> %1
pslist >> %1
echo. ********************************* >> %1


REM Capture both the locally logged on users and users logged on  for
%COMPUTERNAME%
echo. ********************************* >> %1
echo. Current Logged on Users for %COMPUTERNAME% >> %1
echo. >> %1
psloggedon >> %1
echo. ********************************* >> %1


REM Scans the NT event log and reports logon/logoff activity  for
%COMPUTERNAME%
echo. ********************************* >> %1
echo. Current NT Event logg for %COMPUTERNAME% >> %1
echo. >> %1
ntlast >> %1
echo. ********************************* >> %1


REM Identifies last file accessed times  for %COMPUTERNAME%
echo. ********************************* >> %1
echo. Last file accessed times for %COMPUTERNAME% >> %1
echo. >> %1
dir /t:a /o:d /s c:\ >> %1
echo. ********************************* >> %1


REM Identifies last file modified times  for %COMPUTERNAME%
echo. ********************************* >> %1
echo. Last file modified times for %COMPUTERNAME% >> %1
echo. >> %1
dir /t:w /o:d /s c:\ >> %1
echo. ********************************* >> %1


REM Identifies file created times  for %COMPUTERNAME%
echo. ********************************* >> %1
echo. Last file modified times for %COMPUTERNAME% >> %1
echo. >> %1
dir /t:c /o:d /s c:\ >> %1
echo. ********************************* >> %1


REM Captures security event log for %COMPUTERNAME%
echo. ********************************* >> %1
echo. Security Event log for %COMPUTERNAME% >> %1
echo. >> %1
dumpel -l security >> %1
echo. ********************************* >> %1
```

```
REM Captures application event log for %COMPUTERNAME%
echo. ********************************** >> %1
echo. Application Event log for %COMPUTERNAME% >> %1
echo. >> %1
dumpel -l application >> %1
echo. ********************************** >> %1


REM Captures System event log for %COMPUTERNAME%
echo. ************************************* >> %1
echo. System Event log for %COMPUTERNAME% >> %1
echo. >> %1
dumpel -l system >> %1
echo. ********************************** >> %1


REM Lists current dll files for %COMPUTERNAME%
echo. ************************************* >> %1
echo. DLL files for %COMPUTERNAME% >> %1
echo. >> %1
listdlls >> %1
echo. ********************************** >> %1


REM Registry Key TypedURLs for %COMPUTERNAME%
echo. ************************************** >> %1
echo. Registry Key TypedURLs for %COMPUTERNAME% >> %1
echo. >> %1
REG QUERY "HKEY_CURRENT_USER\Software\Microsoft\Internet
Explorer\TypedURLs" /s >> %1
echo. ************************************** >> %1


REM Registry Key USBSTOR for %COMPUTERNAME%
echo. *************************************** >> %1
echo. Registry Key USBSTOR for %COMPUTERNAME% >> %1
echo. >> %1
REG QUERY
"HKEY_LOCAL_MACHINE\SYSTEM\CurrentControlSet\Enum\USBSTOR" /s >> %1
echo. *************************************** >> %1


REM Registry Key Map Network Drive MRU for %COMPUTERNAME%
echo. *************************************** >> %1
echo. Registry Key Map Network Drive MRU for %COMPUTERNAME% >> %1
echo. >> %1
REG QUERY
"HKEY_CURRENT_USER\Software\Microsoft\Windows\CurrentVersion\Explorer\Ma
p Network Drive MRU" /s >> %1
echo. *************************************** >> %1


REM Registry Key UserAssist for %COMPUTERNAME%
echo. *************************************** >> %1
echo. Registry Key UserAssist for %COMPUTERNAME% >> %1
echo. >> %1
```

```
REG QUERY
"HKEY_CURRENT_USER\Software\Microsoft\Windows\CurrentVersion\Explorer\Use
rAssist" /s >> %1
echo. ************************************** >> %1

REM Registry Key Typed URLs for %COMPUTERNAME%
echo. ************************************** >> %1
echo. Registry Key UserAssist for %COMPUTERNAME% >> %1
echo. >> %1
REG QUERY "HKCU\Software\Microsoft\Internet Explorer\TypedURLs" /S >> %1
echo. ************************************** >> %1

REM Registry Key Run MRUs for %COMPUTERNAME%
echo. ************************************** >> %1
echo. Registry Key Run MRUs for %COMPUTERNAME% >> %1
echo. >> %1
REG QUERY
"HKCU\Software\Microsoft\Windows\CurrentVersion\Explorer\RunMRU" /S >> %1
echo. ************************************** >> %1

REM Registry Key Open Command for %COMPUTERNAME%
echo. ************************************** >> %1
echo. Registry Key Run MRUs for %COMPUTERNAME% >> %1
echo. >> %1
REG QUERY "HKCR\exefile\shell\open\command" /s >> %1
echo. ************************************** >> %1

REM Capture System MAC Address for %COMPUTERNAME%
echo. ************************************** >> %1
echo. Current MAC Address Table on %COMPUTERNAME% >> %1
echo. >> %1
arp -a >> %1
echo. ************************************** >> %1
goto End

:Syntax
cls
echo. Specify path and filename for capture information
echo.
echo. Example forensic.bat X:\SystemA.txt
echo.
echo. The will capture selected volatile system
echo. information and save it to a text file on
echo. the X: drive with the file name SystemA.txt
echo.
echo.

:End
```

Once you save this batch file in the Volatile directory on your thumb drive you are to demonstrate it.

16. Go to a test or target system and insert the Volatile flash drive.

17. Open a command prompt and navigate to the correct drive letter of the flash drive.

18. Issue the volatile.bat X:volatile1.txt command where "X" is the drive letter of the flash drive and "volatile1.txt" is the name of the file that you are going to store the contents of the volatile information to be recovered from the target or test system.

The above step may take up to several minutes depending upon the size of the hard disk, the amount of RAM and other variable information available on the system at the time this step is performed. It should be noted that some of this information recovery may be considered intrusive and the batch file may need to be modified to remove anything not included in RAM. Information obtained from a Reg Query operation can be obtained back at the forensics lab, however, it is included here as an example of a forensic compliance audit. Also, not all versions of Windows operating systems have the same level of administrative rights. Some of the commands may not execute properly and may have to be adjusted.

STUDENT SUMMARY:

1. What did you learn from this exercise?

2. Approximately how long did it take for your batch file to execute?

3. Did all of the commands execute properly? Identify any that did not.

4. What might be the legal ramifications of executing this file on a system that you are not authorized to do so?

Evaluators Review of Learners Performance

1   2   3   4   5

Forensics Exercise # 34
Computer Forensics Terms and Definitions

OBJECTIVE:

It is necessary that the computer forensic specialist have an understanding of topics and issues collateral to this profession. This exercise will provide additional insight into the language of computer forensics.

OVERVIEW:

All of the terms associated with this laboratory exercise relate to the field of computer forensics. Fill in the blank for each of the below listed terms. The descriptions of each term are located in the accompanying text manual. Not each term is in the exact order as described in the text manual. This is to invoke a better understanding by reading the term description as opposed to simply filling in the blanks in sequence.

TERMS:

_____ : A cryptographic hash of a message which is used to create a digital signature of that message.

_____ : Methods to ensure users access only those areas, resources or services they are authorized to.

_____ : Liable to being called to account; answerable, accountable.

_____ : The basic unit of information in digital computing. The amount of information stored in one of two possible states, 0 or 1.

_____ : A defined data structure that provides information regarding the basic information and parameters of an operating systems organization of the storage media.

_____ : The exact mirrored backup of a storage device that includes all possible storage areas, including all files and ambient data storage areas.

_____ : Raw facts, information in raw or unorganized form.

_____ : That data that is stored in non-traditional storage areas and format locations.

_____: A unit of information in digital computing that consists of eight bits.

_____: A collection of facts or data.

_____: When a user performs an action they should not have, according to law or policy.

_____: The space between the end of a file and the end of the cluster it is stored in

_____: A certification, Certified Forensic Computer Examiner, sponsored by The International Association of Computer Investigative Specialists, IACIS.

_____: To obtain access to an area, resource or service.

_____: The hiding of a secret message within a non-secret message with the intent of it being extracted at its destination.

_____: A set of tracks on a multi-headed disk, all with the same track number, that can be accessed without moving the head.

_____: A software program, or set of instructions, that permits higher-level software or applications to interact with the lower-level hardware functions of the computer or device.

_____: Recommended practice that allows discretion in a course of action or situation.

_____: The circular disk component of a hard disk that stores the data, operating system and other files.

_____: Also known as E-Discovery is the obligation of parties to a lawsuit to exchange documents that exist only in electronic form such as e-mails, voice messages and instant messages.

_____: A type of boot sector located on a hard disk or other storage device that contains the instructions necessary for starting the operating system boot process.

_____: The International Association of Computer Investigative Specialists.

_____ :   Units of addressable disk space defined by the file system. Also known as Allocation Units.

_____ :   The Windows File Allocation Table for earlier hard disk drives consisting of a 16-bit wide address.

_____ :   The act or process of bringing or contesting a legal action in a court, a judicial proceeding or contest.

_____ :   A degree to which a system, person, process or organization is susceptible to harm, degradation or destruction.

_____ :   A certification, Certified Information Forensics Investigator, sponsored by the IISFA.

_____ :   The Windows File Allocation Table that was introduced in Windows 95 version OSR2 and consists of a 32-bit wide address.

_____ :   Software that enables continued privileged access to a computer while actively hiding its presence from administrators

_____ :   A mathematical scheme for demonstrating the authenticity of a digital message or electronic document.

_____ :   High Performance File System. A file system introduced with IBMs OS/2 version 1.2.

_____ :   Deals with the preservation, identification, extraction and documentation of computer evidence.

_____ :   Software that sends information about web surfing habits to another web site.

_____ :   A thing or things helpful in forming a conclusion or a judgment.

_____ :   The basic principles by which an organization is guided.

_____ :   A level of risk associated with a particular activity at which dangers are acceptable to an evaluator.

_____ :   Extended File Allocation Table introduced by Microsoft and suited well for USB flash drive technology.

_____ : High Technology Crime Investigation Association.

_____ : Referring to files that are not continuous in physical sequence when stored on a media device.

_____ : A self-replicating malware program that uses computer networking resources to send itself to other devices on the network.

_____ : International Information Systems Forensics Association.

_____ : A mathematical function that converts large variable-sized amounts of data into a single index value.

_____ : A unit of information in digital computing that consists of four bits and corresponds to sixteen possible values.

_____ : A computer forensics software suite maintained by the U.S. Department of Treasure for use by law enforcement. It is not available to the general public.

_____ : The wasted space on a disk drive that is not used due to varying sizes of files that are written to the disk.

_____ : A certification, Certified Computer Examiner, sponsored by the International Society of Forensic Computer Examiners.

_____ : A software program usually capable of reproducing itself and able to cause harm to other files on the same computer.

_____ : A network device that forwards data packets or frames from one network segment to another.

_____ : Abbreviation for Malicious Software. Software that was designed with the intent to disable, damage or do other unwanted actions on a computer.

_____ : Information Systems Forensics Association.

_____ : A virtual memory implementation that allows main memory to use secondary storage as primary memory when needed.

_____: A operating system structure that permits the storing, organizing, and retrieval of various files within a storage media.

_____: National Institution of Standards and Technology.

_____: A troubleshooting mode of operation for the operating system. Used to load minimal, or necessary only software to operate the system.

_____: Space that is available, or unallocated by the operating system for storage of active files, information or data.

_____: Master File Table. A list of files and folders in a Windows NTFS based operating system that contains the name, size, time and date for each file.

_____: Space that does not belong to an active or logically assigned partition. Unused or wasted space between partition boundaries.

_____: A step-by-step sequence of activities or course of action.

_____: A destructive program that masquerades as a benign program.

_____: United States Department of Justice. The United States federal department responsible for enforcing all U.S. federal laws.

_____: The folder in the hierarchy that contains all other folders.

_____: A set of data that provides information about other data such as context, content, structure, file and text parameters.

_____: A specifically sized division of the logical structure of a data track.

_____: International Society of Forensic Computer Examiners.

_____: Data that is being, relating to, or affording evidence.

_____: New Technology File System. The primary file system used with Windows NT based operating systems.

STUDENT SUMMARY:

1. What did you learn from this exercise?

2. Consider that you are a corporate computer examiner and you have been notified that you are to testify as to the discoveries on an employee's corporate computer system. The employee has brought civil suit against the company claiming that the information you discovered on their computer was not put there by that employee. You know that the employee's attorney is going to attempt to discredit you, your skills and your methods. Identify five terms, concepts or forensic principles that you feel you would need to review so you improve your appearance of being competent.

Evaluators Review of Learners Performance

1   2   3   4   5

Forensics Exercise # 35
Analyze Case Image File 2005-30

OBJECTIVE:

To advance forensic auditing and examination skills by performing a forensics examination of a media image to determine if any information of evidentiary value is contained within it, and to report your findings.

OVERVIEW:

This exercise will provide the student the opportunity to examine an existing case image file and analyze it for digital contraband or illegal files. The previous case image file, 2005-30, was an introduction to using Autopsy and the concepts and techniques of forensically examining a media image. This exercise will provide you with the opportunity to utilize tools and techniques learned in previous exercises for examination and recovery of data and information. This exercise is expected to take much longer to examine and report as it contains much more information.

STEPS:

1. Acquire the case image file 2005-30 from your instructor.

2. Initialize Autopsy and import the 2005-30 case image file into it using the steps and techniques used in the previous exercise.

3. Index the case image file 2005-30 using appropriate naming conventions.

4. Analyze the image and identify the following from this case image file:

    a. What types of files did you discover in this image?

    b. How did you open these files? Be very specific in how you opened each file.

    c. What are the contents of each of these files? Provide a screenshot if available.

5. Discuss your findings with the instructor. Your instructor has the listing of relevant items in each case image file.

As a reminder, you have been instructed that it is inappropriate to present opinion regarding intentions of the user, or generalized perceptions as to their motives; however, part of being an effective computer forensic examiner is to let the image guide you towards deeper discoveries contained therein.

STUDENT SUMMARY:

1. What did you learn from this exercise?

Evaluators Review of Learners Performance

1   2   3   4   5

Forensics Exercise # 36
Analyze Case Image File 2005-35

OBJECTIVE:

To advance forensic auditing and examination skills by performing a forensics examination of a media image to determine if any information of evidentiary value is contained within it, and to report your findings.

OVERVIEW:

This exercise will provide the student the opportunity to examine an existing case image file and analyze it for digital contraband or illegal files. The previous case image file, 2005-35, was an introduction to using Autopsy and the concepts and techniques of forensically examining a media image. This exercise will provide you with the opportunity to utilize tools and techniques learned in previous exercises for examination and recovery of data and information. This exercise is expected to take much longer to examine and report as it contains much more information.

STEPS:

1. Acquire the case image file 2005-35 from your instructor.

2. Initialize Autopsy and import the 2005-35 case image file into it using the steps and techniques used in the previous exercise.

3. Index the case image file 2005-35 using appropriate naming conventions.

4. Analyze the image and identify the following from this case image file:

   a. What types of files did you discover in this image?

   b. How did you open these files? Be very specific in how you opened each file.

   c. What are the contents of each of these files? Provide a screenshot if available.

5. Discuss your findings with the instructor. Your instructor has the listing of relevant items in each case image file.

As a reminder, you have been instructed that it is inappropriate to present opinion regarding intentions of the user, or generalized perceptions as to their motives; however, part of being an effective computer forensic examiner is to let the image guide you towards deeper discoveries contained therein.

STUDENT SUMMARY:

1. What did you learn from this exercise?

Evaluators Review of Learners Performance

1	2	3	4	5

Forensics Exercise # 37
Analyze Case Image File 2005-40

OBJECTIVE:

To advance forensic auditing and examination skills by performing a forensics examination of a media image to determine if any information of evidentiary value is contained within it, and to report your findings.

OVERVIEW:

This exercise will provide the student the opportunity to examine an existing case image file and analyze it for digital contraband or illegal files. The previous case image file, 2005-40, was an introduction to using Autopsy and the concepts and techniques of forensically examining a media image. This exercise will provide you with the opportunity to utilize tools and techniques learned in previous exercises for examination and recovery of data and information. This exercise is expected to take much longer to examine and report as it contains much more information.

STEPS:

1. Acquire the case image file 2005-40 from your instructor.

2. Initialize Autopsy and import the 2005-40 case image file into it using the steps and techniques used in the previous exercise.

3. Index the case image file 2005-40 using appropriate naming conventions.

4. Analyze the image and identify the following from this case image file:

    a. What types of files did you discover in this image?

        d. How did you open these files? Be very specific in how you opened each file.

        e. What are the contents of each of these files? Provide a screenshot if available.

5. Discuss your findings with the instructor. Your instructor has the listing of relevant items in each case image file.

As a reminder, you have been instructed that it is inappropriate to present opinion regarding intentions of the user, or generalized perceptions as to their motives; however, part of being an effective computer forensic examiner is to let the image guide you towards deeper discoveries contained therein.

STUDENT SUMMARY:

1. What did you learn from this exercise?

Evaluators Review of Learners Performance

	1	2	3	4	5

Forensics Exercise # 38
Computer Forensics and Computer Examiner Certification

OBJECTIVE:

To become more familiar with the industry certifications in the profession of computer and digital forensics so the student can focus their learning objectives.

OVERVIEW:

You should have discussed several computer forensics certifications in class and their sponsoring organizations. As this field continues to evolve in the corporate environment, more emphasis will be placed on industry certifications. You are to research several of these certifications and determine which, if any, hold significance to your career goals.

Certification

Testing

Industry Experience in Computer and Digital Forensics

Training in Computer and Digital Forensics

Hardware, Software and Operating System Experience

STEPS:

1. Your supervisor tells you your company is going to be showcased in an upcoming news article and to better represent the firms talent pool he wants all computer forensic examiners to add some certifications to their credentials. Perform an on-line search of available computer forensics certifications. Identify the certification and the sponsoring organization. State the requirements for each certification. Begin with the ACE and CCE forensics certifications.

CERTIFICATION	SPONSORING ORGANIZATION	CERTIFICATION REQUIREMENTS
CCE		
ACE		

STUDENT SUMMARY:

    1. What did you learn from this exercise?

    2. Perform a search and identify if computer forensic examiners must be certified or licensed in your state.

        A. Computer Forensic Examiners must be licensed in my state of residence:

            True   False

    3: Identify the state licensing statute or information link where you acquired this information from.

    4. Identify the specific requirements for computer forensic examiners to legally conduct examinations, acquisitions and investigations in your state. Identify where this information is stated in government records, i.e. statutes, government websites, etc.

Evaluators Review of Learners Performance

1   2   3   4   5

Forensics Exercise # 39
Reporting your Findings: Writing Reports and Documentation

OBJECTIVE:

To guide the learner towards the ability to adequately present findings from a computer forensic examination.

OVERVIEW:

Report writing is a critical aspect of the computer forensics field. Being able to document and present your findings is critical to your work being recognized as competent. This exercise is designed to help focus your information into such a format.

STEPS

Step 1: Handling of the evidence. The forensic examiner must be able to identify the following:

- What the evidence is
   - -DVD
   - -Hard Drive
   - -Compact disc
   - -Thumb drive
   - -Internal SSD
   - -External SSD

- Be able to describe the evidence.

- Be able to identify the steps taken to preserve and protect the evidence.

- Be able to describe how the integrity of the evidence was maintained.

- Be able to describe the method used to create a forensic image, copy or duplicate of the evidence or media.

- Be able to explain the steps performed that verified the forensic image is an exact duplicate.

- Describe how the target media was prepared.

- Explain how you ensured that no left over data existed on the target media prior to imaging.

Software:

- State the exact software used to perform the examination.

- Identify who the software is licensed to.

- Explain what the software is designed to do.

Definitions:

- Explain any terms used in your report. A non-technical person must be able to understand the meaning of swap file, slack space, unallocated space, RAM slack, metadata, etc.

Reports:

- The report should be excruciatingly detailed.

- You should outline and describe the steps performed. This can save a tremendous amount of trouble in the event that you are subpoenaed 1-2 years later for a court appearance and will permit you to be better able to describe how you recovered the data.

- The report must be written in a logical sequence. Simply saying that you acquired some evidence and secured it is inadequate. You also need to explain that you removed the evidence from a secure storage location for analysis.

Conclusions/Opinions

- All conclusions or opinions must be founded upon sound forensic principals. Theories must be tested and documented with the outcome. Example, if a disk was formatted, explain why you know it was formatted.

- If your report is to be continuous, cut and paste the relevant documents into the report body. If you do not want to make the report continuous then include any recovered files or documents as an attachment and include a reference such as "see exhibit #."

- Document the chain of custody for each piece of evidence and provide the documentation in your report.

- Document the disposition of all evidence.

- Convert all evidence to a viewable and presentable format.

- If the operating system uses the FAT file system, examine the File Allocation Table with an acceptable hex editor.

- You are not to make judgments of the evidence. Your responsibility is discover the data and information, not interpret user motives.

- Do not say that you destroyed any handwritten notes you made.

- Include any and all passwords you find in your report.

STEP 2:

Review the sample forensic examination report on the next page.

COMPUTER FORENSICS INVESTIGATION

CASE 2019-110, Mr. Dell

Prepared for Future Hard Drives Corporation

DATE
December 6, 2019

Examiner:

Mr. D.B. Cooper

My Computer Forensics, LLC

CISSP, MCSE, CCE

Table of Contents:

Case History:

- This examiner was called by the Human Resources Manager of the Future Hard Drives Corporation, Mr. Donald Dell, on the morning of November 15, 2019. He asked that we examine the office computer of an employee of the company, whose name was not disclosed. There was suspicious activity noted on the work machine of this employee on November 11, 2019, and the machine was secured until this examiner and the IT Manager of Future Hard Drives, Mr. Donald Smith, entered at 9:30 AM on November 15.He gave no further information about the employee except that the employee's access to the office was removed. It was requested that we secure and remove the drive from the machine along with any other relevant items.

Investigation Log:

- ## 9:30 AM 11/15/2019: Interview with Mr. Donald Smith, IT Manager at Future Hard Drives Corporation:

  Mr. Smith reported to this investigator that suspicious activity was noted on the company's network on November 11, 2019, and was subsequently traced by him to this machine. He also stated to us that the company has an acceptable use policy, which every employee has signed. We have been given a copy of the Acceptable Use Policy for Future Hard Drives, and it has been attached to this report. Mr. Smith confirmed that no one has entered the office where the machine in question was located since the activity was detected, and the office was locked. He stated that, as far as Future Hard Drives knows, the machine in question has no Remote Access.

- **9:40 AM, 11/15/2019: On site of Future Hard Drives Corporation, office of the evidence machine:**

  The office area of the office looked as follows upon arrival of this examiner.

  Exhibit 1

- Identified System as a Dell Optiplex GX270, which is the standard issue machine at the company.
- The PC serial number was CN-OR3611-47985-43J-65642RMR41. The system was not operational.
- There was a ZIP disk sitting on the desk next to the machine, with writing scratched out on the label. Future Hard Drives gave us permission to remove this disk into our custody and analyze it (Exhibit 2).

Exhibit 2

- **9:45 AM, 10/25/2019:** Disconnected the machine's power source, removed the cover, photographed the inside, then removed the hard drive. The drive was placed into a static-free evidence bag, labeled Case 2019-110, Future Hard Drives Corporation-Dell. A receipt for removal of property was signed by and given to Mr. Smith, IT Manager, as was the Chain of Custody form. A copy of each is attached to this report. No other items were seen in the office that would be known to contain electronic data or information related to the investigation, and no other items were removed.

Exhibit 3

- **10:00 AM 11/15/2019: Transport of Hard Drive and ZIP disk to My Computer Forensics Analysis Lab.**

- **10:30 AM 11/15/2019: Arrival at Analysis Lab, imaging of drive and disk for analysis:**

  Upon arrival at the My Computer Forensics Analysis Lab, the subject hard drive was readied for analysis by the attachment of a write-blocking device. This investigator then made a bit-by-bit image of the subject drive using AccessData's Forensic ToolKit Imager, 4.2.1, build 05.04.04, registered to My Computer Forensics, LLC. Analysis of the drive revealed it to be a 1TB Quantum Fireball P hard drive, model LM10.2, and serial number SG-0030YM-12542-083-04FF, formatted as two NTFS partitions (one hidden.)

- **The following is a photograph of the subject drive taken before imaging: (Exhibit 4)**

Exhibit 4

Evidence List Summary:

- ### The following screenshot shows a listing of all items recovered during analysis (Exhibit 5)

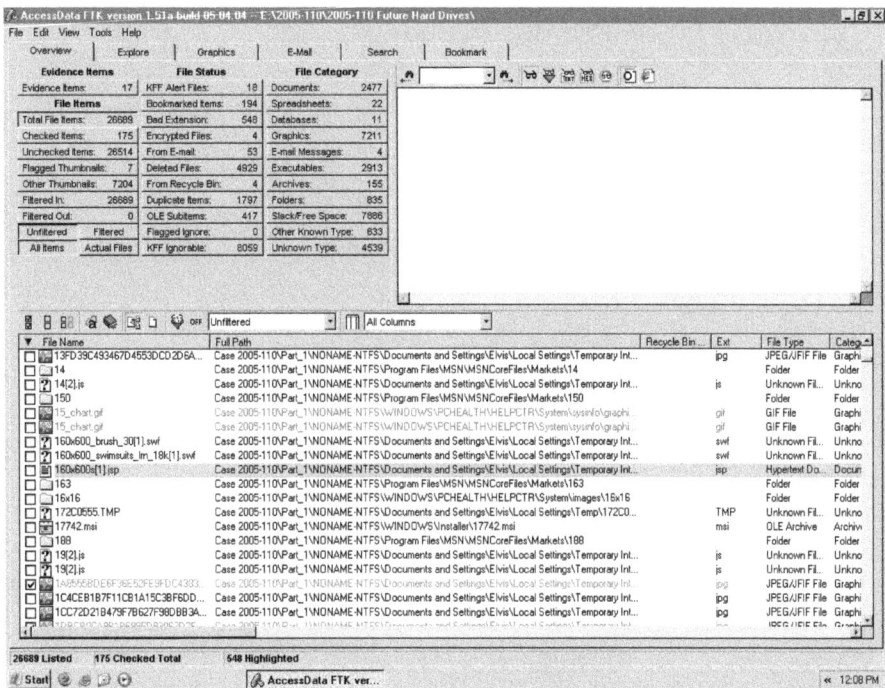

Exhibit 5

- The ZIP disk was also prepared for imaging by connecting it first through a Write-Blocking device, but subsequent efforts to acquire data using BadCopy Pro, version 3.0 build 1108, from the disk were unsuccessful (Exhibits 6 & 7).

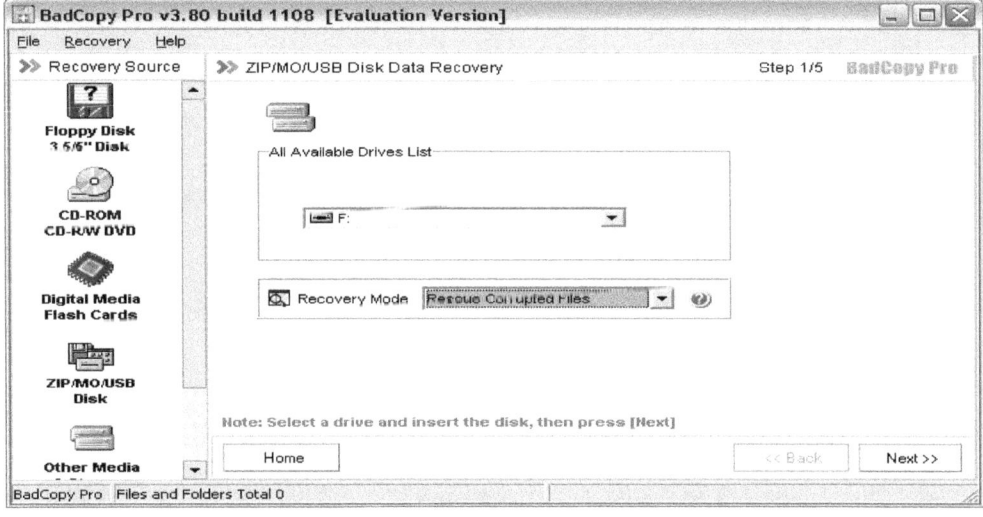

Exhibit 6

231

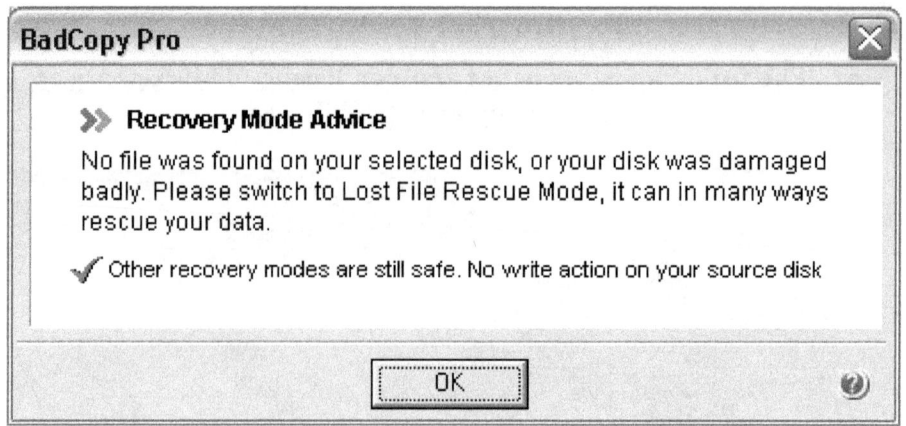

Exhibit 7

Evidence:

✓ Upon examination, the hard drive was found to contain 4 encrypted files (Exhibit 8).

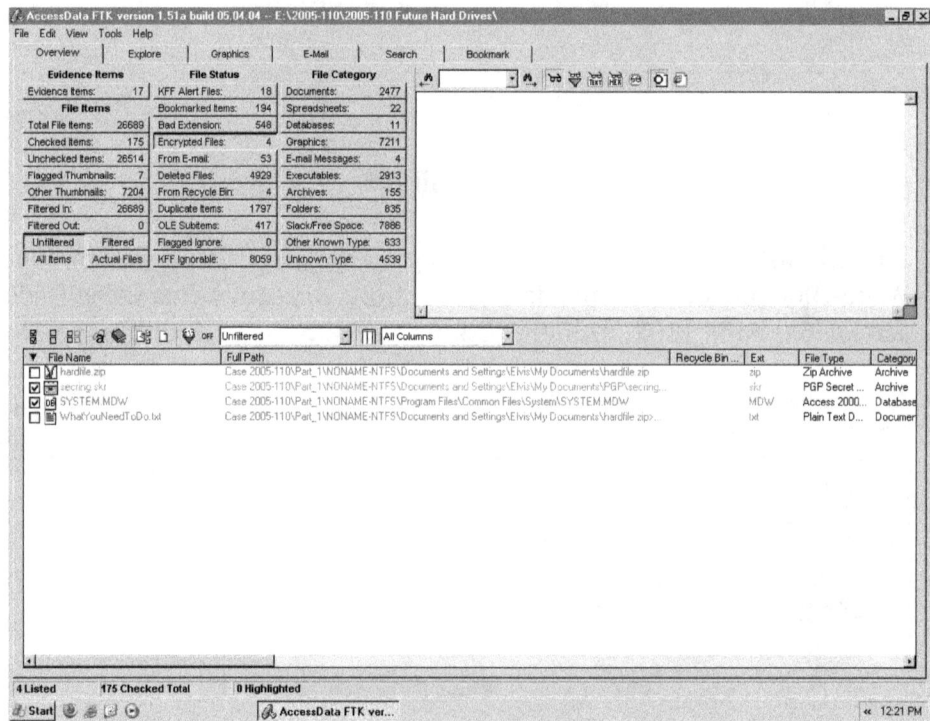

Exhibit 8

✓ The encrypted files were analyzed using Password Recovery ToolKit. The results of the password recoveries are as show in Exhibit 9.

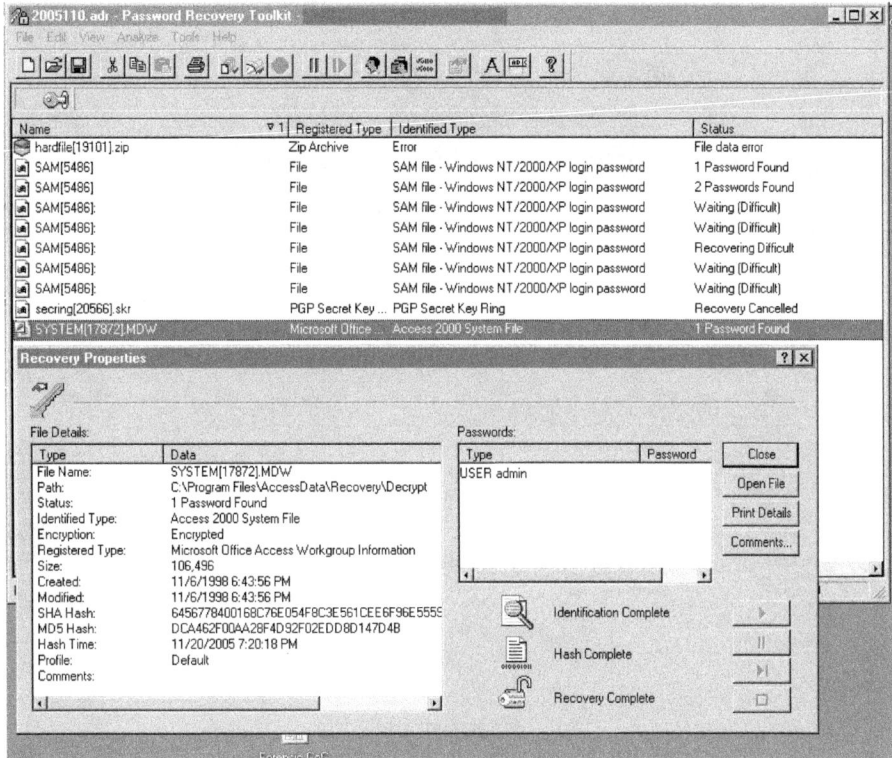

Exhibit 9

✓ The SAM (Security Accounts Manager) database for the machine was recovered using AccessData's Registry Viewer and loaded into PRTK, and several login passwords were recovered (Exhibits 10 & 11).

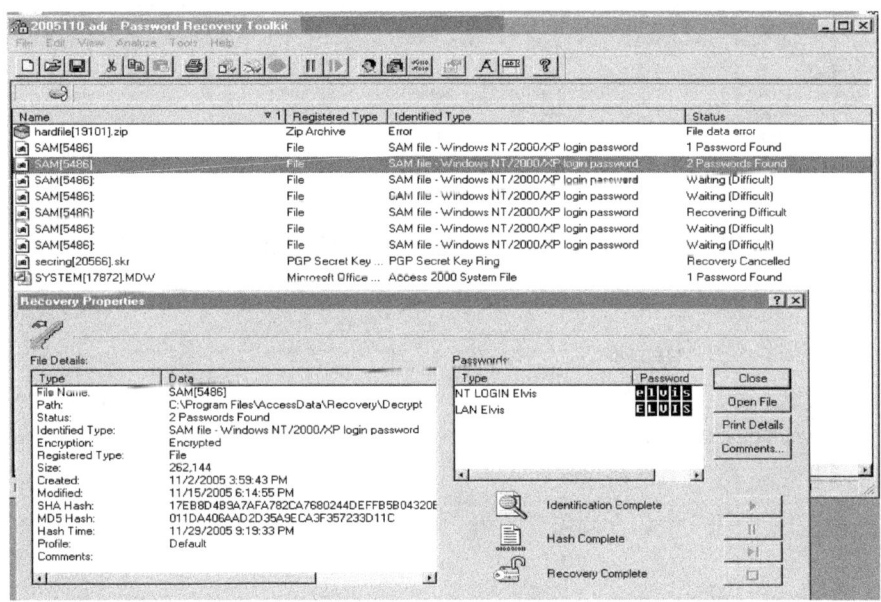

Exhibit 10

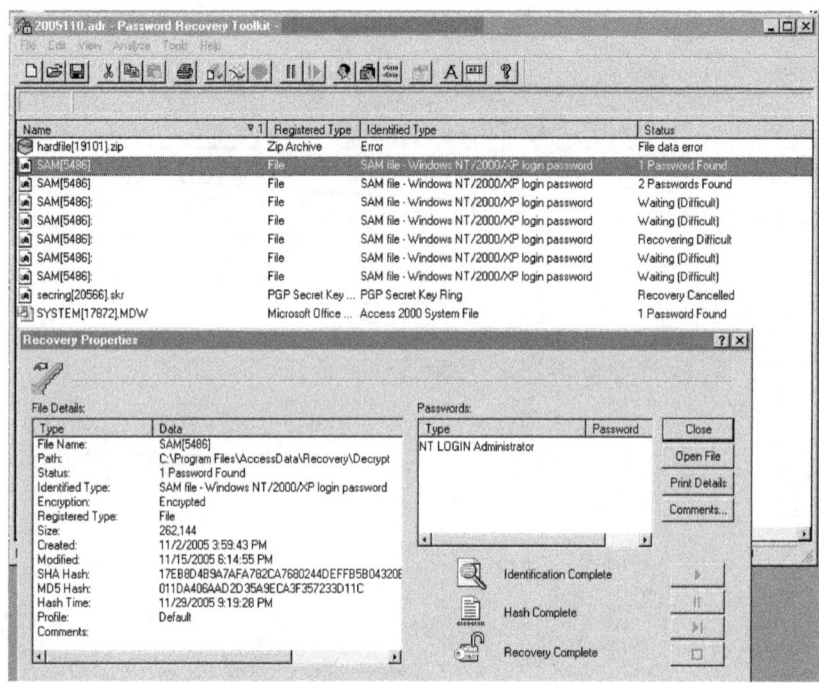

Exhibit 11

✓ Upon analysis by PRTK, the file hardfile.zip showed a data error and was not recoverable using this tool (Exhibit 12).

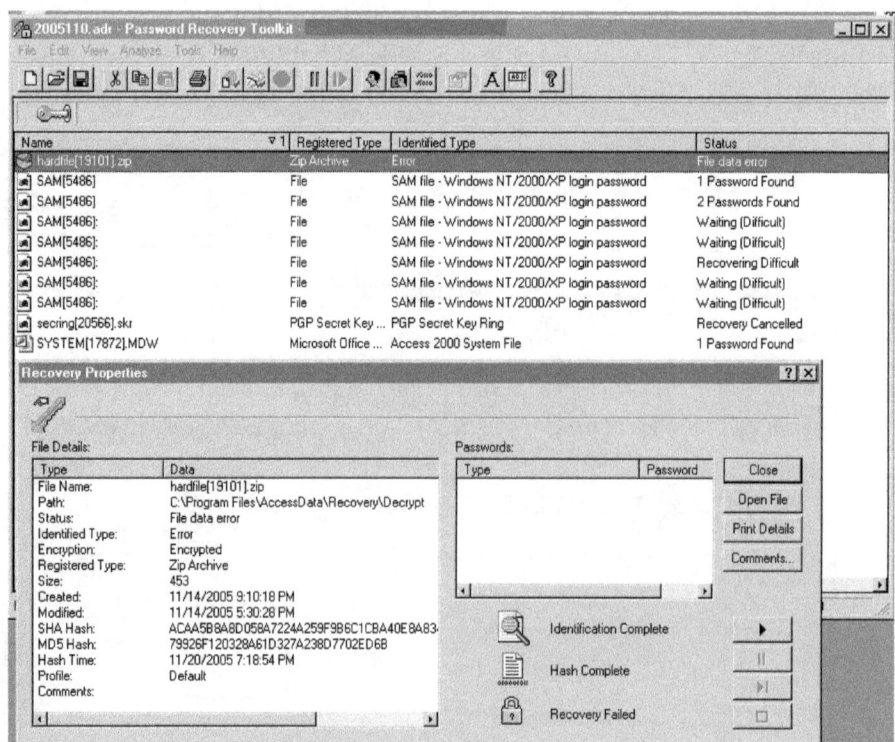

Exhibit 12

✓ Another encrypted file, entitled secring.skr (A PGP database of user keys), was analyzed continuously with Password Recovery ToolKit for seven days, and then for several more days using Distributed Network Attack 2.0, but the recovery attempts were unsuccessful using those tools. The file continues to be analyzed by PRTK (Exhibit 13).

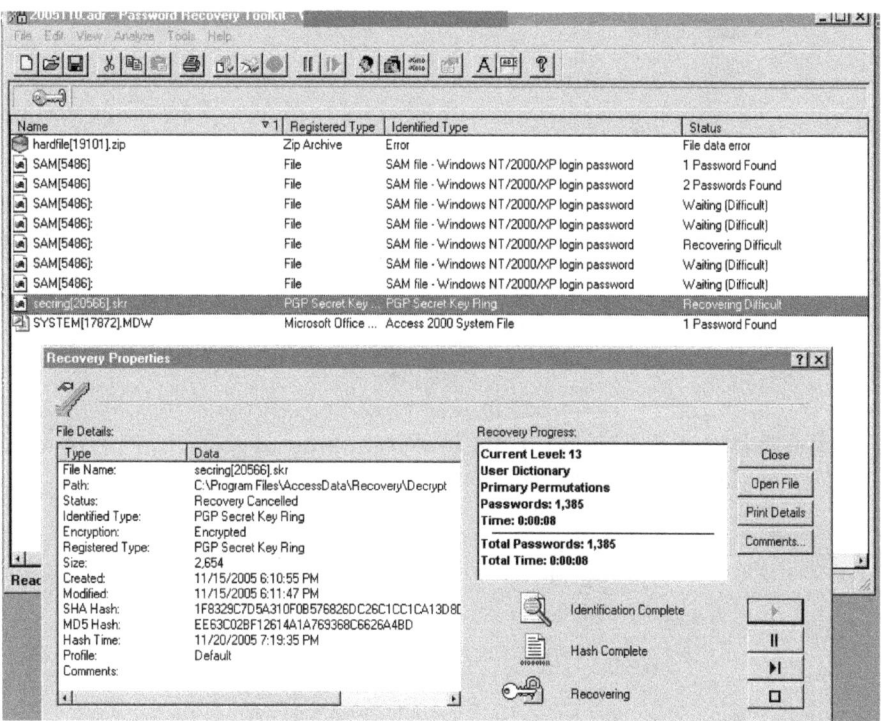

Exhibit 13

✓ Upon analysis of the file hardfile.zip, using HexWorkshop 4.2, it was discovered that the file had been altered by one-half byte (the hexadecimal digit, 8), making the file visible but corrupted. Using the Hex Editor, this investigator changed the digit, and saved the file under a new name. The following is a screenshot of the original file from the machine (Exhibit 14).

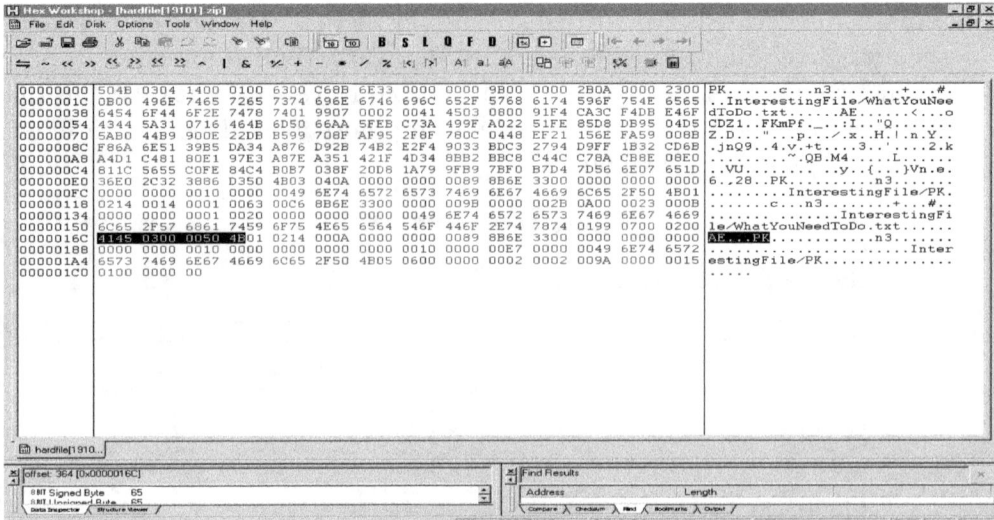

Exhibit 14

A screenshot of the file with the half-byte altered so that it matches the string earlier in the file (Exhibit 15).

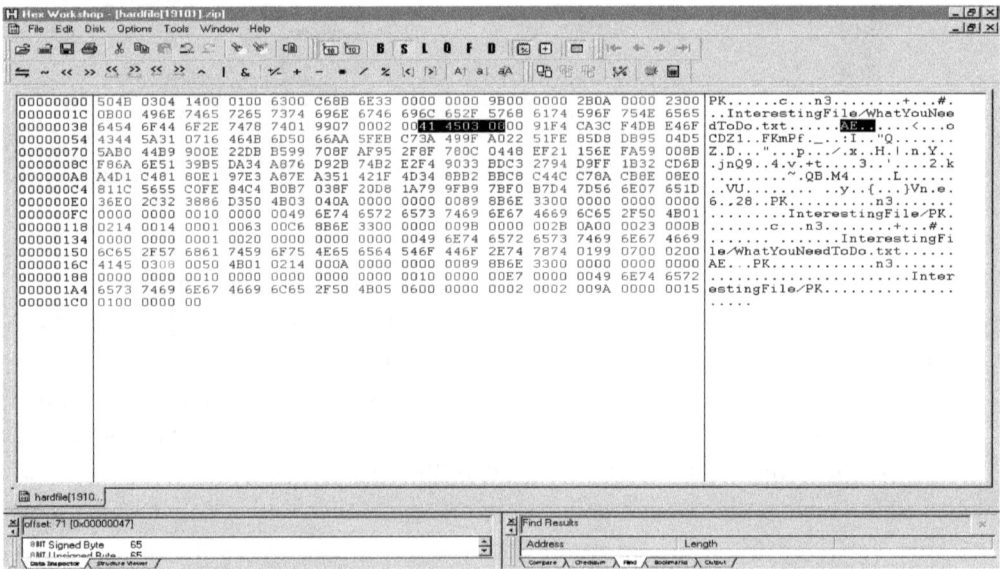

Exhibit 15

✓ The file can now be viewed, and the contents accessed, however, the Hashes are not the same (because it was necessary to reconstruct the file header to restore the file to an executable state) and the contents of the Zip archive can still not be opened, as the file WhatYouNeedToDo.txt (within the folder InterestingFile) is encrypted. PRTK cannot recover the password as the file is still corrupted, and the individual file cannot be exported from the archive without the password. This file (both the original and the altered version) have no evidentiary value.

✓ During analysis of the encrypted files, several virus warnings were given, alerting us to the presence of several Trojan executables on the image copy of the evidence machine, specifically IISXploit, and Sub-Seven, (Exhibit 16).

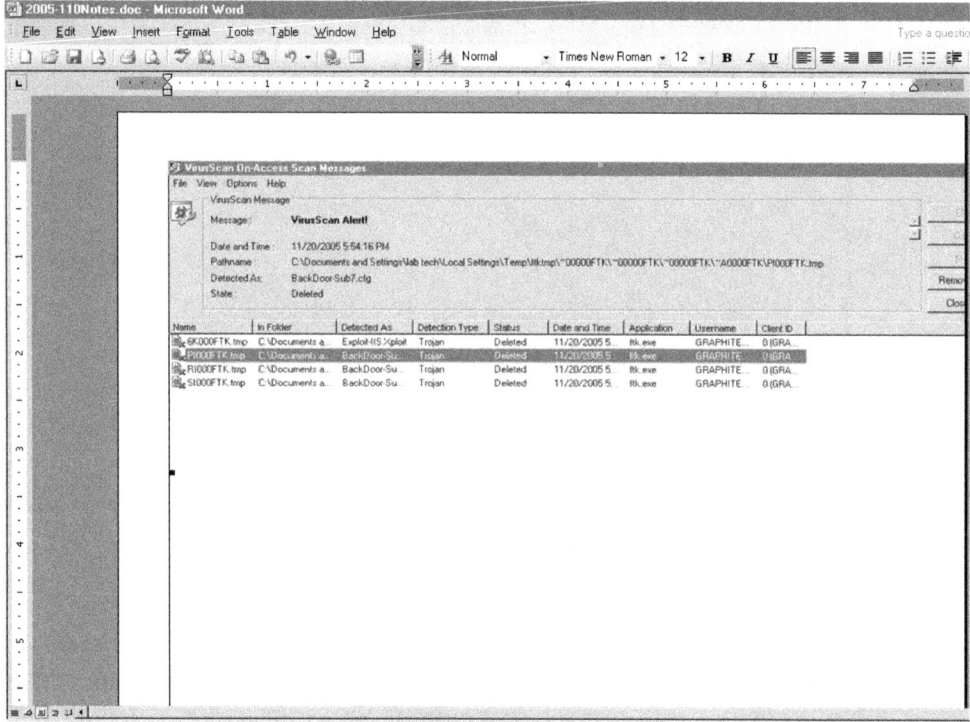

Exhibit 16

✓ An email was discovered that was addressed to billfates@hotmail.com (Exhibit 17). It had attachments to it, beyondexecv2.exe and nc.exe (NetCat), both remote monitoring and backdoor tools:

237

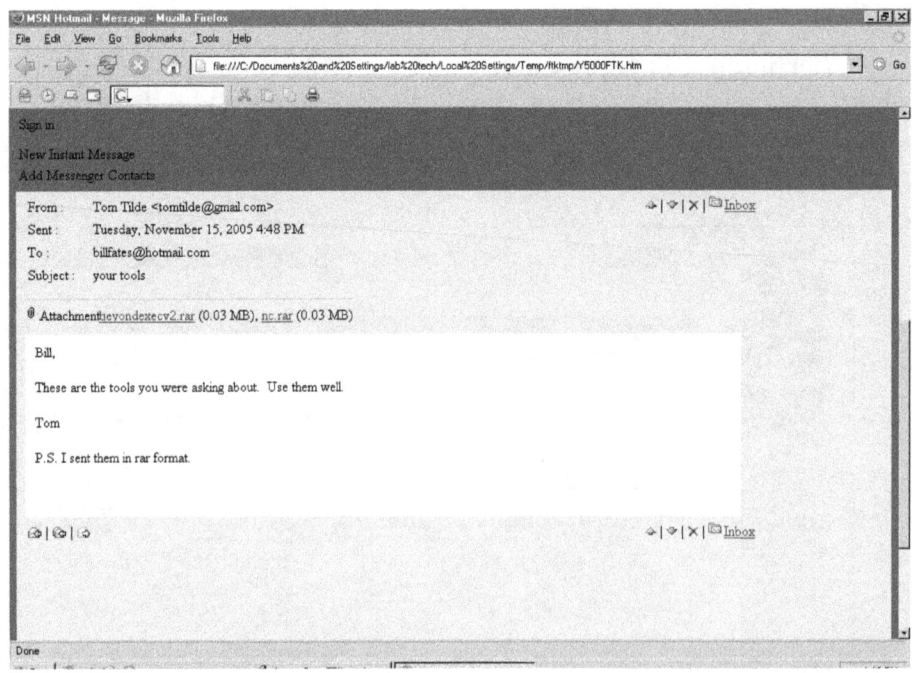

Exhibit 17

✓ Despite the information given to us by the IT Manager, Mr. Smith, that the machine was securely locked in an inaccessible office from the evening of November 11 through the morning of November 15, 2019, and that the machine probably had no remote access, sever logfiles of last-visited websites were found, showing that the user Elvis was logged in and visiting web pages during that time period (Exhibits 18 & 19).

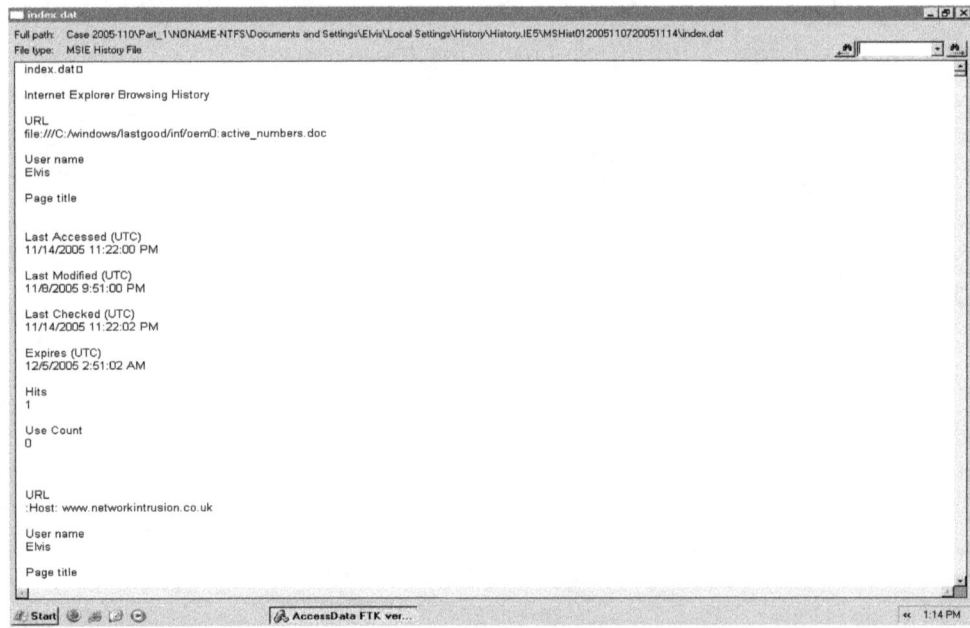

Exhibit 18

238

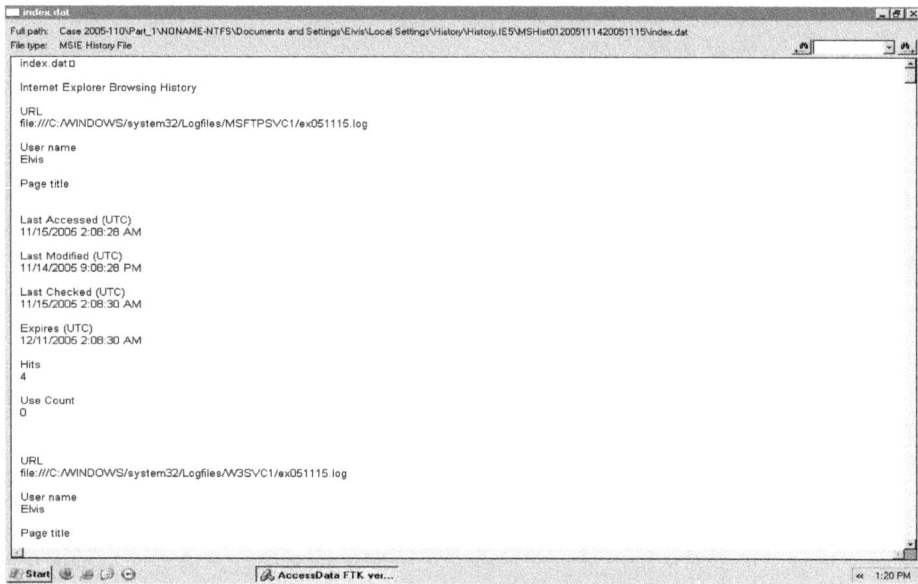

Exhibit 19

✓ A plain text document, called ##.txt, was discovered in Elvis' Recent documents. The phone number referenced within this document reaches the answering machine of Hacker Quarterly (Exhibit 20).

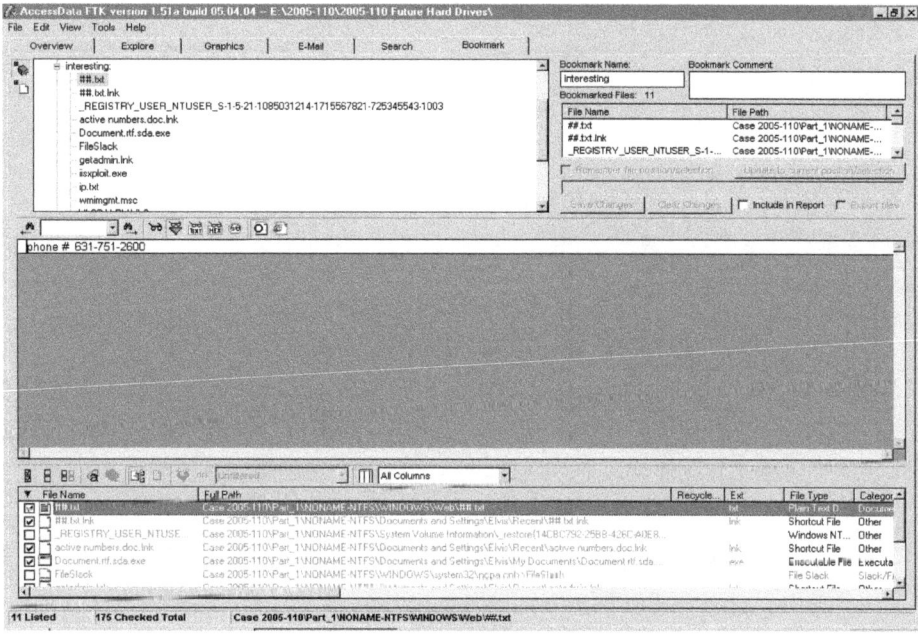

Exhibit 20

✓ This examiner discovered a file titled document.rtf.sda.exe, that when viewed with the Hex Editor looked like an executable file. However, when viewed with a detached viewer, the user is asked for its PGP password.

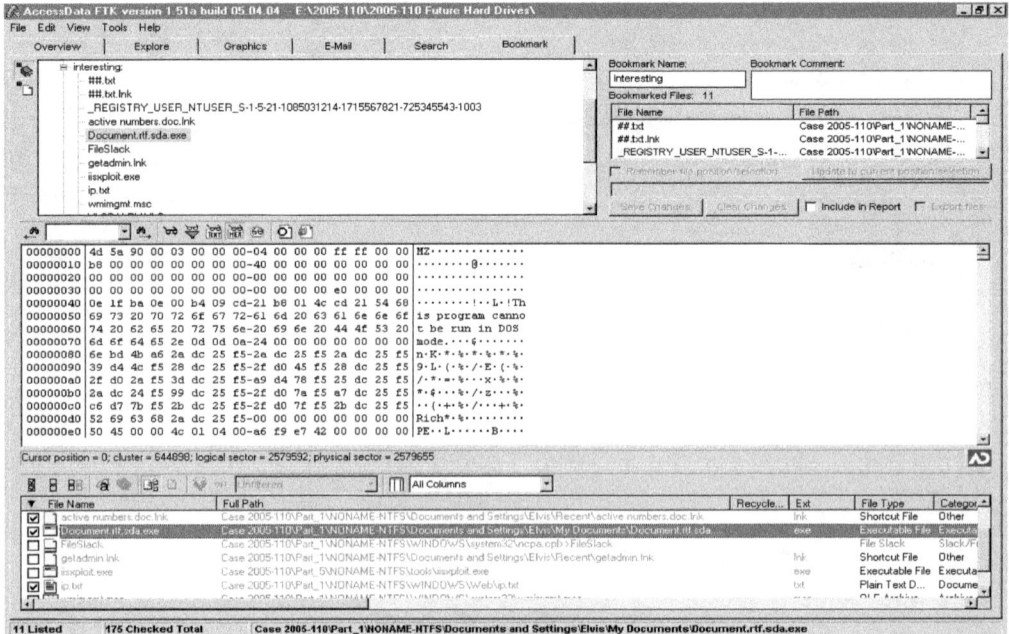

Exhibit 21

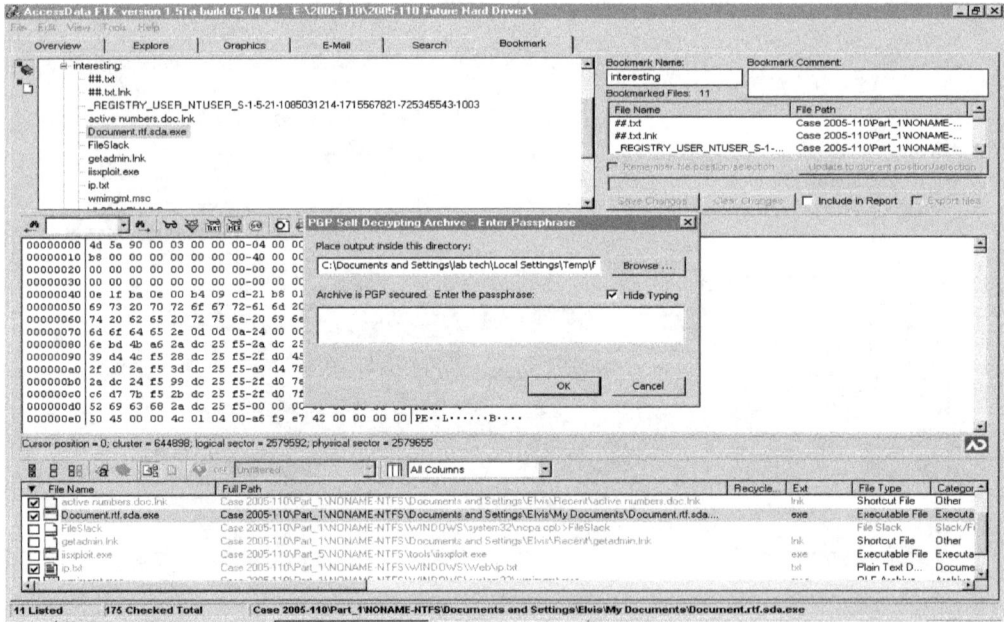

Exhibit 22

✓ When this file is exported into PRTK, the software does dot recognize it as an encrypted file, because of the .exe extension, and so will not begin a recovery of the password. This examiner was able to open this file, however by using the password "password", which was one of multiple guesses based upon commonly used passwords. The contents of the encrypted file referenced the scanning of the IP addresses as shown in exhibit 23.

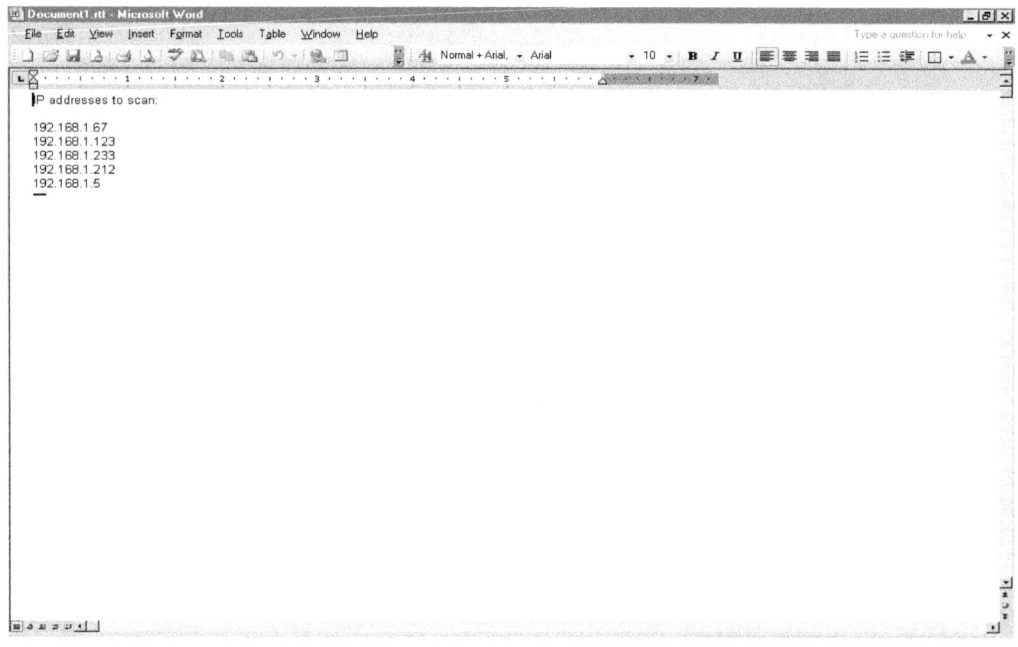

Exhibit 23

✓ A file, called ip.txt, was found, also containing IP numbers as shown in exhibit 24.

Exhibit 24

✓ Upon further examination of the file and directory structure, several types of malicious or obfuscation tools were found. They fall into these categories: Steganography (such as Unstegano, Steganography, JPHide and Seek, and StegDetect/StegBreak) as shown in exhibits 25 & 26.

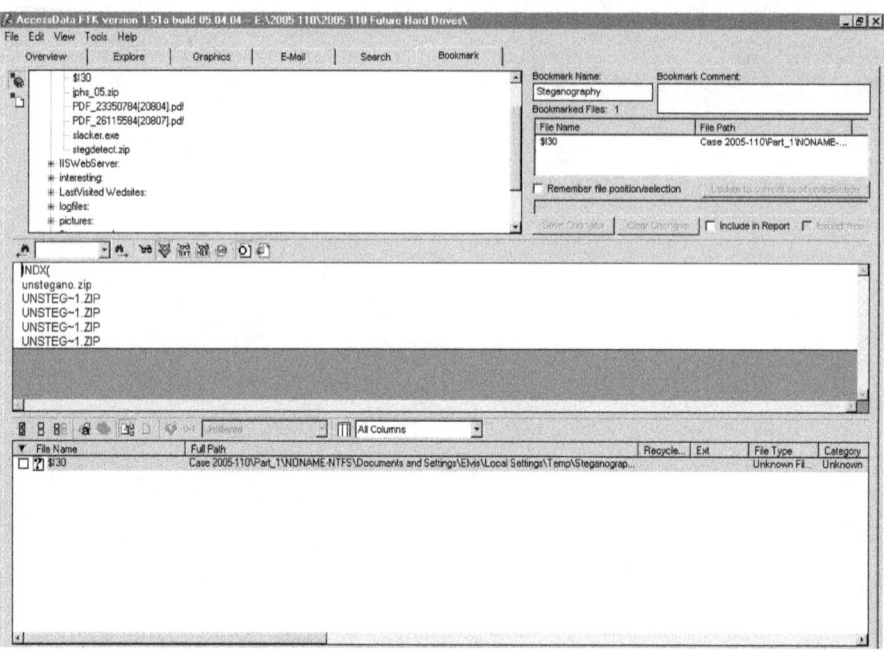

Exhibit 25

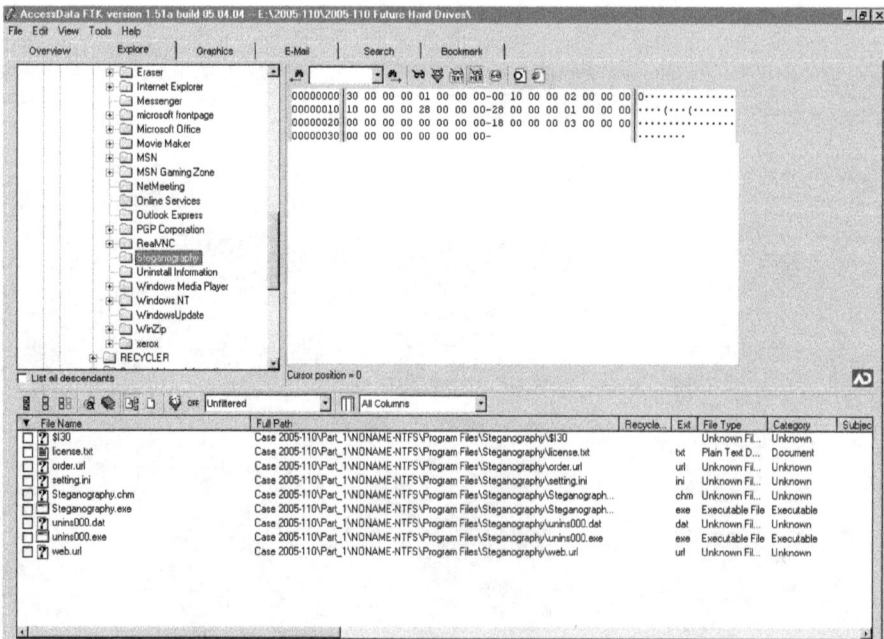

Exhibit 26

✓ Obfuscation or Covering/Hiding Tools such as Eraser and PGP (Exhibit 27).

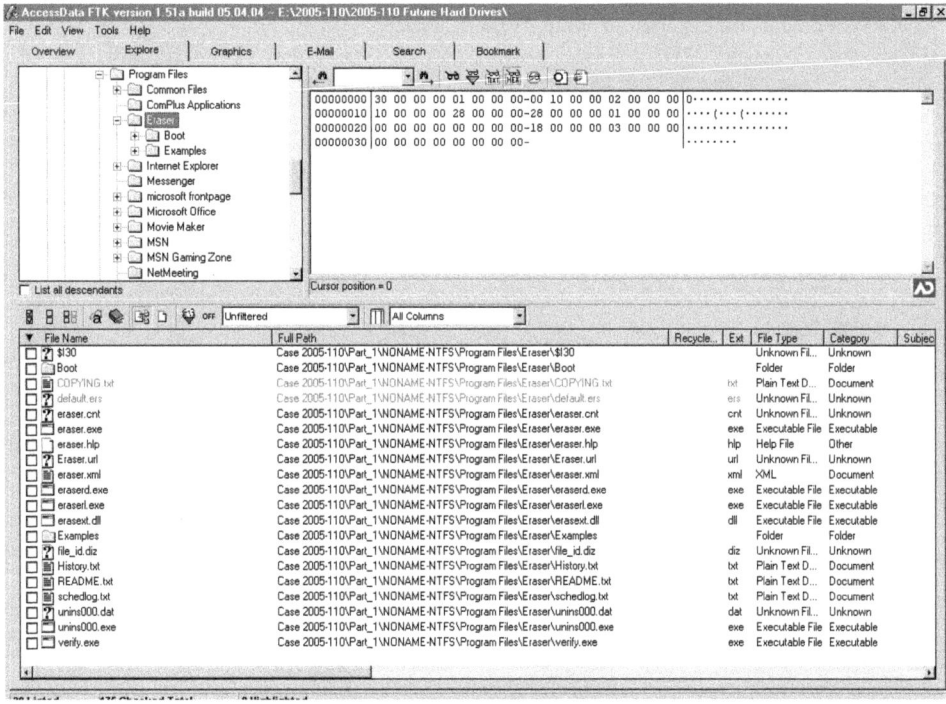

Exhibit 27

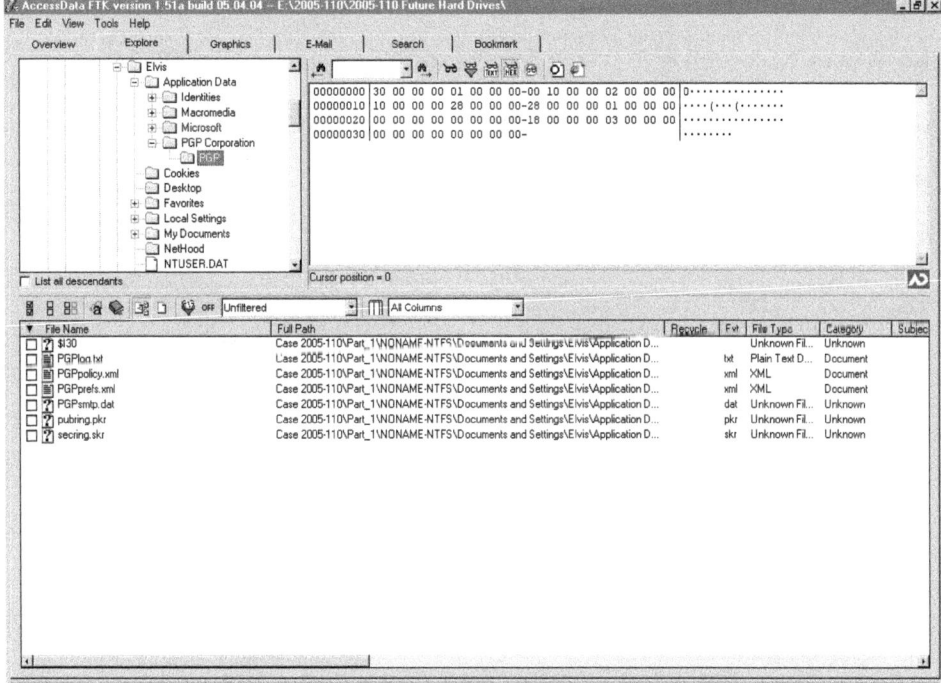

Exhibit 28

✓ Password Cracking, Network Monitoring, and BackDoor programs such as nMap, PWDump, Cain and Abel, SubSeven, AntiFirewall, NetCat, Ethereal, and VNC were discovered as shown in exhibit 29.

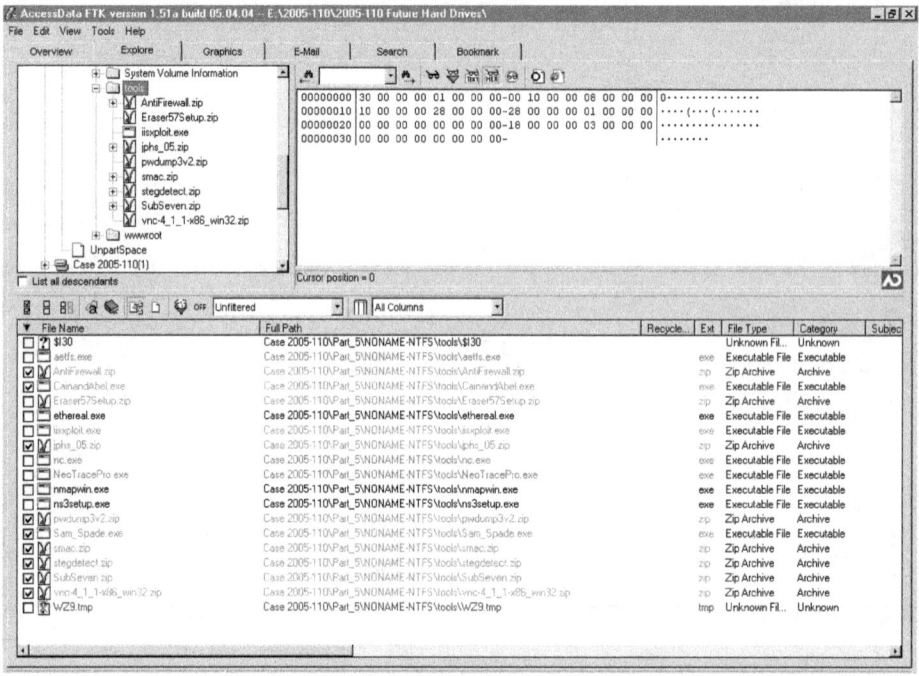

Exhibit 29

✓ References to searches for "AntiForensics" were discovered (Exhibit 30).

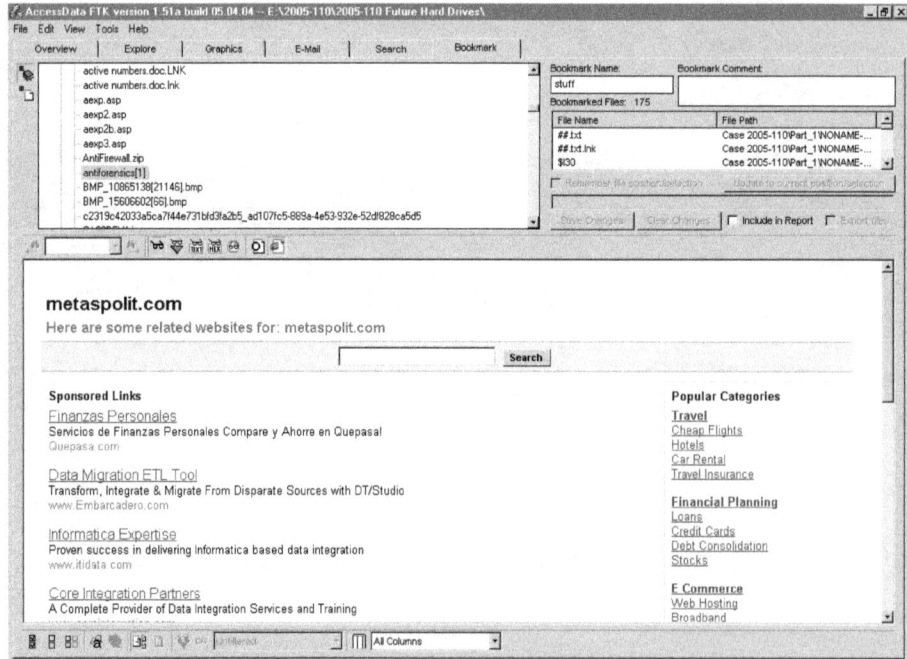

Exhibit 30

✓ Because Steganography tools were located on the suspect machine, a search of all .jpeg images was conducted using xSteg, Steganography, and JPHide and Seek (all registered to FHD). One file was located containing steganographic data, it is titled mountains356.jpg. The original file size was 3Kbytes as found elsewhere in the image however after modification the file size increased to 65Kbytes (Exhibit 31).

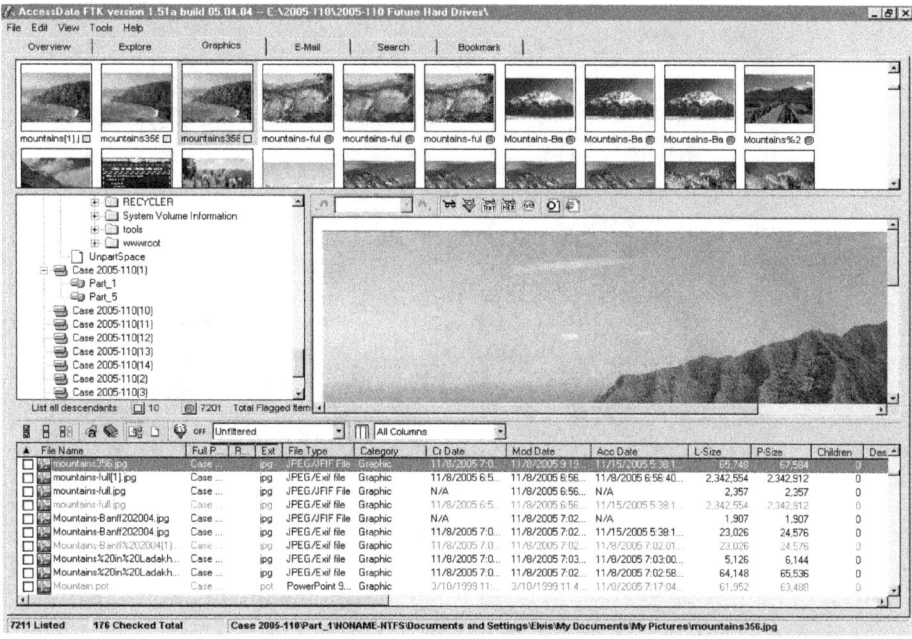

Exhibit 31

✓ Using Steganography, the hidden file (mainlist.2) was extracted (Exhibit 32).

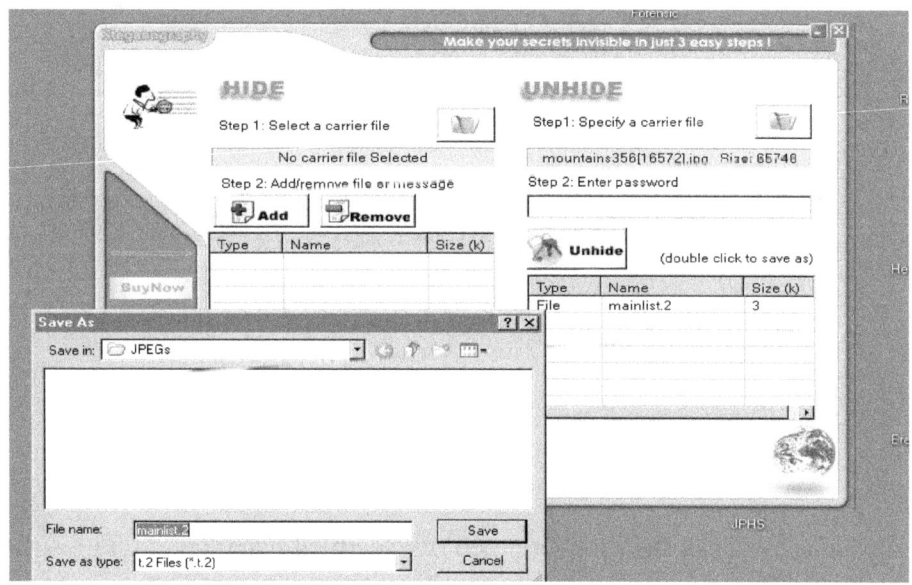

Exhibit 32

✓ It was determined by looking at the file headers of mainlist.2 with HexWorkshop, that this file was part of a larger file that had been broken up into several pieces with software called AEFTS, or Archiving Encrypting Tiny File Splitter (Exhibit 33).

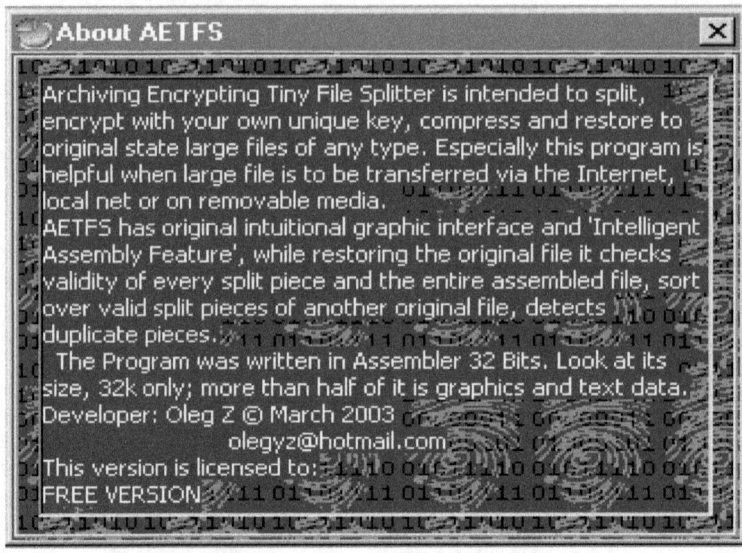

Exhibit 33

✓ Three more pieces of the file were located, in various places on the evidence machine (Exhibit 34).

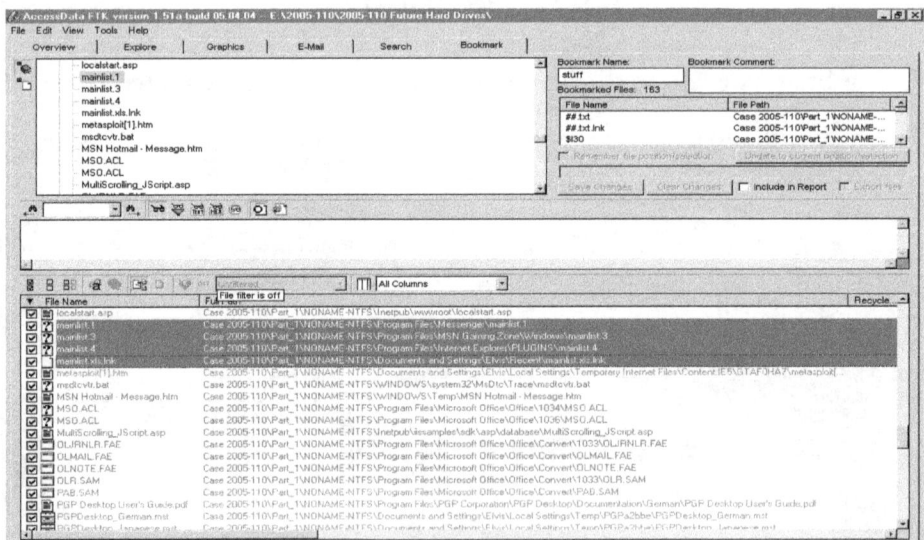

Exhibit 34

✓ The four pieces of the file were then reassembled using the AETFS software (no password was assigned), and the results of the reassembly are as follows (an Excel spreadsheet of active, cancelled and unknown credit card numbers):

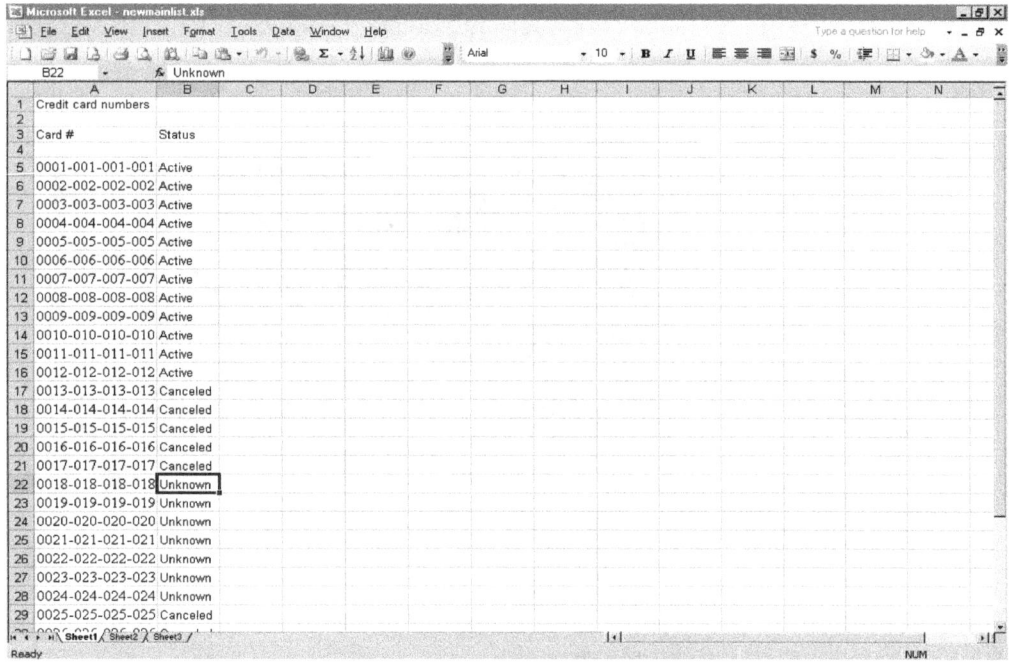

Exhibit 35

✓ When further examining the directory structure of the second partition on the machine, this investigator noted the presence of a wwwroot folder, which indicates that Microsoft Internet Information Services (IIS, or a Web Server) has been configured to run on the machine. This directory is created when IIS is installed, and holds all of the Web Server files and logs (Exhibit 36).

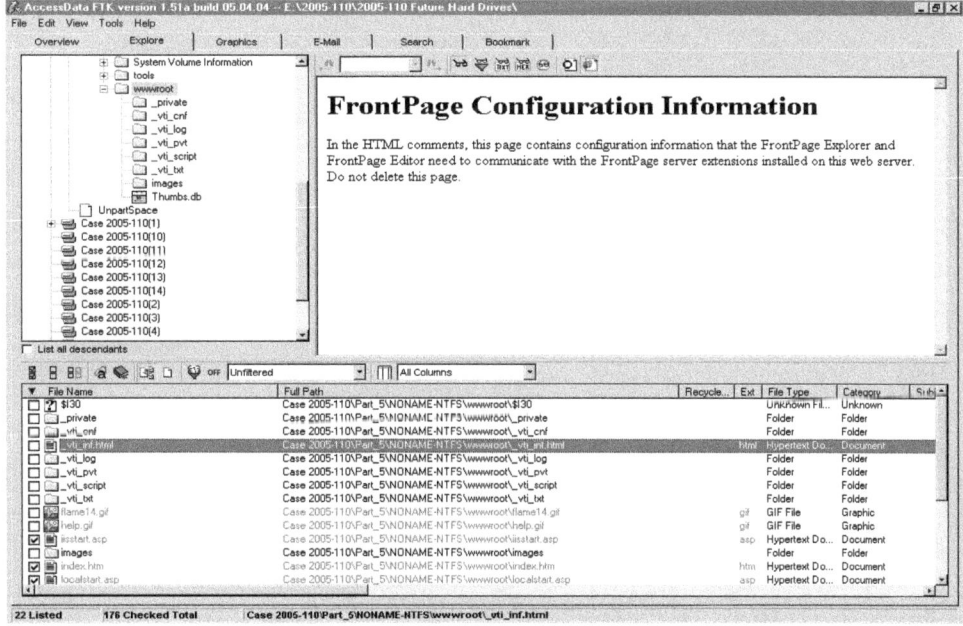

Exhibit 36

247

✓ The front page of the under-construction web site was located (Exhibit 37).

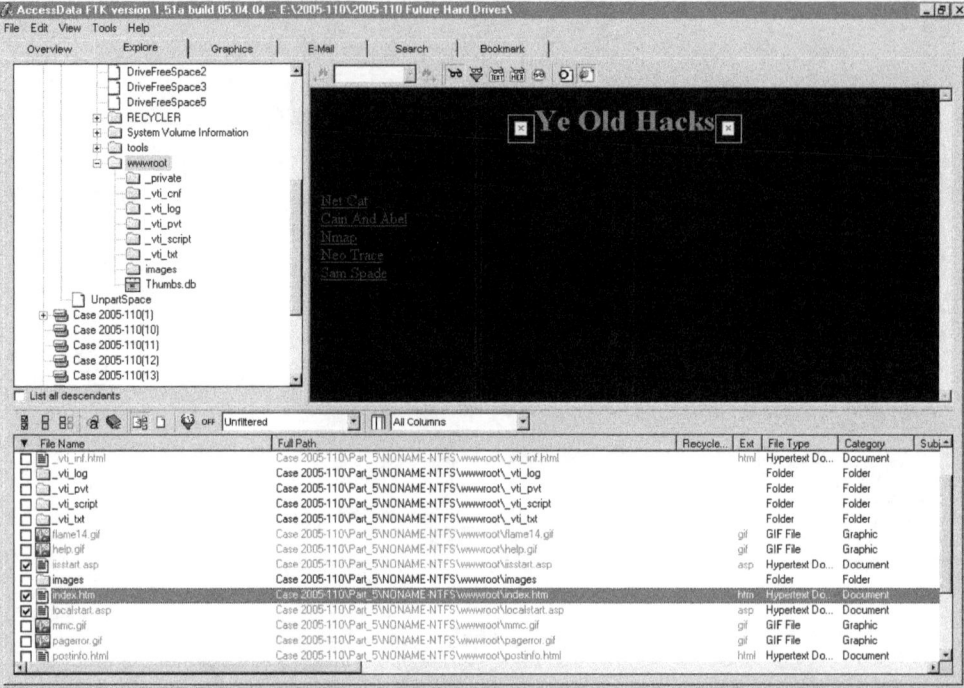

Exhibit 37

✓ And several log files documenting IIS activity on the machine were found, including several from days when no one was expected to be using the machine (Exhibit 38).

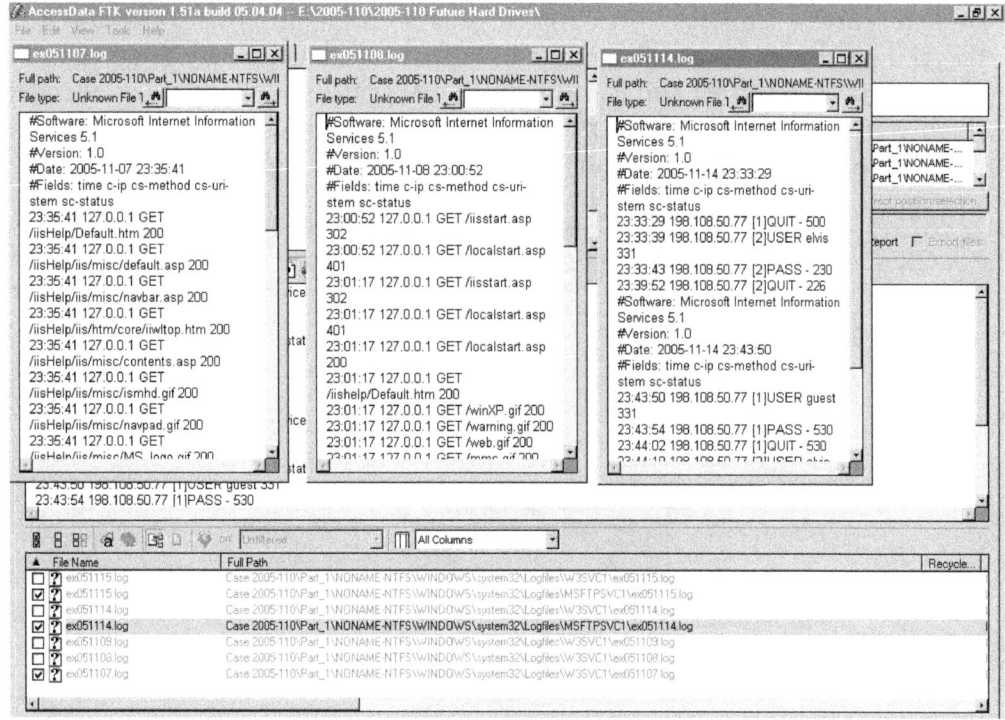

Exhibit 38

✓ One logfile was located documenting that user account Elvis logged in and sent a variety of malicious executables to several different IP addresses (Exhibit 39).

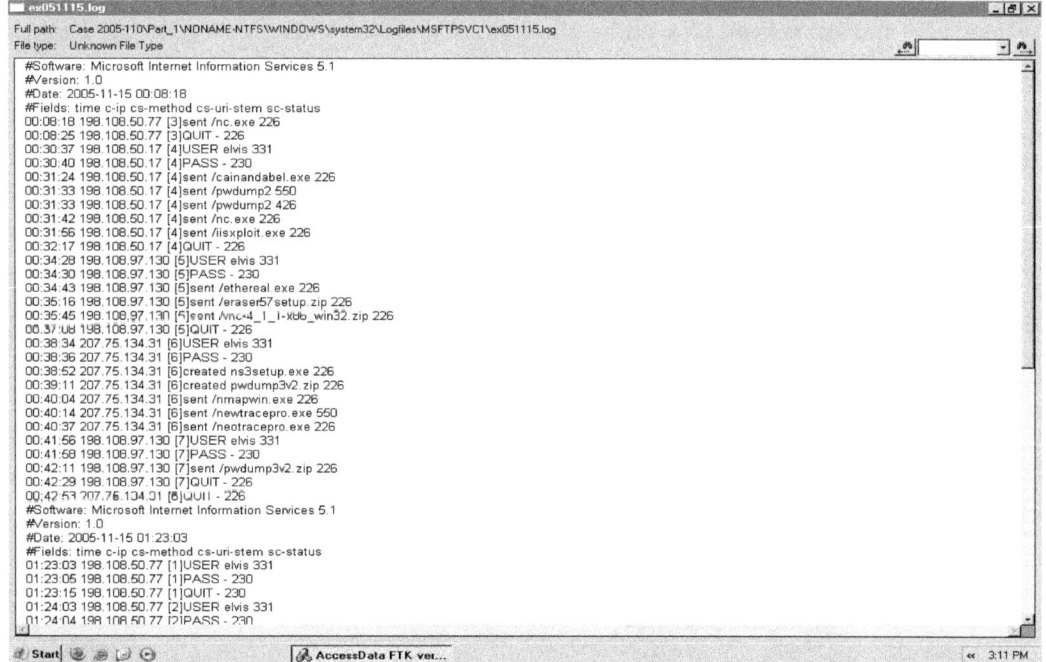

Exhibit 39

✓ The machine's registry was examined, as well as the files that were stored on the second partition, the one that contained all of the malicious programs and the root of the web server, and it was determined that this partition had been hidden from any other viewer of this machine, besides the user Elvis. This hidden state is indicated by the Dollar sign in front of folders (Exhibit 40).

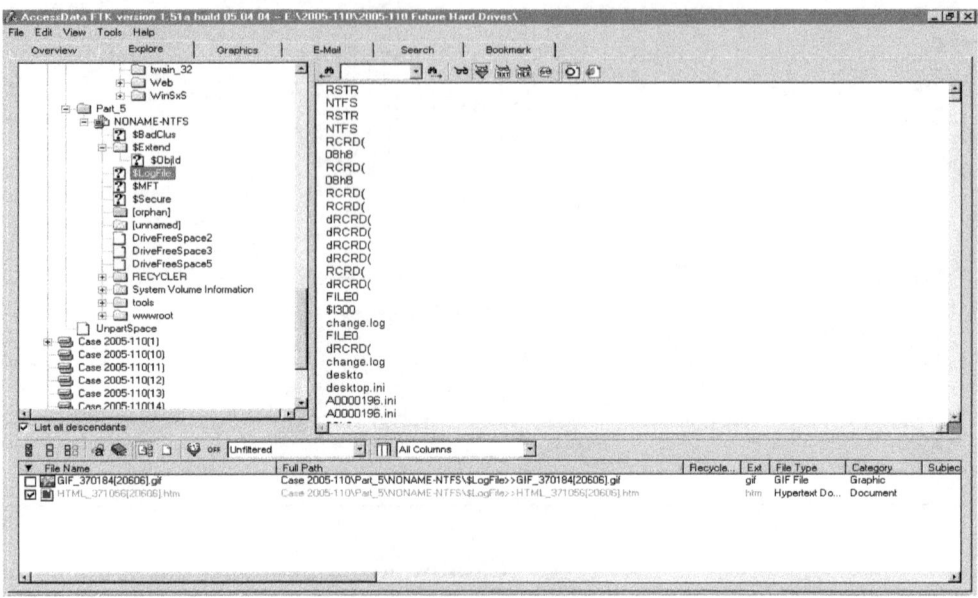

Exhibit 40

✓ While operational this volume was given the label E:, and contained the Web server, and ftp server, as well as all of the malicious files previously mentioned (Exhibits 41 & 42).

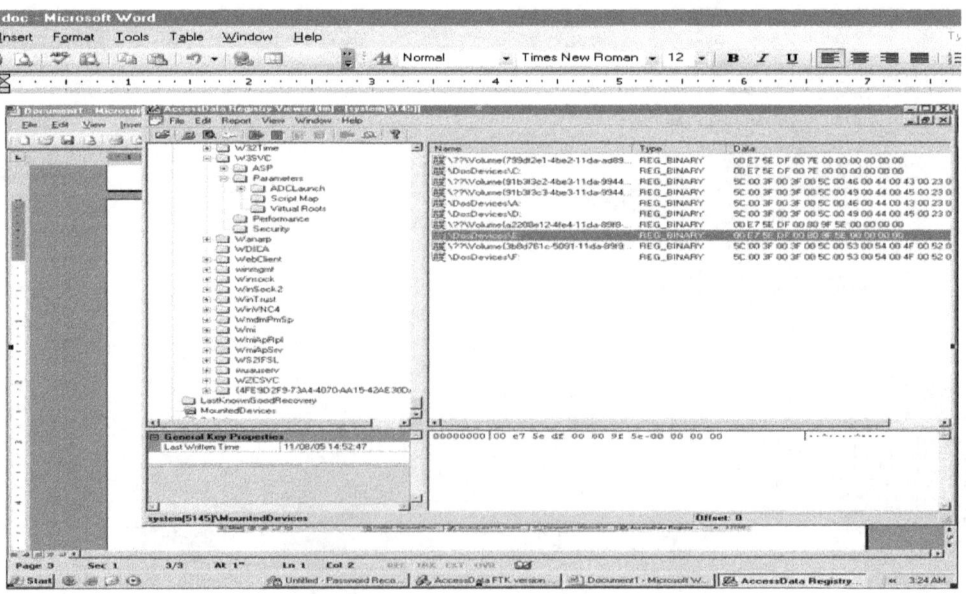

Exhibit 41

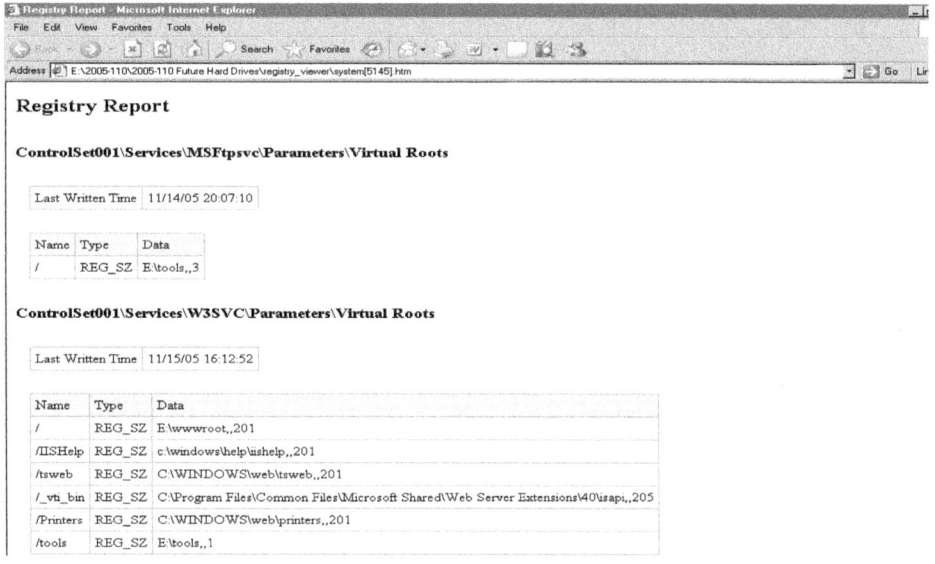

Exhibit 42

✓ This investigator also located a file containing an Alternate Data Stream when examining the registry. It was located in the MUI cache of the user Elvis' NTUser.dat file. The MUI cache (Short for Multilingual User Interface), is a .dll library folder associated with Windows operation. As you see in the screenshot below, nc.exe, the NetCat monitoring program, is streamed with Windows (as indicated by the colon). This means that every time that Windows starts up on the machine, NetCat begins running as well. The significance of the program running in an alternate data stream, is that it cannot be detected as it is running, as it does not appear in task manager, and does not change the listed file size of the program that it is streamed with (Exhibit 43).

Exhibit 43

✓ A suspicious "hosts" file was identified. Hosts files are used by Windows to map a domain name to an IP address without having to use Domain Name Servers. In the following file, several banking sites' domain names are all mapped to the same IP address (Exhibit 44).

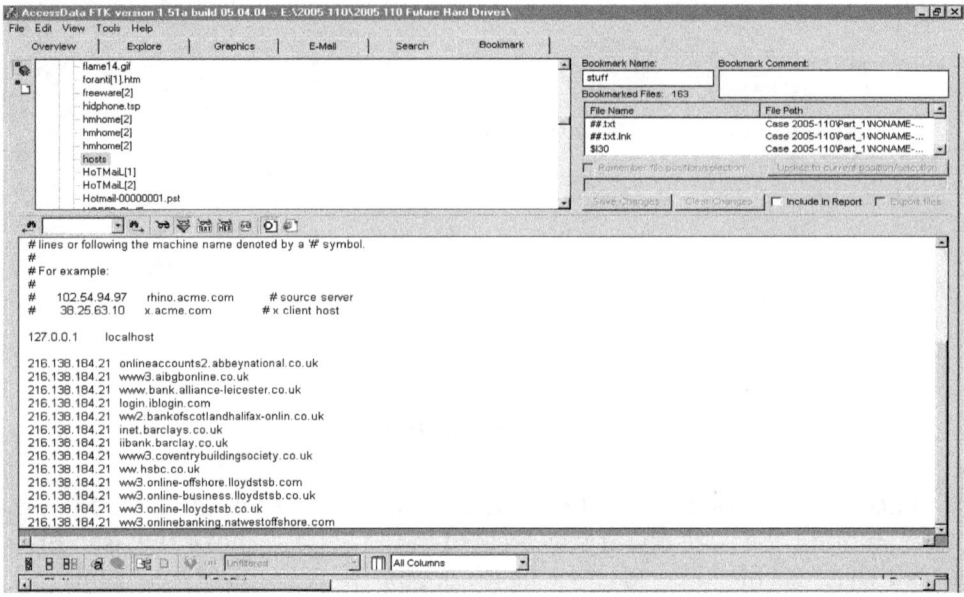

Exhibit 44

Investigational Summary

Examination of the suspect drive showed the presence of the following items:

1. Four encrypted files, two of which, hardfile.zip and WhatYouNeedToDo.txt, were not recoverable due to data corruption. A third, SYSTEM.MDW, was an empty database. The fourth, secrng.skr, is still being processed through PRTK for a password.
2. A SAM database file, which was decrypted using PRTK, giving us the password for a user of the machine, Elvis.
3. An email to billfates@hotmail.com, with the backdoor tools, NetCat and BeyondExec attached.
4. Logfiles contradicting Mr. Smith's assertion that noone used the machine after November 11, 2019, and that no one has remote access to the machine.
5. A file called ##.txt, containing a phone number that reaches the answering machine of Hacker Quarterly, (phone number registered to Cathy and Howard Tripod, of Stony Brook, NY).
6. An rtf file containing "IP numbers to scan" and a text file listing IP numbers.
7. Numerous instances of Steganography, Obfuscation, Password Cracking, BackDoor and Network Monitoring Tools, including Cain and Abel, SubSeven, BeyondExec, SamSpade, Eraser, JPHide and Seek, Steganography, xSteg, StegBreak, and StegDetect, NetCat, nMap, neoTrace, PGP, PWDump, Ethereal, VNC, and AntiFirewall.
8. A steganographic file, mountains356.jpg, revealed to contain one piece of a file, broken up into four parts by AETFS, and scattered around the machine.
9. The above-mentioned file, mainlist, originally an Excel file, that when reassembled by AETFS, contained a list of credit card numbers.
10. Evidence that an IIS Web Server was running on the machine, and that a web site called "Ye Olde Hacks" was being constructed on it, and that they were running on a hidden partition on the machine.
11. A logfile documenting that user "Elvis" sent several malicious files and executables to several IP addresses.
12. An Alternate Data Stream containing the nc.exe program.
13. A suspicious "Hosts" file, redirecting a variety of banking websites' domain names (when entered in this machine's browser) to one IP address, 216.138.184.21, block registered to Norlight Telecommunications.

Based on the evidence uncovered, the IT Manager at Future Hard Drives Corporation was contacted at 8:00 AM on November 28, 2019, and informed that there is a likelihood that the suspect's machine did indeed have remote access, and had been accessed while it was secured. He was advised that he should monitor his network carefully for suspicious web traffic. A user of the suspect machine had configure the computer to run a hidden Web and FTP server. He was then informed that he would have the full forensic report the next day.

Case Log of Forensic Examination of Subject Drive

```
11/16/2019 11:41:42 AM -- FTK Version 1.51a build 05.04.04
        Examiner's Machine:
        Phys Mem:  Total: 1,072,676,864  Available: 771,297,280  Used:
301,379,584
        Virt Mem:  Total: 2,147,352,576  Available: 1,967,243,264  Used:
180,109,312
        Page File Available: 2,393,894,912
        ------------------------------------------------------
11/16/2019 11:41:42 AM -- New case started by examiner James T. Bond
FTK version 1.51a build 05.04.04
        Investigator: James T. Bond
        Case Name: 2005-110 Future Hard Drives
        Case Number: 2005-110
        Case Folder: E:\2005-110\2005-110 Future Hard Drives
        Description:
        Case Log Options (NOT Case Agent Logging Options):
          Log case and evidence events: Yes
          Log error messages: Yes
          Log bookmarking events: Yes
          Log searching events: Yes
          Log special searching events: Yes
          Log other events: Yes
          Log extended information: No
        Processes to be performed:
          File Extraction: Yes
          File Identification: Yes
          MD5 Hash: Yes
          SHA1 Hash: Yes
          KFF (Known File Filter): Yes
          Entropy Test: Yes
          Full Text Index: Yes
          Prerender Thumbnails: Yes
          File Listing Database: Yes
          HTML File Listing: No
          Decrypt EFS Files: Yes
        Default Case Refinement Settings:
          Add files only if they satisfy BOTH the file status and the
          file type criteria as follows:
            File Status Criteria:
              Deletion status: any
              Encryption status: any
              From email status: any
              Duplicate status: any
              OLE stream status: any
            File Type Criteria:
              documents: yes
              spreadsheets: yes
              databases: yes
              graphics: yes
              email messages: yes
              executables: yes
              archives: yes
              folders: yes
```

```
              other recognized: yes
              unknown: yes
        Default Index Refinement Settings:
          Don't index KFF ignorable files
          Index files only if they satisfy BOTH the file status and the
          file type criteria as follows:
            File Status Criteria:
              Deletion status: any
              Encryption status: any
              From email status: any
              Duplicate status: any
              OLE stream status: any
            File Type Criteria:
              documents: yes
              spreadsheets: yes
              databases: yes
              graphics: yes
              email messages: yes
              executables: yes
              archives: yes
              folders: yes
              other recognized: yes
              unknown: yes

        Comment:
        Evidence-specific Case Refinement Settings:
          Add all files
        Evidence-specific Index Refinement Settings:
          Index all files
11/16/2019 11:41:42 AM -- Starting to add evidence items...
11/16/2019 11:41:57 AM -- Completed adding Case 2005-110\NONAME-Unknown
```

A full listing of the FTK Case Activity Log may be viewed when reviewing the full FTK Forensic Report.

<u>Case Summary and Documentation</u>

The investigation and analysis of the suspect's drive was performed, using a dedicated analysis drive, with Access Data's Forensic Tool Kit, Version 1.51a, build 05.04.204, registered to My Computer Forensics, LLC, with its accompanying Imager and Password Recovery Toolkit. The investigator also utilized HexWorkshop 4.2 for verification of file formats, and Distributed Network Attack 2.0, from Access Data, registered to My Computer Forensics, LLC, to attempt recovery of an encrypted document. For recovery of Steganographic data, the investigator used JPSeek 2.0, xSteg, StegDetect and StegBreak 4.0, and Steganography. For reassembly of the segmented file, the investigator used AETFS version 1.2. All software is registered to My Computer Forensics, LLC, and documentation can be obtained for all software from the Lab Administrator of WMy Computer Forensics.

Drive image documentation and verification is as follows:

Physical Evidentiary Item (Source) Information:
 Drive Interface Type: USB
 Drive Model: QUANTUM FIREBALLP LM10.2 USB Device
 [Drive Geometry]
 Bytes per Sector: 512
 Cylinders: 1,240
 Sectors per Track: 63
 Sector Count: 19,925,880
 Tracks per Cylinder: 255
 Source data size: 9729 MB
 Sector count: 19925880
 MD5 checksum: b27e58c248ae82901d6ba141bef60f05
 SHA1 checksum: ebb026dbe65e1aebaba939c38c3bb3af65d13002

The full FTK report was encrypted using File Encryption XP, registered to My Computer Forensics, LLC, using a 384-bit Blowfish algorithm, and stored in the secure storage area at the My Computer Forensics lab facility. The report can be viewed upon documented request of an authorized individual.

Reprinted with Permission

Exhibit A – Sanitization Policy

- All machines will be maintained with the latest anti-virus and anti-spyware patches from McAfee and PestPatrol.

- Any drive to be used for a forensic examination will be reformatted with a complete format before being used

- All forensic machines will use an appropriate hardware based write blocker.

All forensic analysis workstations will not be connected to the Internet or to the company network in order to prevent any risk of being hacked.

Exhibit B – Forensic Handling Policy 8-15-18

- To prevent cross contamination between cases and prior to use in any analysis or recovery, the working drive must be forensically sterile by performing a full reformat. The working drive is the drive used to store the target image. The working drive will have no other images files stored on it. After completion of each case, image files may be stored on an alternate data base system.

- Chain of Custody documentation must be maintained and accompany any forensic recovery. Image files, original media or any other information is not to be disclosed to any third party unless required by law.
- Storage of original media must be consistent with local law enforcement procedures. All original media is to be stored in the on-site storage safe and protected from fire, water and environmental concerns.
- All stored original media must be labeled by forensic case number

Exhibit C – Hash Image Validation Policy 8-15-18

All recovered image information must be validated as having an equivalent hash value with that of the original unless the file required reconstruction. In such a circumstance the detailed steps of how the file was reconstructed must be included in the final report for verification by a third party. The hash value may be either MD5 or SHA-1 and must be included in the final report.

Forensics Exercise # 40
Being Interviewed in a Forensics Investigation

OBJECTIVE:

To become familiar with the interview process with the opportunity to meet with a law enforcement official to learn how they conduct interviews, the types of interviews and how they process and report the results.

OVERVIEW:

Interviewing is a critical component of understanding the environment and events surrounding the system to be analyzed. From a successful interview of those involved, key search terms may be identified.

THIS EXERCISE MAY BE PERFORMED INDIVIDUALLY BY THE STUDENT OR COLLECTIVELY AS A PRESENTATION TO THE CLASS

STEPS:

1. Contact someone you may know in law enforcement or someone who has worked in law enforcement and request they share with you interview processes. Note, however, that some law enforcement may not be as receptive to share interview techniques. Explain that you are focusing on computer forensics and not criminal cases. If you cannot locate an official that is receptive to this assignment, contact your instructor for an alternative one.

2. Take detailed notes on your meeting. Ask the following questions to the individual

   a. What type of training or experience does the law enforcement official have to conduct an interview?

   b. How many interviews has the person conducted?

   c. What are the majority of the categories or nature of the interviews, i.e. drug, robbery, assault, cyber-crime, etc?

   d. What rights does the person being interviewed have?

   e. How are they made aware of those rights?

f. Identify other questions you ask:

_____

_____

_____

_____

3. Complete the following information.

    a. The name of who you met with

    _____

    b. Their title or position.

    _____

    c. Name of the company / law enforcement agency where they work

    _____

4. When the interview is complete, thank the individual for their participation.

5. Write a letter thanking them for their time and assistance. Include a copy of the letter with this assignment.

STUDENT SUMMARY:

1. What did you learn from this exercise?

Evaluators Review of Learners Performance

1   2   3   4   5

Forensics Exercise # 41
Conducting a Personal Interview in a Forensics Investigation

OBJECTIVE:

To become familiar with the interview process with the opportunity to conduct a mock interview.

OVERVIEW:

Interviewing is a critical component of understanding the environment and events surrounding the system to be examined. The interviewee may provide additional search terms that may not have been previously considered or identified. It is important that the student working in industry understand they are not law enforcement and many of the techniques used by law enforcement are not applicable in corporate cases. However, the student may decide to integrate as much of what they learned from their interview with law enforcement without raising their risk of civil or criminal exposure. The intent of this exercise is for the student to improve their insight into professional and relevant interviewing while remembering they may not be sworn law enforcement officials, and to consider corporate and civil responsibilities during the interview.

THIS EXERCISE MAY BE PERFORMED INDIVIDUALLY BY THE STUDENT OR COLLECTIVELY AS A PRESENTATION TO THE CLASS

STEPS:

1. This exercise should be performed after you have completed the student exercise Being Interviewed in a Forensics Investigation.

2. Have someone agree to a mock interview. They will need to spend about ¼ to ½ hour of their time performing a task on the computer system.(You assign them the task). The task may be performing a Google search, working on a database, checking their e-mail.

3. From a distance, observe the interviewee and not their actions on the computer.

4. When they have completed the task, ask them if you can meet with them to conduct an interview of their activities. Conduct the interview as you would a real interview in your corporation. Even though this is a mock interview, do not make up information to fill the unknowns. Complete the following information.

a. What time did you arrive at the location / computer?

b. Was the computer on or off when you arrived?

c. Was anything on the screen at the time?

d. Where they any other personnel in the room at the time?

e. What were they doing?

f. What specific actions did they perform on the computer?

g. How much time did they spend on this particular computer?

Try to make the person being interviewed feel comfortable and relate that this is a learning experience for you, the student. Include as many relevant questions as necessary to obtain as accurate a history of actions as possible. Be as prepared as you can prior to the interview.

5. When the interview is complete, thank the individual for their participation.

6. If you did not include the interviewee's answers to the above questions, record them in the Student Summary portion and any additional questions that you may have added and their responses.

7. Compare their responses to what you observed and recorded.

A. Did they correlate?

B. How close or different were they?

STUDENT SUMMARY:

1. What did you learn from this exercise?

2. What are the three components of the Reid Technique™ of interviewing and interrogaration?

   1. _____ 2. _____ 3. _____

3. Perform a search and identify the Reid Nine Steps of Interrogation.

   1. _____

   2. _____

   3. _____

   4. _____

   5. _____

   6. _____

   7. _____

   8. _____

   9. _____

4. Additional notes from the interview.

Evaluators Review of Learners Performance

1   2   3   4   5

Forensics Exercise # 42
Evidence Handling Policy

OBJECTIVE:

To become familiar with an example of an Evidence Handling Policy.

OVERVIEW:

Adequate evidence handling policies must be adhered to and are required to maintain consistency in the integrity of the forensic process. Inadequate handling can result in misplaced evidence or the wrong evidence being examined.

STEP: 1

1. Review the example of the Evidence Handling Policy.

EVIDENCE HANDLING POLICY 2019.30.A

To prevent cross contamination between cases and prior to use in any analysis or recovery, the working drive must be forensically sterile by performing a full reformat. The working drive is the drive used to store the target image. The working drive will have no other images files stored on it. After completion of each case, image files may be stored on an alternate data base system.

Chain of Custody documentation must be maintained and accompany any forensic recovery. Image files, original media or any other information is not to be disclosed to any third party unless required by law.

Storage of original media must be consistent with local law enforcement procedures. All original media is to be stored in the on-site storage safe and protected from fire, water and environmental concerns.

All stored original media must be labeled by forensic case number

Using an instructor provided policy template, develop an Evidence Handling policy and show it to your instructor.

STUDENT SUMMARY:

1. What did you learn from this exercise?

2. Describe what you believe may be the consequences of not having or abiding by a Chain-of-Custody form or policy.

3. Describe what you believe may be the consequences of not having or abiding by a sanitization policy.

4. Describe what you believe may be the consequences of not having or abiding by an evidence storage policy.

Evaluators Review of Learners Performance

1   2   3   4   5

Forensics Exercise # 43
Chain of Custody

OBJECTIVE:

To become accustomed to documenting secure handling, processing, storage and transportation of devices in order to demonstrate integrity in handling and storage.

OVERVIEW:

Handling of evidence must be documented. If the evidence is handled or moved it must be recorded who handled the evidence, why they handled it, where it was moved, what was done to it, and the dates and times it was handled. This includes going to and from the forensics lab for analysis or display in court.

STEPS:

1. Attached are samples of Chain of Custody forms. Use this form as an example in your future case image file examinations or create one that fits the needs of your organization. Make sure the form has a creation and revision date listing on the form.

Chain of Custody

Case: <u>5-25-19-001</u>

Item #	Date	Released By	Received By	Purpose of Change of Custody
		Chain of Custody		
11-25-19-A	10/25/19 9:35 A.M.	SIGNATURE: **Mr. Big Shot** NAME/GRADE/TITLE	SIGNATURE: **D. B. Cooper** NAME/GRADE/TITLE **Forensic Examiner**	**Recovered hard disk drive from XYZ Company, office of Mr. Not So Big Shot** **DRIVE INFO:** **Make:** Connor **Model #:** CFS541A **Serial#:** CF214457A **Labeled Drive Parameters:** 1048 Cylinders 16 heads 63 sectors per track **Placed drive into secure container and labeled with Case # 11-25-04-001. Transported to forensics lab.**
11/25/19-B	10/25/19 11:00 A.M.	SIGNATURE: NAME/GRADE/TITLE	SIGNATURE: **D. B. Cooper** NAME/GRADE/TITLE **Forensic Examiner**	**Arrived at forensics lab. Inserted target drive into forensic system for recovery.**
11/25/19-C	10/25/19 4:10 PM	SIGNATURE: NAME/GRADE/TITLE	SIGNATURE: **D. B. Cooper** NAME/GRADE/TITLE **Forensic Examiner**	**Completed recovery of drive image. Returned drive to secure container and placed into secure storage.**
		SIGNATURE: NAME/GRADE/TITLE	SIGNATURE: NAME/GRADE/TITLE	

Figure 43-1

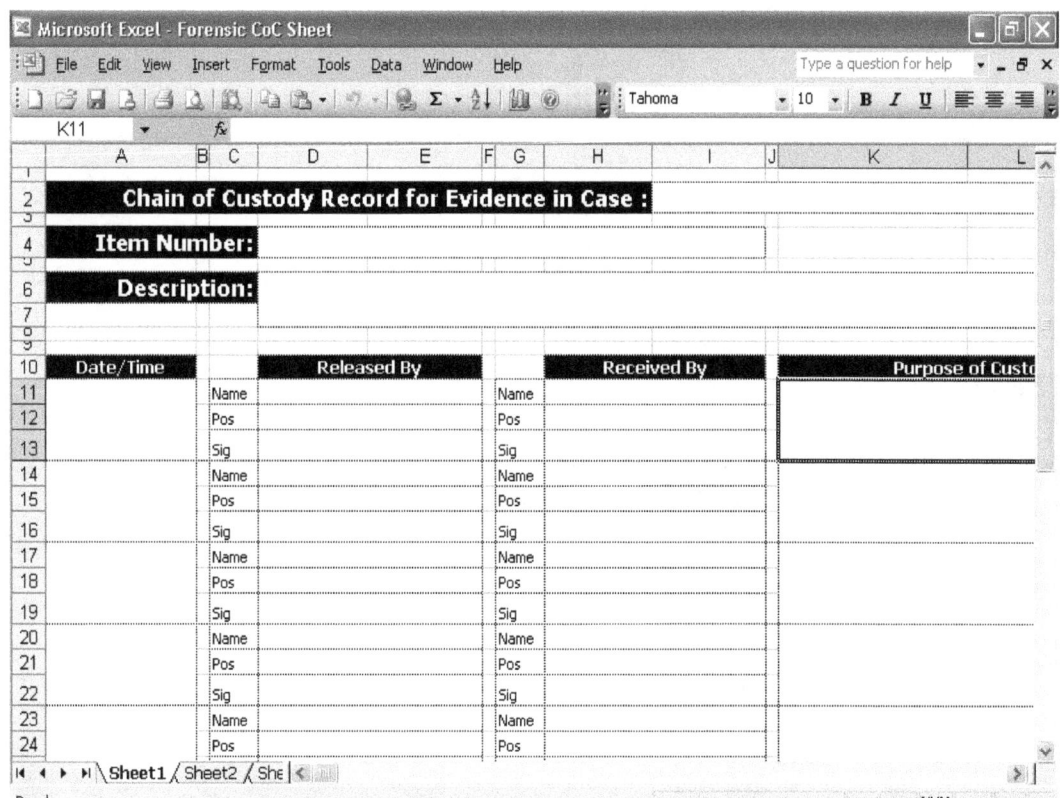

Figure 43-2

STUDENT SUMMARY:

1. What did you learn from this exercise?

Evaluators Review of Learners Performance

1   2   3   4   5

Forensics Exercise # 44
Creating a Receipt

OBJECTIVE:

To understand the importance of creating a documented the receiving or providing of evidence.

OVERVIEW:

As with the chain of custody documentation, proof of receiving or providing evidence must be maintained. This exercise provides an example of a self generated receipt.

STEPS:

1. Review the RECEIPT OF EQUIPMENT form and use the one presented here or create one tailored to your organizational needs.

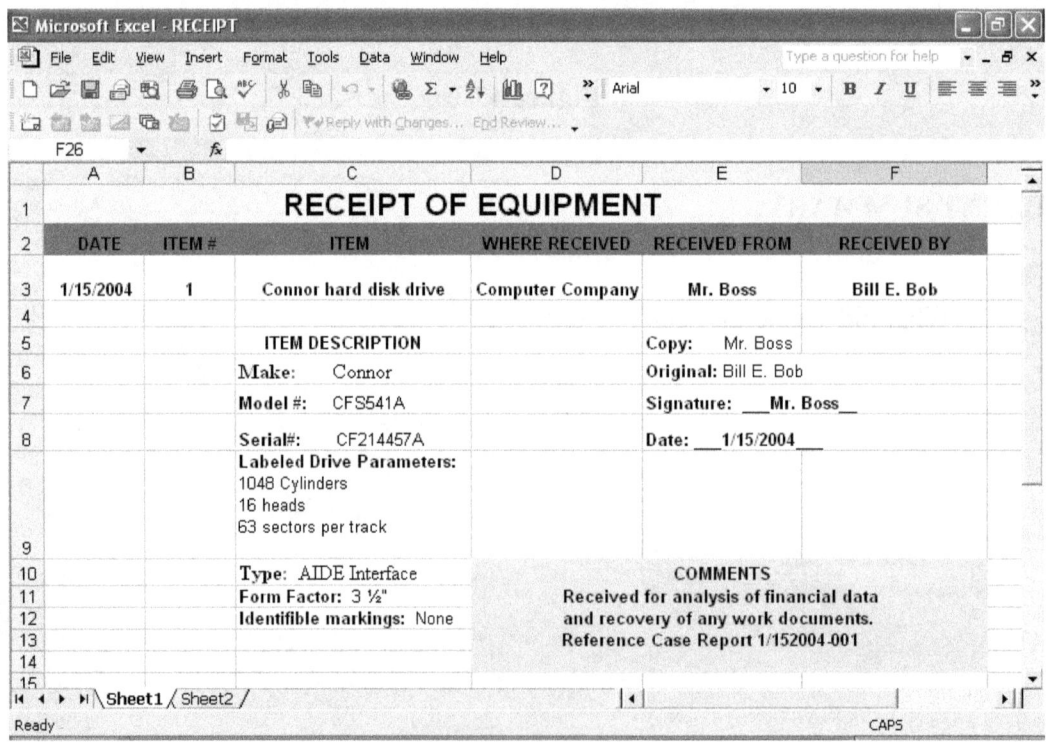

Figure 44-1

CASE SCENERIO:

You are in the office of the Vice President of Finance and you have just been provided with his company laptop computer, an IBM Think Pad Type 9549, Serial # 78-MM219 05/19. You are instructed to take this computer back to the forensics lab for analysis. Create both a receipt and a chain of custody document for this case. Submit it with this exercise.

Evaluators Review of Learners Performance

1   2   3   4   5

Forensics Exercise # 45
Legal Terms and Definitions

OBJECTIVE:

To have the learner become familiar with common legal terms associated with computer forensics and identify if the topic falls under civil, criminal, regulatory law, or other.

OVERVIEW:

The learner needs to have more than just a Hollywood understanding of legal terms and issues. Reconstruction and recovery of data sometimes yields information that may be associated with legal issues. It is to your advantage to become familiar with some of the language of the legal profession. This exercise is not intended to make you a lawyer; however, you do need a base understanding of the common terms associated with the law and forensics. An excellent reference for this material is the Blacks Law Dictionary. You may also ask someone who is familiar with the various types of laws and record their responses here being careful to state your source and whether or not you verified their responses. This exercise will be discussed in class.

THIS EXERCISE MAY BE PERFORMED INDIVIDUALLY BY THE STUDENT OR COLLECTIVELY AS A PRESENTATION TO THE CLASS

STEPS:

1. Research and write next to each term below, CI for Civil Law, CR for Criminal Law, L for Legislative or Regulatory, or Other if the term pertains to something else.

2. Research the following legal terms and provide a "brief" explanation of each.

TERM	CI, L, R, O	DESCRIPTION / EXAMPLE
Arrest Warrant		
Burden of Proof		
Confession		
Complaint		
Competent Evidence		
Consent		
Court Order		
Crime		
Criminal Law		
Cross Examination		
Culpable		
Cyber Squatting		
Damages		
Decree		
Defamation		
Defendant		
Disclosure		

TERM	CI, L, R, O	DESCRIPTION / EXAMPLE
Discovery		
Eavesdropping		
Electronic Signature		
Embezzlement		
Entrapment		
Espionage		
Evidence		
Evidence Handling		
Evidence of Tampering		
Exculpatory		
Exhibit		
Expert		
Felony		
Force Majeure		
Forgery		
Fraud		
FOIA		
Frivolous Suit		
Fruit of the Poisonous Tree		
Habeas Corpus		
Harassment		
Harm		

TERM	CI, L, R, O	DESCRIPTION / EXAMPLE
Hearing		
Hearsay		
Inadmissible		
Incompetence		
Indemnify		
Independent Contractor		
Informed Consent		
Infringement		
Inside Information		
Intangible		
Intellectual Property		
Intent		
Joint Venture		
Judgement		
Jurisdiction		
Knock and Announce		
Lewd		
Liability		
Liable		
Libel		
Lis Pendens		
Malfeasance		

TERM	CI, L, R, O	DESCRIPTION / EXAMPLE
Malice		
Malpractice		
Mediation		
Minor		
Miranda Warning		
Misdemeanor		
Misrepresentation		
Mitigate		
Negligence		
Nominal Damages		
Non-Competition Agreement		
Non-Disclosure Agreement		
Oath		
OSHA		
Offer		
Order		
Pain and Suffering		
Paralegal		
Patent		
Plagiarism		
Plaintiff		
Power of Attorney		

TERM	CI, L, R, O	DESCRIPTION / EXAMPLE
Precedent		
Presumption of Innocence		
Preliminary Injunction		
Pro Se		
Property		
Prosecute		
Public Domain		
Punitive Damages		
Quantum Meruit		
Quitclaim		
Reasonable Doubt		
Red Herring		
Reformation		
Retainer		
Search Warrant		
Sexual Harassment		
Slander		
Small Claims Court		
Spam		
Statute		
Statute of Limitations		
Subponea		

TERM	CI, L, R, O	DESCRIPTION / EXAMPLE
Summons		
Testify		
Theft		
Tort		
Trade Name		
Trade Secret		
Trademark		
Trespass		
U.S. Copyright Office		
Unfair Competition		
Unjust Enrichment		
Warrant		
Warranty		
With Prejudice		
Witness		
Work for Hire		

STUDENT SUMMARY:

1. What did you learn from this exercise?

2. You have been contracted by an attorney to examine the contents of a hard disk drive and look for evidence of an automobile sale where the seller misrepresented the condition of the vehicle being sold. What type of law does a situation like this fall under, Civil, Criminal, Legislative or Regulatory, Other, or none of these?

3. You have been contracted by a company to examine the contents of a hard disk drive and look for evidence of a an employee using their computer for the sale of stolen items on the Internet. What type of law does a situation like this fall under?

   Would this be under the jurisdiction of the local, state or federal authorities? Explain why!

Evaluators Review of Learners Performance

1   2   3   4   5

277

Forensics Exercise # 46
Analyze Case Image File 2005-45

OBJECTIVE:

To analyze a particular media to determine if any information of evidentiary value is contained within and to report on it. Write a Case Image Report for this case using forms and concepts learned in previous exercises.

OVERVIEW:

This exercise will provide the student the opportunity to examine an existing case image file and analyze it for digital contraband or illegal files. This exercise is expected to take much longer than previous ones and it is expected the student will report their findings as a complete examination report, to include the following:

- Cover Page
- Table of Contents
- Chain-of-Custody
- Receipt
- Summary of Case
- Listing of All Evidence Items
- Case Summary
- Case Log Information
- Any pertinent pictures or images
- Any pertinent documents or files
- Any Applicable Policy References

STEPS:

1. Acquire the case image file 2005-45 from your instructor.

2. Initialize Autopsy and import the 2005-45 case image file into it using the steps and techniques used in the previous exercise.

3. Discuss your findings with the instructor and provide a complete case report. Your instructor has the listing of relevant items in each case image file.

Your case report will serve as your student summary.

Evaluators Review of Learners Performance

1   2   3   4   5

278

Forensics Exercise # 47
Analyze Case Image File 2005-50

OBJECTIVE:

To analyze a particular media to determine if any information of evidentiary value is contained within and to report on it. Write a Case Image Report for this case using forms and concepts learned in previous exercises.

OVERVIEW:

This exercise will provide the student the opportunity to examine an existing case image file and analyze it for digital contraband or illegal files. This exercise is expected to take much longer than previous ones and it is expected the student will report their findings as a complete examination report, to include the following:

- Cover Page
- Table of Contents
- Chain-of-Custody
- Receipt
- Summary of Case
- Listing of All Evidence Items
- Case Summary
- Case Log Information
- Any pertinent pictures or images
- Any pertinent documents or files
- Any Applicable Policy References

STEPS:

1. Acquire the case image file 2005-50 from your instructor.

2. Initialize Autopsy and import the 2005-50 case image file into it using the steps and techniques used in the previous exercise.

3. Discuss your findings with the instructor and provide a complete case report. Your instructor has the listing of relevant items in each case image file.

Your case report will serve as your student summary.

Evaluators Review of Learners Performance

1   2   3   4   5

Forensics Exercise # 48
Analyze Case Image File 2005-55

OBJECTIVE:

To analyze a particular media to determine if any information of evidentiary value is contained within and to report on it. Write a Case Image Report for this case using forms and concepts learned in previous exercises.

OVERVIEW:

This exercise will provide the student the opportunity to examine an existing case image file and analyze it for digital contraband or illegal files. This exercise is expected to take much longer than previous ones and it is expected the student will report their findings as a complete examination report, to include the following:

- Cover Page
- Table of Contents
- Chain-of-Custody
- Receipt
- Summary of Case
- Listing of All Evidence Items
- Case Summary
- Case Log Information
- Any pertinent pictures or images
- Any pertinent documents or files
- Any Applicable Policy References

STEPS:

1. Acquire the case image file 2005-55 from your instructor.

2. Initialize Autopsy and import the 2005-55 case image file into it using the steps and techniques used in the previous exercise.

3. Discuss your findings with the instructor and provide a complete case report. Your instructor has the listing of relevant items in each case image file.

Your case report will serve as your student summary.

Evaluators Review of Learners Performance

1   2   3   4   5

OBJECTIVE:

To analyze a particular media to determine if any information of evidentiary value is contained within and to report on it. Write a Case Image Report for this case using forms and concepts learned in previous exercises.

OVERVIEW:

This exercise will provide the student the opportunity to examine an existing case image file and analyze it for digital contraband or illegal files. This exercise is expected to take much longer than previous ones and it is expected the student will report their findings as a complete examination report, to include the following:

- Cover Page
- Table of Contents
- Chain-of-Custody
- Receipt
- Summary of Case
- Listing of All Evidence Items
- Case Summary
- Case Log Information
- Any pertinent pictures or images
- Any pertinent documents or files
- Any Applicable Policy References

STEPS:

1. Acquire the case image file 2009-05-07 from your instructor.

2. Initialize Autopsy and import the 2009-05-07 case image file into it using the steps and techniques used in the previous exercise.

3. Discuss your findings with the instructor and provide a complete case report. Your instructor has the listing of relevant items in each case image file.

Your case report will serve as your student summary.

Evaluators Review of Learners Performance

1   2   3   4   5

Forensics Exercise # 50
Analyze Drug Trafficking Case

OBJECTIVE:

To analyze a particular media to determine if any information of evidentiary value is contained within and to report on it. Write a Case Image Report for this case using forms and concepts learned in previous exercises.

OVERVIEW:

This exercise will provide the student the opportunity to examine an existing case image file and analyze it for digital contraband or illegal files. This exercise is expected to take much longer than previous ones and it is expected the student will report their findings as a complete examination report, to include the following:

- Cover Page
- Table of Contents
- Chain-of-Custody
- Receipt
- Summary of Case
- Listing of All Evidence Items
- Case Summary
- Case Log Information
- Any pertinent pictures or images
- Any pertinent documents or files
- Any Applicable Policy References

STEPS:

1. Acquire the drug trafficking case image file from your instructor.

2. Initialize Autopsy and import the drug trafficking case image file into it using the steps and techniques used in the previous exercise.

3. Discuss your findings with the instructor and provide a complete case report. Your instructor has the listing of relevant items in each case image file.

Your case report will serve as your student summary.

Evaluators Review of Learners Performance

1   2   3   4   5

Forensics Exercise # 51
Student Challenge Case Image File

OBJECTIVE:

To analyze a particular media that has been created by a fellow student or the instructor. This case image file should be created in accordance with proper sanitization procedures or guidelines for media preparation. This exercise is intended to bridge the understanding of the student between how case images are created and how they are analyzed and examined.

STEPS:

1. Acquire a small capacity storage device such as a thumb drive.

2. Prepare a target media to be examined by completing the following steps.

    a) Make sure there are no left over files on the media by performing several sanitizing steps. To do these perform the following:

    b) Format the media a minimum of two times. Verify the format operation is a full format and not a quick format.

    c) Run a cyber-scrubbing operation on the media device using a multi-overwrite tool such as Eraser.

3. Using a computer system that has not been used for personal or confidential items, shut down the system to completely clear out any RAM artifacts. Leave the system in an unpowered state for approximately two minutes.

4. Power-up the system and insert the media device or thumb drive.

5. Create five layers of folder / directory structure. Name each folder with a name of your choosing.

6. Copy multiple system files into each folder. These can be any system file and are used only to add variety and quantity of files to the case image you are creating.

7. Create a text document with a specific message of your choice. (Use discretion). Once you have completed the text document change the text color to white. This will make the lettering white on white, which will not be visible to the human eye. Name the file with a name of your choosing.

8. Password protect this file with a two letter password and save the file to one of the folders.

9. Open WinHex or some other hexadecimal editing program and modify the first five characters of the file header.

10. Delete the file you just created. (Do not erase it, only delete it).

11. Create a Spreadsheet document with a specific message of your choice. Place the text somewhere in the middle of the Spreadsheet and make the lettering white on white. Name the file with a name of your choosing.

12. Password protect this file with a two-letter password and save the file to one of the folders.

13. Open WinHex or some other hexadecimal editing program and modify the first five characters of the file header.

14. Acquire the case image file from either your instructor or another student.

15. Perform the steps necessary to create an image file of the target media using all precautionary steps to protect the media.

16. Once the case image file has been created, examine it using Autopsy.

17. Provide a full assessment report of your findings.

STUDENT SUMMARY:

1. What did you learn from this exercise?

2. What did you learn from creating your own case image file? Do you feel you have a better insight or increased confidence from creating and examining case image files?

Evaluators Review of Learners Performance

1   2   3   4   5

Forensics Exercise # 52
Instructor Challenge Case Image File

OBJECTIVE:

To analyze a particular media to determine if any information of evidentiary value is contained within and to report on it. Write a Case Image Report for this case using forms and concepts learned in previous exercises.

OVERVIEW:

This exercise will provide the student the opportunity to examine an existing case image file and analyze it for digital contraband or illegal files. This exercise is expected to take much longer than previous ones and it is expected the student will report their findings as a complete examination report, to include the following:

- Cover Page
- Table of Contents
- Chain-of-Custody
- Receipt
- Summary of Case
- Listing of All Evidence Items
- Case Summary
- Case Log Information
- Any pertinent pictures or images
- Any pertinent documents or files
- Any Applicable Policy References

STEPS:

1. Acquire the Instructor Challenge case image file from your instructor.

2. Initialize Autopsy and import the Instructor Challenge case image file into it using the steps and techniques used in the previous exercise.

3. Discuss your findings with the instructor and provide a complete case report. Your instructor has the listing of relevant items in each case image file.

Your case report will serve as your student summary.

Evaluators Review of Learners Performance

1   2   3   4   5

Forensics Exercise # 53
Class Challenge Case Image File

OBJECTIVE:

To analyze a particular media to determine if any information of evidentiary value is contained within and to report on it. Write a Case Image Report for this case using forms and concepts learned in previous exercises.

OVERVIEW:

This exercise will provide the student the opportunity to examine an existing case image file and analyze it for digital contraband or illegal files. This exercise is expected to take much longer than previous ones and it is expected the student will report their findings as a complete examination report, to include the following:

- Cover Page
- Table of Contents
- Chain-of-Custody
- Receipt
- Summary of Case
- Listing of All Evidence Items
- Case Summary
- Case Log Information
- Any pertinent pictures or images
- Any pertinent documents or files
- Any Applicable Policy References

STEPS:

1. Acquire the Class Challenge case image file from your instructor.

2. Initialize Autopsy and import the Class Challenge case image file into it using the steps and techniques used in the previous exercise.

3. Discuss your findings with the instructor and provide a complete case report. Your instructor has the listing of relevant items in each case image file.

Your case report will serve as your student summary.

Evaluators Review of Learners Performance

1   2   3   4   5

Exercise Supplemental
Identifying FRED System Requirements for your

OBJECTIVE:

To identify several manufacturers of FRED systems and select one that based on company needs.

OVERVIEW:

This exercise will provide the student the opportunity to search and review various forensic recovery systems.

You are the IT manager for a mid-size corporation and have been assigned the task of building a computer and digital forensics lab. Your company designs, manufacturers and markets high capacity solid-state drives. Your company leadership is concerned about the loss of intellectual property though unauthorized use of employee computers. The concern is that company policy has not been universally adhered to as network monitoring frequently reveals employee visits to unauthorized and potentially dangerous websites. Your company compliance monitor has upgraded the acceptable use policy to include the following:

    a. No expectation of privacy on company computers
    b. Frequent forensic audits of company computers
    c. Revising of the company confidentiality and non-disclosure agreements

STEPS:

1. Identify three FRED type systems and compare their performance attributes.

2. Select one of the three and explain why you chose it.

3. Submit your response on the next page.

4. Complete the missing information below.

FRED System # 1

FRED Make and Model: _____

Manufacturer: _____

Specifications:
    Interfaces: _____
    Write Blockers/Types: _____
    Cores in Processor: _____
    Processor Speed: _____
    RAM Specifications: _____
    Hard Disk Capacities: _____
    SSD Capacities: _____
    Operating System: _____
    Software Included Types: _____
    Cost for System: _____

FRED System # 2

FRED Make and Model: _____

Manufacturer: _____

Specifications:
    Interfaces: _____
    Write Blockers/Types: _____
    Cores in Processor: _____
    Processor Speed: _____
    RAM Specifications: _____
    Hard Disk Capacities: _____
    SSD Capacities: _____
    Operating System: _____
    Software Included Types: _____
    Cost for System: _____

FRED System # 3

FRED Make and Model: _____

Manufacturer: _____

Specifications:
    Interfaces: _____
    Write Blockers/Types: _____
    Cores in Processor: _____
    Processor Speed: _____
    RAM Specifications: _____
    Hard Disk Capacities: _____
    SSD Capacities: _____
    Operating System: _____
    Software Included Types: _____
    Cost for System: _____

Evaluators Review of Learners Performance

1   2   3   4   5

ERRATA SHEET

For any errors in this manual, please send an e-mail to

infoccdn@gmail.com

In the subject line put: Errata Sheet for Computer Forensics Volume I

You can then enter the following information in the body of the e-mail:

Type of error:

       Spelling   Grammar   Other

Describe the error:

Page/s where error is located:

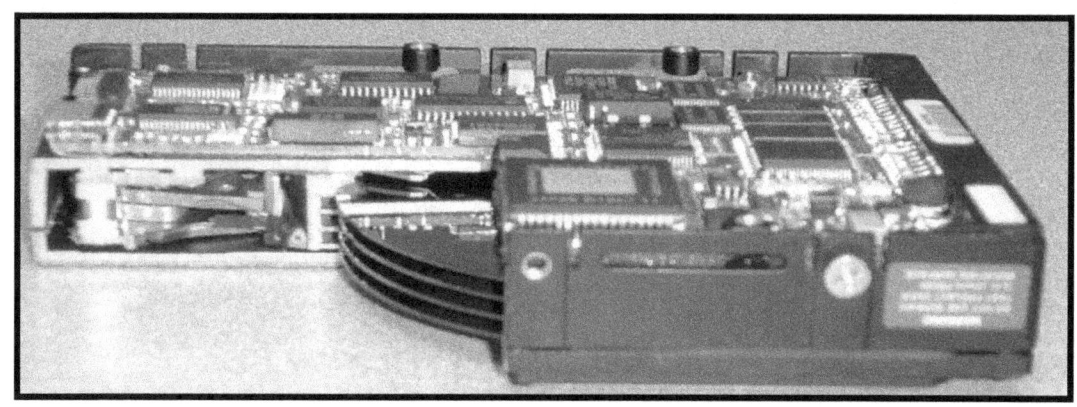

CPSIA information can be obtained
at www.ICGtesting.com
Printed in the USA
LVHW051510080520
655247LV00022B/1739